What People Are Saying About
Chicken Soup for the African American Soul ...

"Warning! This book will definitely make you feel better!"

Suzanne de Passe
television producer

"Sharing and celebrating the inner and outer victories of a courageous, creative and heart-centered people, this collection of human experience won't leave a dry eye in the house! It represents a milestone in storytelling that will endure, just as its people have."

Michael Beckwith
author, founder and spiritual director,
Agape International Spiritual Center

"Foundation in life is critical both spiritually and naturally; undoubtedly *Chicken Soup for the African American Soul* will help the seeker of foundation bridge the gap between the two worlds. It is a must-read for all."

Bishop Gilbert Coleman Jr.
Bishop Of Freedom World Wide Covenant Ministries

"Heartwarming and uplifting, powerful and real—*Chicken Soup for the African American Soul* will stir your emotions and soothe them at the same time."

Dr. Jeff Gardere
author, *Smart Parenting for African Americans*
and *Love Prescription, Healing Our Hearts Through Love*

"Soul travel needs traffic signals, stop signs, cautionary crossings, testimonies, the spoken and written word to guide us along the way. This book provides that and more. From soup to nuts, *Chicken Soup* is now African American inspired, taste-tested and it's so-o-o good!"

Dr. Gwendolyn Goldsby Grant
advice columnist, *Essence Magazine*
and author, *The Best Kind of Loving*

CHICKEN SOUP FOR THE AFRICAN AMERICAN SOUL

Celebrating and Sharing Our Culture One Story at a Time

Jack Canfield
Mark Victor Hansen
Lisa Nichols
Tom Joyner

Health Communications, Inc.
Deerfield Beach, Florida

www.hcibooks.com
www.chickensoup.com

We would like to acknowledge the many publishers and individuals who granted us permission to reprint the cited material. (Note: The stories that are in the public domain or that were written by Jack Canfield, Mark Victor Hansen, Lisa Nichols or Tom Joyner are not included in this listing.)

A Journey on Cane River. Reprinted by permission of Lalita Tademy. ©2001 Lalita Tademy.

I Know Why the Caged Bird Sings by Maya Angelou ©1969 and renewed 1997 by Maya Angelou. Used by permission of Random House, Inc.

Five Garbage Bags and a Dream. Reprinted by permission of Darrell Jerome Andrews. ©2002 Darrell Jerome Andrews.

Something Unbelievable. Reprinted by permission of Mary A. Spio. ©2003 Mary A. Spio.

(Continued on page 379)

Library of Congress Cataloging-in-Publication Data

Chicken soup for the African American soul : celebrating and sharing our culture one story at a time / Jack Canfield . . . [et al.].

   p. cm.

ISBN 0-7573-0142-8 (trade pbk)

1. African Americans—History—Anecdotes.   2. African Americans—Biography—Anecdotes.   3. African Americans—Social conditions—Anecdotes.
I. Canfield, Jack, 1944–

E184.6.C47 2004
973'0496073—dc22

2004054006

Publisher: Health Communications, Inc.
         3201 S.W. 15th Street
         Deerfield Beach, FL 33442–8190

R-09-04

Cover art by Keith Mallett
Cover design by Larissa Hise Henoch
Inside formatting by Dawn Von Strolley Grove

This book is dedicated to the village that has danced and sang, that has fought and cried, that has shouted and laughed aloud, and that has attained magnificence through healing, love and family—the village that has lived the journey to tell the story.

Contents

2. CELEBRATING FAMILY

3. TRIUMPH AND RESILIENCE

4. ACCEPTING ME, LOVING YOU

Acknowledgments

The path to *Chicken Soup for the African American Soul* has been made all the more beautiful by the many "companions" who have been there with us along the way. Our heartfelt gratitude to:

Our families, who have been chicken soup for our souls! Inga, Travis, Riley, Christopher, Oran and Kyle Canfield for all their love and support.

Patty, Elizabeth and Melanie Hansen, for once again sharing and lovingly supporting us in creating yet another book.

The entire Nichols family—for being so close and dedicated to each other; you have been the foundation of unconditional love that was required. Lisa's son, Jelani, for sharing his mom with her work. Agnes, James Sr., James Jr., Leslie and Eva for being her biggest cheerleaders ever. Your comfort, guidance, strength and integrity have helped to bring this book into existence. Denise and Duane, for your unwavering commitment to this project. To Lisa's church family and fellow disciples, your prayers and support have made all the difference.

Our senior editor, Eve Eschner Hogan—her level of professionalism and compassion, along with hundreds of dedicated hours, have set this book up to be a huge success. Thank you also to her husband, Steve, for his constant understanding and support of her work. Thank you to her family for cheering us on and lending their hearts to this project.

Our publisher, Peter Vegso, for his vision and commitment to bringing *Chicken Soup for the Soul* to the world.

Patty Aubery and Russ Kamalski, for being there on every step of the journey, with love, laughter and endless creativity.

Barbara LoMonaco, for nourishing us with truly wonderful stories and cartoons.

D'ette Corona, for listening and being there to answer questions along the way. You've truly made this task more efficient and more fun!

Patty Hansen, for her thorough and competent handling of the legal and licensing aspects of the *Chicken Soup for the Soul* books. You are magnificent at the challenge!

Laurie Hartman, for being a precious guardian of the *Chicken Soup* brand.

Veronica Romero, Teresa Esparza, Robin Yerian, Jody Emme, Trudy Marschall, Michelle Adams, Dee Dee Romanello, Shanna Vieyra, Lisa Williams, Gina Romanello, Brittany Shaw, Dena Jacobson, Tanya Jones, Mary McKay and David Coleman, who support Jack's and Mark's businesses with skill and love.

Bret Witter, Allison Janse, Elisabeth Rinaldi and Kathy Grant, our editors at Health Communications, Inc., for their devotion to excellence.

Terry Burke, Tom Sand, Lori Golden, Kelly Johnson Maragni, Randee Feldman, Patricia McConnell, Kim Weiss, Paola Fernandez-Rana and Teri Peluso, the marketing, sales, administration and PR departments at Health Communications, Inc., for doing such an incredible job supporting our books.

Tom Sand, Claude Choquette and Luc Jutras, who

manage year after year to get our books transferred into thirty-six languages around the world.

The art department at Health Communications, Inc., for their talent, creativity and unrelenting patience in producing book covers and inside designs that capture the essence of Chicken Soup: Larissa Hise Henoch, Lawna Patterson Oldfield, Andrea Perrine Brower, Anthony Clausi and Dawn Von Strolley Grove.

Keith Mallet, "A picture is worth a thousand words" and your images manage, in a glimpse, to capture and portray the powerful and heartfelt message contained within the book. You are a true master artist and we are honored to have your work grace the cover.

All the *Chicken Soup for the Soul* coauthors, who make it so much of a joy to be part of this *Chicken Soup* family.

Special thanks to our newest friends and partners Suzanne de Passe and Reg Harris of De Passe entertainment for taking this project under their wings.

Our glorious panel of readers who helped us make the final selections and made invaluable suggestions on how to improve the book:

Jarralynne Agee, Kathy Atkinson, Michol Brandon, Andrea Brown, Timolin Colbert, Cenyce Carter, Lorene Carter, Latoya Carter-Qawiyy, La'Rea Cecil, Linda Chavis, Pamela Clements, Linda Coleman, Inetta Cooper, Katrina Croswell, Sherry Curry, Linda Delaney, Christina Dixon, Ray Driver, Mary Edwards, Stephanie Embry-Horace, Valerie Flack, Jane Foley, BJ Foster, Greg Franklin, V-Nessa Gabriel, C. L. Gilmore III, K. D. Green, Chawn Green-Farmer, Tecaral Haggerty, Carrie Hall, Linda Harmon, Monte Howard, Shelau Howard, Pamela Hudson, Jesse Ianniello, Anne Jaffe, Cassandra Johnson, Deborah Johnson, Ally Kemp, Duane Kemp, Mia Landrin, Rebecca Law, Anges Lewis, Del Lewis, Anita Lovely, Candace Montague, Angel Mason, Tyi Moultry, Bonita Neal, James

Nichols, Leslie Nichols, Subrina Nichols, Brian Olowude, Donna Polk, Latoya Carter Quigley, Gloria Quinney, Leroy Robinson, Tia Ross, Tee C. Royal, Vanette Ryanes, Stacey Seay-Duvall, Marla Seller, Devri Smith, Jim Smith Jr., Alicia Spivey, Vernitta Supall, Chandra Sparks Taylor, Charlene Taylor, R. L. Ayo Terrie-Branch, Eva Thomas, LaRosa Thomas, Rudelle Thomas, Teresa Thomas, Mr. Walker, Rhonda Welsh, Tamille Williams, Felisicia Williams, Mary Williams and Rasheeda Wint.

A major thank you to the amazing Volunteer Development Team, too numerous to mention each by name, who joined forces to keep a constant flow of incoming stories, who spread the word far and wide and offered constant words of support and encouragement. Thank you to those who spent their valuable time soliciting stories, doing research, circulating flyers or simply participating in our conference calls. You are truly the "village" that brought this project together and we could not have done this without your prayers and support!

Special thanks to the volunteers who went way above and beyond: Annette Harris, Denise Thackson, Ray Driver, Deborah Bellis, Deborah Johnson, Duane Kemp, Minister Mary Edwards, Felisicia Williams, Susan Madison, Kevin Ross, Ahmondra McClendon, Carol Ross-Burnett, Aisha Johnson, Natasha Williams, Alice Johnson, Marci Eanes, Greg Husskinson, Angel Mason, Linda Coleman-Willis, Jerry Craft, Gail Swanson and Sue Gibson.

Mrs. Ella Lindsey, Rita Cameron-Wedding and Tony Bernez who, through love and simply being who they are, powerfully contributed to this book long before its beginning and without even knowing it.

Selina Heaton, Patricia Stevens, Winnie Briney and their husbands who have allowed us to adopt them in each project that Motivating the Teen Spirit takes on.

Berny and Lynn Dohrmann of Income Builders International. The networking opportunity IBI provided was like a puzzle that brought together all the key pieces to make this book happen. Barry Spilchuk, for being an integrity gate keeper for God's work.

And, most of all, everyone who submitted their heartfelt stories, poems, quotes and cartoons for possible inclusion in this book. While we were not able to use everything you sent in, we know that each word came from a magical place flourishing within your soul. May the spirit of nature carry you gently towards peace!

Because of the size of this project, we may have left out the names of some people who contributed along the way. If so, we are sorry, but please know that we really do appreciate you very much.

We are truly grateful and love you all!

Foreword

When I was asked to co-author *Chicken Soup for the African American Soul*, I had to say yes, if nothing else just to shock my old schoolteachers. I mean, it isn't every day that a C-student (at best) like me gets this kind of opportunity. But it's amazing what we can do if given the chance. The odds get even better if that chance is backed up with encouragement, support, guidance and high expectations for success.

I got all those things in my little town of Tuskegee, Alabama. I grew up in a community full of black folks with something to prove. The people in my community were always busy upgrading everything from their cars to their add-on dens; in fact, whoever sold wood paneling to Tuskegeeans should have been filthy rich! In spite of the segregation and racism that loomed over the South at that time, they set high standards for themselves and their families. They weren't settling for "as good as;" they wanted to do better! And more importantly, they believed they could.

I've done a lot of thinking over the years about my hometown and its "can-do" spirit, and I've wondered what made it so unique. For one thing, much of its population was made up of men and women, like my parents, who moved there to participate in the Tuskegee Airman program, which was really an experiment that set out to prove that black men could fly planes! They were young, college-educated, success-oriented people who were willing to take a chance. Everybody, of course, didn't make it as an airman. My daddy washed out of the program, but worked until he retired at the V.A. hospital. My mother was hired as a secretary for the program, but what she really did was use her writing skills to make her bosses look a lot smarter than they were!

But much of the can-do spirit possessed by the people that lived there can be credited to my alma mater, Tuskegee Institute, a black college founded by Booker T. Washington. It was the heart and soul of the town.

As I began reading what the writers contributed to *Chicken Soup for the African American Soul*, I was reminded of how our lives can be shaped and inspired by the wisdom, success, pain and sorrow of others.

Growing up I'd spent countless hours watching and listening to men and women who shared their stories. Like the writers of this book, those who contributed to my life ran the gamut from people of prominence to guys running their mouths at the barbershop. If I'd had the forethought I would have carried around a notebook and jotted down some of what I heard and saw and put it in a book. It would have included Tuskegee Airman Chappie James, George Washington Carver, Mrs. Ritchie (Lionel's mom), Booker T. Washington, Rosa Parks and many more. I didn't realize it then but Tuskegee really was a happening place. Everybody that was anybody in black America, or Negro America as it was considered back then, made a stop in Tuskegee to speak or perform, and my family made sure we were right there to see people such as Malcolm X, Leontyne Price and James Brown—not all on the same bill, of course!

The Tom Joyner Foundation, which raises money to help students who have run out of money at Historical Black Colleges and Universities (HBCU), is an outgrowth of what I gained from a town that gave me the confidence and desire to believe that I could be anything I wanted to be. My wish is for every black child to get the chance to go college. That's a tall order. A more realistic one is making sure that those who have chosen to attend HBCUs get what's needed to keep them there—support, encouragement and expectation of success. Like chicken soup, the meal and the book, a variety of ingredients ensure a winning outcome.

My role as host of the *Tom Joyner Morning Show* allows me to reach millions of African American radio listeners daily. We have fun together, but we also try to make a difference by encouraging our audience to take a more proactive role in their health, education and the political process. That's what a community is all about, and whether our community consists of 15 hundred or 15 million, our responsibility to our neighbors doesn't change.

I see this book as an extension of our efforts to reach the souls of black folks all around the country, and I'm very proud to be a part of this project.

Chicken Soup for the African American Soul includes stories of inspiration, humor and wisdom that we all can relate to. There are perspectives from everyone from Colin Powell to Yolanda King. From Sojourner Truth to Snoop Dogg. . . . Okay, Snoop Dogg is not included, but you get the picture. There are also great quotations from Frederick Douglass, Rosa Parks, Reggie Jackson, Jesse Jackson, Ralph Waldo Emerson, and the list goes on and on. The pot is full and seasoned just right! You can take a big helping all at once or dip a little at a time.

Enjoy the book! I hope it warms your soul as much as it warmed mine.

Tom Joyner

Introduction

I pray each day, that I not stand in my way, so that I can do what I have been created to do . . . I keep remembering it isn't just about me, it's about who I touch.

Lisa Nichols

When I was first asked to submit a proposal to coauthor *Chicken Soup for the African American Soul,* I had two challenges that needed to be resolved before I could move forward with this awesome project and opportunity. First, I had a challenge with considering myself a writer. I believed my college English professor when she failed me in her class, saying, "Lisa, you are the weakest writer I have ever met in my entire life." I promptly began a career in speaking and successfully avoided any profound writing. Therefore, the thought of being a coauthor for *Chicken Soup for the African American Soul*—to be read by the millions of people who love and respect the series—did not ring possible in my mind. During six months of procrastinating, a close friend repeatedly said, "Lisa, if you can speak powerfully, then you can write powerfully." I finally chose to break through my self-doubt and self-dialogue and pursue the opportunity. I started by writing my own stories and, much to my relief, I discovered that my English teacher had inaccurately assessed me.

I now know who I am to be responsible for this project:
Education, preparation, motivation,
With a dedication to my community.
Public speaking is my occupation,
School of hard knocks is my certification.
People of color are my orientation,
Yes, folks, you can speak to me later for clarification.

I speak bold, I speak strong, I am three wrapped in one
Malcolm X's desire for cultural cultivation,
Martin Luther King's yearning for total liberation,
And I do it all with a smile, with God's motivation.
There is a great mother figure wrapped around my
    tongue,
She helps clarify the three-n-one,
She leads me, she guides me,
She lets me know which way to go
Beside my three-n-one sits Mrs. Maya Angelou.
I'm Lisa Nichols and I am on my way.
Listen closely, you will hear me another day,
For I represent the strong people of color
    that are here to stay.

My second challenge was that I needed to know this wasn't just "another book" for Jack Canfield and Mark Victor Hansen and that these men (both white guys) had an authentic emotional or heart connection to what this book offered to African Americans. I needed to know that the production of this book offered something significant in terms of celebration, healing and the opportunity to share our culture, and that it would contribute to our children, literacy, economics and other areas of systemic change and advancement. My life has been about personal and cultural empowerment, so before I could enter into a contractual agreement to dedicate every free moment and several years of my life to this project, I had to look Jack Canfield and Mark Victor Hansen in the eyes and personally understand their intentions. After meeting several times with Jack, his conviction and personal passion for this project were clear to me. His amazing fight to teach African American children their history and worth started over twenty years ago when he was a teacher in an all-black school in Chicago. His eyes clearly said that though his commitment to stand for change had returned to him some great personal pains and hurt, he would do it all again to make a difference—as would we. Then I met Mark and saw firsthand, that through his life of celebrating, learning and spiritual growth, he understands our cultural differences but chooses to focus on our human similarities. I could comfortably say I saw character, integrity, authentic compassion and respect in both of my soon-to-be colleagues. Knowing a percentage of the proceeds from book sales would be given to the Tom Joyner Foundation to financially assist African American college students, I had what I needed to move forward. The result is this phenomenal collection of stories—in our words—celebrating and sharing our culture.

Chicken Soup for the African American Soul is a tribute to a culture that prides itself on survival, resiliency, healing, prayer and perseverance. These stories offer an opportunity for African Americans and our friends of other cultures to understand who we are. This book is not only a tribute to what *has been* in our history, but also to what *still can be* in our future. This volume of *Chicken Soup* is

Share with Us

We would love to hear your reactions to the stories in this book. Please let us know what your favorite stories were and how they affected you.

We also invite you to send us stories you would like to see published in future editions of *Chicken Soup for the Soul.* Please send submissions to:

www.chickensoup.com
Chicken Soup for the Soul
P.O. Box 30880
Santa Barbara, CA 93130
fax: 805-563-2945

You can also access e-mail or find a current list of planned books at the *Chicken Soup for the Soul* Web site at *www.chickensoup.com.* Find out about our Internet service at *www.clubchickensoup.com.*

We hope you enjoy reading this book as much as we enjoyed compiling, editing and writing it.

1

FROM
STRONG
ROOTS

The ultimate measure of a man is not where he stands in moments of comfort and convenience, but where he stands at times of challenge and controversy.

Dr. Martin Luther King Jr.

A Journey on Cane River

Success always leaves footprints.

Booker T. Washington

Growing up, I knew for an absolute fact that no one on the planet was stronger than my mother. So when she told me stories of who *she* admired growing up, I paid attention. She was clearly in awe of her grandmother Emily. She described her grandmother as iron-willed and devilish, physically beautiful and demanding of beauty from others, determined to make her farmhouse in central Louisiana a fun place to be on Sundays when family gathered, and fanatical and unforgiving about the responsibilities generated from family ties.

My mother drew parallels between her grandmother Emily and Jacqueline Kennedy. "Emily was class," she would say, describing her physical attributes: her long, graceful neck, her tiny, tiny waist. "Emily was class, Emily was elegant, *just like* Jackie."

How my mother came by this first-name familiarity with the president's wife I couldn't begin to imagine, but as I grew older and listened carefully to other stories about my great-grandmother Emily that was the least of my bafflement. The pieces wouldn't fit. On the one hand, Emily, refined, graceful, elegant, soft-spoken, classy. On the other, Emily, a woman from the backwoods of Louisiana, possibly born a slave right before the Civil War, unapologetic about dipping snuff, buzzed on her home-made muscadine wine each and every day. Not exactly "just like Jackie."

Emily intrigued me and the puzzle of this woman simmered on the back burner of my conscious mind for decades, undoubtedly triggering questions about who I was as well. Not until 1995 did the search really start to heat up, for the simple reason that I was no longer gainfully employed and suddenly had massive quantities of time on my hands. I had been a corporate executive, vice president and general manager of Sun Microsystems in Silicon Valley, when I decided to change my life by stepping off into the great unknown. I quit my job. Not a sabbatical. No looking back or second-guessing. Just walked away.

"When does your new job start?" asked my mother. Actually, what I heard was, "How could you possibly walk away from a good job you got only because I sacrificed to put you through school, and by the way, I spent fourteen hours in labor to get you here in the first place." She didn't really say the last part, at least not out loud, but that is what it *felt* like she said.

"I refuse to take a job for at least a year," I replied, trying to sound confident. "I need to listen to the silence, find the inner me, reengineer myself outside of the confines of corporate America."

My mother had no patience with this drivel. "Who's going to pay you to do that?"

"I've saved enough for a year or two."

"Can you get your old job back?"

"I don't want my old job. It's gone. There's something else I'm supposed to be doing," I said. "I just don't know what it is yet."

"You're *supposed* to have a job."

I let the silence build. For some things, there is no response.

"So what are you going to do for the next year?" she pushed.

Here was the critical moment where a persuasive argument could win her to my side, put her mind to rest, reassure her of my ability to adapt.

"I don't know," I said, which unbeknownst to me would become my mantra of the next few years.

I couldn't explain it because I didn't understand it, but I felt compelled to leave my job and research my ancestry. Gradually, and then overwhelmingly, I slipped into the dark, shadowy, addictive parallel universe of genealogy. Entire days disappeared from my life when I entered the bowels of the National Archives to pore over census records. Secretive trips to Louisiana to chase down fragile leads in local courthouses, newspaper archives and libraries followed. I began to lie to my friends, telling them I was "just relaxing, taking it easy, enjoying my newfound free time."

Meanwhile, the relentless search for dead relatives consumed weeks and then months. I lost all sense of shame, carrying tape recorders into nursing homes to interview people who couldn't remember what they had for breakfast but could spin sharp tales of events from eighty years ago. I craved one more fact, one more connection, one more story, but one was never enough. I had to have more, to know more about the people in my family, dead for a hundred years. I was hooked.

So hooked, I traced my mother's line to a place in

Louisiana called Cane River, a unique area that before the Civil War housed one of the largest and wealthiest collections of free people of color in the United States. I decided to hire a specialist on Cane River culture, a genealogist who could read the Creole French records that I could not. The task I assigned her was to find my great-grandmother Emily's grandmother.

"Let's get the facts we know on the table, starting with her name," the genealogist said.

"I don't know." (The mantra echoed.)

"No first name or last name?"

"No."

"Okay. Was she from Cane River?"

"Maybe," I said encouragingly. "Her daughter was."

"Okay. Was she slave or free?"

"I don't know. I can't find any trace of her in the free census records, but I'm not sure."

The genealogist seemed doubtful, but she took the job anyway. I was, after all, paying her by the hour just to look.

No job, no paycheck, so how long could this foolish obsession to find my unnamed great-great-great-great-grandmother last? Turns out, for eighteen months, by the hour, until the genealogist recovered a document that banished any doubt I would write a historical novel based on the characters revealed. In a collection of ten thousand unindexed local records written in badly preserved Creole French, she found the bill of sale for my great-great-great-great-grandmother Elisabeth, who was sold in 1850 in Cane River, Louisiana, for eight hundred dollars.

I wondered whether my great-great-great-great-grandmother spent as much time envisioning her descendants as I had spent envisioning her life. I held the bill of sale in my hands, awed and humbled, curious what any one of the women who came before me, born slaves, would think of one of their own having the opportunity to become an executive at a Fortune 500 company. Could any of them have even dreamed of that possibility in 1850 as they changed hands at auction from one property owner to another? I wondered what they would think of the world we live in today. What would Elisabeth have thought of my quitting my job and spending far more than her selling price to find *any* evidence she had existed?

At this point, I had no choice. I had to write their story and document their lives—my history. They were, after all, real flesh-and-blood people. I pieced their lives together the best I could from over a thousand documents uncovered in my years of research, re-creating what life must have been like for them during the 1800s and 1900s. The result was *Cane River*, a novelized account covering one hundred years in America's history and following four generations of Creole slave women in Cane River, Louisiana, as they struggled to keep their families intact through the dark days of slavery, the Civil War, Reconstruction, and the pre-civil rights era of the Jim Crow South.

The rest—the dog-work of writing the novel, finding an agent, finding a publisher and doing the book tour—was as grueling and exciting as discovering my ancestry. Within days of being sent to several publishers, Warner Books purchased the novel. Once again, my family was on the auction block but this time in a more satisfying way, honoring instead of dishonoring. Things had certainly changed over the last hundred and fifty years. I wished I could show my great-great-great-great-grandmother Elisabeth the price our family commanded this time.

Three months after the publication of *Cane River*, the phone rang as I was packing for yet another book-signing trip.

"Hello, this is Oprah."

"Yeah, right!" I said, wondering which of my friends was playing this cruel practical joke. I waited for laughter that never came. *"This is* Oprah," the distinct and ever-so-familiar voice said again.

As recognition registered, I mustered my most professional corporate voice in the midst of my total embarrassment and surprise. "Hello, Ms. Winfrey. What can I do for you today?" My heart pounded so hard I could hardly hear what followed.

She had called to tell me she selected my novel for her book club, which ultimately led to *Cane River* spending seventeen weeks on the *New York Times* bestseller list and a readership broader than I dared dream.

My mother has conceded once, and only once, that quitting my job wasn't as disastrous as she had feared. But she still thinks I should be out interviewing for a corporate position, as a backup. The women in my family are strong, and strength is a mother's legacy. Worry, on the other hand, now that's a mother's prerogative.

Lalita Tademy

Ain't I a Woman?

If we study the lives of great men and women carefully and unemotionally we find that, invariably, greatness was developed, tested and revealed through the darker periods of their lives. One of the largest tributaries of the River of Greatness is always the Stream of Adversity.

Cavett Robert

Well children, where there is so much racket there must be something out of kilter. I think that 'twixt the Negroes of the South and the women at the North, all talking about rights, the white men will be in a fix pretty soon. But what's all this here talking about?

That man over there says that women need to be helped into carriages, and lifted over ditches, and to have the best place everywhere. Nobody ever helps me into carriages, or over mud-puddles, or gives me any best place! And ain't I a woman?

Look at me! Look at my arm! I have ploughed and

planted, and gathered into barns, and no man could lead me! And ain't I a woman? I could work as much and eat as much as a man—when I could get it—and bear the lash as well! And ain't I a woman? I have borne thirteen children, and seen most all sold off to slavery, and when I cried out with my mother's grief, none but Jesus heard me! And ain't I a woman? Then they talk about this thing in the head; what's this they call it? [Member of audience whispers, "Intellect."] That's it, honey. What's that got to do with women's rights or Negroes' rights? If my cup won't hold but a pint, and yours holds a quart, wouldn't you be mean not to let me have my little half measure full?

Then that little man in black there, he says women can't have as much rights as men, 'cause Christ wasn't a woman! Where did your Christ come from? Where did your Christ come from? From God and a woman! Man had nothing to do with Him!

If the first woman God ever made was strong enough to turn the world upside down all alone, these women together ought to be able to turn it back, and get it right side up again! And now they is asking to do it, the men better let them.

Obliged to you for hearing me, and now old Sojourner ain't got nothing more to say.

Sojourner Truth (1797–1883)

I Know Why the Caged Bird Sings

If there is no struggle, there is no progress.

Frederick Douglass

The last inch of space was filled, yet people continued to wedge themselves along the walls of the Store. Uncle Willie had turned the radio up to its last notch so that youngsters on the porch wouldn't miss a word. Women sat on kitchen chairs, dining-room chairs, stools and upturned wooden boxes. Small children and babies perched on every lap available and men leaned on the shelves or on each other.

The apprehensive mood was shot through with shafts of gaiety, as a black sky is streaked with lightning.

"I ain't worried 'bout this fight. Joe's gonna whip that cracker like it's open season."

"He gone whip him till that white boy call his Momma."

At last the talking was finished and the string-along songs about razor blades were over and the fight began.

"A quick jab to the head." In the Store the crowd grunted. "A left to the head and a right and another left."

One of the listeners cackled like a hen and was quieted. "They're in a clench, Louis is trying to fight his way out." Some bitter comedian on the porch said, "That white man don't mind hugging that niggah now, I betcha." "The referee is moving in to break them up, but Louis finally pushed the contender away and it's an uppercut to the chin. The contender is hanging on, now he's backing away. Louis catches him with a short left to the jaw."

A tide of murmuring assent poured out the doors and into the yard. "Another left and another left. Louis is saving that mighty right. . . ." The mutter in the Store had grown into a baby roar and it was pierced by the clang of a bell and the announcer's "That's the bell for round three, ladies and gentlemen."

As I pushed my way into the Store I wondered if the announcer gave any thought to the fact that he was addressing as "ladies and gentlemen" all the Negroes around the world who sat sweating and praying, glued to their "master's voice."

There were only a few calls for R.C. Colas, Dr Peppers, and Hire's root beer. The real festivities would begin after the fight. Then even the old Christian ladies who taught their children and tried themselves to practice turning the other cheek would buy soft drinks, and if the Brown Bomber's victory was a particularly bloody one they would order peanut patties and Baby Ruths also.

Bailey and I lay the coins on top of the cash register. Uncle Willie didn't allow us to ring up sales during a fight. It was too noisy and might shake up the atmosphere. When the gong rang for the next round we pushed through the near-sacred quiet to the herd of children outside.

"He's got Louis against the ropes and now it's a left to the body and a right to the ribs. Another right to the body, it looks like it was low. . . .Yes, ladies and gentlemen, the referee is signaling but the contender keeps raining the blows on Louis. It's another to the body, and it looks like Louis is going down." My race groaned. It was our people falling. It was another lynching, yet another Black man hanging on a tree. One more woman ambushed and raped. A Black boy whipped and maimed. It was hounds on the trail of a man running through slimy swamps. It was a white woman slapping her maid for being forgetful. The men in the Store stood away from the walls and at attention. Women greedily clutched the babes on their laps while on the porch the shufflings and smiles, flirtings and pinching of a few minutes before were gone. This might be the end of the world. If Joe lost we were back in slavery and beyond help. It would all be true, the accusations that we were lower types of human beings. Only a little higher than the apes. True that we were stupid and ugly and lazy and dirty and unlucky and, worst of all, that God Himself hated us and ordained us to be hewers of wood and drawers of water, forever and ever, world without end.

We didn't breathe. We didn't hope. We waited.

"He's off the ropes, ladies and gentlemen. He's moving towards the center of the ring." There was no time to be relieved. The worst might still happen.

"And now it looks like Joe is mad. He's caught Carnera with a left hook to the head and a right to the head. It's a left jab to the body and another left to the head. There's a left cross and a right to the head. The contender's right eye is bleeding and he can't seem to keep his block up. Louis is penetrating every block. The referee is moving in, but Louis sends a left to the body and it's the upper cut to the chin and the contender is dropping. He's on the canvas, ladies and gentlemen."

Babies slid to the floor as women stood up and men leaned toward the radio.

"Here's the referee. He's counting. One, two, three, four, five, six, seven. . . . Is the contender trying to get up again?"

All the men in the Store shouted, "NO."

"—eight, nine, ten." There were a few sounds from the audience, but they seemed to be holding themselves in against tremendous pressure.

"The fight is all over, ladies and gentlemen. Let's get the microphone over to the referee. . . . Here he is. He's got the Brown Bomber's hand, he's holding it up . . . Here he is. . . ."

Then the voice, husky and familiar, came to wash over us—"The winnah, and still heavyweight champeen of the world. . . . Joe Louis."

Champion of the world. A Black boy. Some Black mother's son. He was the strongest man in the world. People drank Coca-Colas like ambrosia and ate candy bars like Christmas. Some of the men went behind the Store and poured white lightning in their soft-drink bottles, and a few of the bigger boys followed them. Those who were not chased away came back blowing their breath in front of themselves like proud smokers.

It would take an hour or more before the people would leave the Store and head for home. Those who lived too far had made arrangements to stay in town. It wouldn't do for a Black man and his family to be caught on a lonely country road on a night when Joe Louis had proved that we were the strongest people in the world.

Maya Angelou

Five Garbage Bags and a Dream

I attended high school in Syracuse, where I was not the greatest academic achiever. I did okay. My sports ability, however, attracted a great deal of attention from small colleges in the region. I received letters from most of the New York state schools. I chose Wagner College.

College was an eye-opening experience for me. I played football, and started with a lot of potential. Two of my friends and I were the top incoming freshman players. All of us were excited about school and all that it had to offer, but I didn't realize how unprepared I was for life away from home, and I began to lose focus during the first year. I started to fall away from the values that caused me to be invited to the school in the first place. Freedom from home became freedom to do what I wanted to do, and this was the beginning of a hard fall; I ended up quitting the football team. I chose not to focus too intensely on academics, and after my first year, I quit school with no plans to return.

It was very difficult being the first person in the family to pursue a bachelor's degree. I had no one from whom to seek advice. Once back home, I took a job as a dishwasher and stayed for almost one year. Being a dishwasher wasn't my quest in life; it was, though, what I had to settle for. The job wasn't difficult and the pay was low. Nevertheless, it afforded plenty of time to think about my future. In my earlier years I had a plan: I was going to make it big playing sports (admittedly, 95 percent of my community had this plan, also). Once I made it big, I was going to use my name to become a motivational speaker, affecting the lives of youth and adults worldwide. I began to dream about this on a regular basis. I realized that as much as I loved sports, it was merely a means to an end—I wanted to speak publicly. My biggest problem was that I didn't have a clue how to make this happen. I started to tell myself, *I have to go back to school; it'll be the only way I can effectively pursue my dream.*

I happened to run into a high school friend a few days later, who told me he attended a little school outside of Philadelphia called Cheyney University—the nation's oldest black college. Cheyney was a good school and their focus was on helping students graduate.

This seemed a perfect opportunity. I contacted the school, the coach and others, to discuss attending the college. Then I set up a going-away party at my mother's home. My family and friends were excited for me and my future. One thing they didn't realize—I was going to this school on faith. I hadn't registered, and I didn't have any money.

When I say I didn't have any money, I really mean I had no money—only enough for a one-way ticket and food along the way. I didn't even have luggage. Instead, I used garbage bags—five to be exact. But I had a dream to obtain my college degree and follow my passion. So, I packed my garbage bags with all of my possessions and said my good-byes. I had no family in Pennsylvania and no idea where I was headed. I'd never visited the campus nor even seen pictures of it. I'd never been to

Philadelphia. I only knew one thing: *Where I was going had to be better than where I was.* For me, it was now or never. I refused to continue living a life of mediocrity and blaming people for my failures. I realized that if I was going to make it, I had to go.

I took a bus, and then a train, to the 69th Street Station. When I got off the train, I was almost hit by a trolley car— my first time ever seeing one! As a result, I dropped my bags, three of which ripped open. The people at the station stared at me. I got on the bus to Cheyney and took up two seats with all of my stuff, still determined.

On campus, long lines led to the registrar's office, and I was hot and hungry. At the last possible hour, just before closing, I arrived at the front of the line. The lady in the registrar's office asked to see my identification; she intended to pull up my registration and then talk about payment. I told her I didn't have either.

"Did I hear you correctly when you said you didn't have payment and you're not registered?"

"Yes, ma'am, that's what I said."

"Have you lost your marbles?"

"Yes, ma'am, that's why I'm here today."

"How do you plan on paying for your education?"

"Ma'am, I don't have any money, but *you* do," I responded.

She looked at me with amazement. "You expect us to pay for your education?"

"Yes, ma'am, and I know you can do it."

"Anybody who has the heart to do something as crazy as this must be serious about his education. Where did you come from?"

"Syracuse, New York, ma'am. I came here with everything I own in these five garbage bags, and I plan on going to school. I'm here to succeed. I know I'm going to make it."

She looked at me for a long moment, "Wait here for one second."

After talking with the business director, she asked, "Do you have a place to stay tonight?"

"No."

"Go and see the dormitory director; she'll put you up for the night, and we'll discuss this first thing in the morning."

"Thank you." I picked up my bags and went.

"You're the young man who's become the talk of the day," the dormitory director greeted me.

"Yes, ma'am, I will graduate from this school, and one day be the talk of this university."

She smiled. "I like you, young man. We'll put you up for the night, and somehow we'll help you get into this school tomorrow."

The next day, I returned to the business office to learn of my fate. At the end of the day, a miraculous thing happened: The business manager found some available funds through a scholarship called the Wade Wilson Scholarship. I also received Pell Grant money and registered as a student at Cheyney University. Four years later, I graduated with a degree in business administration.

I left home with five bags and a dream. I had no money, no connections and no family—nothing except passion. As a result of both my determination and some helping hands, I am now a motivational speaker, author and trainer helping thousands of people pursue their own passions in life. My message is simply this: Don't be afraid of the unknown when pursuing your dreams. Many times they are waiting, hoping you will find them.

Darrell "Coach D" Andrews

Something Unbelievable

Never be limited by other people's limited imaginations. If you adopt their attitudes, then the possibility won't exist because you'll have already shut it out. You can hear other people's wisdom, but you've got to re-evaluate the world for yourself.

Dr. Mae Jemison, astronaut

When I turned sixteen, my Ghanian parents decided to make the ultimate sacrifice. They sold all of our earthly possessions and bought me a plane ticket back to America where we'd lived years earlier. I would have a better life than those before me.

When I returned to the States, I had fire in my blood. I was ready to take on the world. I was unstoppable. I arrived at Charlotte International Airport in North Carolina, and then traveled south to Florence, South Carolina, where I would finish high school. In those early hours, North Carolina seemed like Las Vegas to me, with all the lights, billboards, neon cowboys on taverns, twitching crucifixes on small Southern churches, and streets with names like Avalon and Magnolia. I was mesmerized, amazed, inspired. In one of the first letters I wrote to my family, I called it a sight to behold. On the first day of school, I sat in the front row of my English class just as I had done so many times back home. The teacher was an aging Southern belle named Ms. Smith with leathery skin and blue eyes turning gray with age. Her voice was pleasant and her twang delectable. I remember her well, but not just for the accent. With about six minutes of the first class remaining, Ms. Smith announced that an African was amongst us. The students looked around for a real-life *National Geographic* experience. I honestly didn't know she was talking about me. After all, I'd never been called "the African."

"Come on now! Introduce yourself to the class and tell them what your name means!" Ms. Smith insisted.

She walked over to my desk and told me to stand up. Everyone stared. I was mortified. I knew they were looking for tribal marks, some proof of my ethnicity.

"Good day," I said proudly, after a moment's hesitation. "I bring greetings to you all from Ghana. I am Mary Akua Spio."

My words fell like laughing gas bombs. With each syllable, the class laughed louder and louder. My manner of speech apparently amused the entire class. And my outfit didn't help matters any. In my attempt to look American, I wore cowboy boots and a large belt, similar to the one boxers receive when they win a match. Huge and shiny.

"Mary? What about Obtunde or something like that? What? Did you change your name at the airport?" one student yelled out.

"You speak English good for an Afkan," another student quipped. *Doesn't she mean, "I speak English well"?* I thought to myself.

I became a piñata for the class's questions and insults. "What did you do with the tree you lived in when you left Africa?" I remember one student yelling. Hoping to return control to the class, Ms. Smith interrupted. "So, Mary, what are your dreams? What do you want to be in the future?" Blinking back tears, I answered, "A rocket scientist." Once again the class exploded into laughter. "Oh dear! That's like saying you want to be the Easter Bunny! You ought to study something like physical education, where you get a chance to swing around, just like back home. Besides, you gotta be real smart to be any kind of scientist!" Ms. Smith was now having her own fun with me.

Soon after, the bell rang and everyone dispersed. I sat frozen for a few minutes, feeling numb, filled with disbelief. Later that day, I met with the guidance counselor and things grew worse. Without giving me any evaluative tests, she concluded I wasn't smart enough to take classes like physics and calculus. The counselor's words were the final jabs through my soul. In an instant, all my dreams seemed to go down the drain.

Although I had completed physics and calculus courses in Ghana, I was put back into basic algebra. Teachers and counselors told me my primary focus should be getting rid of my African accent. I felt hopeless. If they were right, if my IQ really was low, what could my future possibly hold?

After graduation, I left South Carolina for New York and got a job at McDonald's. I knew I could flip burgers and mop floors, but I wanted to be so much more. After hearing a commercial I enlisted in the air force and served for almost five years, earning enough money to attend college full-time. I studied hard, received an additional scholarship and headed off to Syracuse University to study electrical engineering.

Several years later, I found myself trudging through the brutal Syracuse winds, arms and legs frozen cold from the icy snow. It was time for my senior design review, the event every engineer dreads. The design review panel consists of a couple of professors and representatives from the engineering industry, and they can be an intimidating bunch. We stood in the back of the class, squirming impatiently, as we watched the review panel approach our lab stations one by one. I was reminded of Don Shaw, our lab instructor, and the inspections we had endured for semesters. During Don's inspections, he would always stop at Lab Station 10 and ask, "Do you know whose lab station this is?" He'd then answer his own question with a mouth full of theatrics. "This is the lab station of Eileen Collins, the first space shuttle commander! Yes, this is the station that Eileen used." Even though I had used Lab Station 10 for more than three years, everyone still called it the Space Commander's Lab Station.

As the review panel approached Lab Station 10, the head of the panel asked in a booming voice, "Whose lab station is this?" I could hear my heart pounding as I made my way to the front of the classroom. This time the question would have far greater implications than ever. I hesitated for a few seconds, biting my lips, tears not far from my eyes, and I answered their question with these words, "Ahem. . . mine." I glanced over at Don Shaw, wondering if he had a better answer for the review board. Smiling through tears of his own, he nodded in encouragement.

The panel drilled me about my design. I tried to remain calm throughout the endless torture. I spoke slowly, answering their questions, but soon the words flowed with the inspiration and reason behind my senior design project. My words were not perfect, but this time I knew they were beautiful. I felt it. Everyone in the room did. In that instant, nothing else mattered. The African had spoken; this time they were proud. They were happy to see her. I felt the unique reverence for life that only a death-defying (or life-defining) moment can create. I didn't want to stop speaking. I wanted to be heard forever. Then came the announcement that I'll never forget: "Congratulations, you are this year's winner of the IEEE (Institute of Electrical and Electronics Engineering) Design and Implementation Award!" The class cheered. People came over to talk to me. Some people asked me questions about the project, while others asked me about things they had been dying to know since our freshman year. Still others expressed their deep respect and admiration. Later that week, I learned I would be graduating number one in my electrical engineering class. It was an honor and a blessing.

After leaving Syracuse University, I continued on to Georgia Tech for graduate studies in deep space communications. I have since worked on heat-seeking probes for the NASA SETI (Search for Extraterrestrial Intelligence) program, designed orbits for rockets bearing communication satellites, sent a rocket into space with my signature on it, and engineered technology that allowed George Lucas to deliver *Star Wars* episode II digitally. The Boeing Company recently bought and patented four of my inventions in deep space science.

Ms. Smith was right. The Easter Bunny and a rocket scientist do have something in common: the unbelievable. Today, I walk through life proud of the African heritage of which I was once ashamed. Who knows what that class back in South Carolina felt in the instant they almost crushed my dreams? Maybe, through the teasing, they caught a glimpse of the woman I would ultimately become: Mary A. Spio, independent inventor and American rocket scientist. Something unbelievable.

Mary Spio

Miz Moore

*How simple a thing it seems to me that to know
ourselves as we are, we must know our mothers'
names.*

Alice Walker

I grew up in a time when you could leave the doors
unlocked while you took a walk to the A&P for groceries—
back when there were real grocery stores in a black neighborhood. Back when you knew most of the neighbors and
who their children were. Back when folks seemed to be
mindful of who was hangin' out with your kids. Back when
you knew that if your children did something they should-
n't have, someone in the neighborhood would let their
momma or daddy know for sure. And back when everybody knew "Miz Moore."

Miz Moore had six children of her own, but at some
point she became Momma to almost every child in the
neighborhood. Everyone, that is, except the bully and the
"evil one" (today they'd probably call him a sociopath). We
lived in a neighborhood where nearly every household

had two working parents struggling to make sure the newly acquired mortgages were paid. Newly acquired, because when we first moved in, there were only two black families in the neighborhood. Within five years, few white families remained. Miz Moore made the conscious decision to stay home and raise her children. To compensate, she did lots of things to save money, from returning milk bottles for a refund to canning or freezing anything she could get. She would pick vegetables out of someone's overabundant garden and turn them into something fantastic. We looked forward to the chow chow or relish she made to go with a pot of beans and a skillet of hot cornbread. We'd shuck bushels of fresh corn for hours on the back porch, peel tomatoes or whatever else for canning in anticipation of her making something special, like homemade ketchup, or her special grape juice.

Carol Jane, our next-door neighbor and best friend of my younger sister, used to love to come over every day and ask for a couple of thick, salty slices of Miz Moore's homemade canned dill pickles, sometimes staying to talk over whatever was on her mind. Most kids who knew her thought Miz Moore could solve any problem. I distinctly remember the day when Larry, Carol's older brother, went limping over, blood pouring from his knee, with a couple of his friends. He and his friends had been playing with a BB gun, and he'd been shot. The problem was that his mother had ordered him not to play with guns. He sat there with his leg propped up in the green vinyl-covered chrome dining room chair, trying to convince Miz Moore she could somehow fix his knee, even though it was clear the shots had caused some major damage, far more than a Band-Aid's worth.

He kept saying over and over, "Miz Moore, you can fix anything; I know you can."

After several minutes, she convinced him that she had to call his mother—a nurse. Miz Moore was a peacekeeper, a friend, a bit of a superwoman. Once, she stood at the end of the walk, her five-foot-two frame drawn to full height. She shook her finger at a considerably taller and mean neighborhood child, telling him to get on back down the street after he had chased down another boy. He had run for his life and stood behind her, shaking his fist at the retreating figure as though he could actually do something.

She was a child advocate before it became popular. Back then, child abuse was not treated as the crime it is today. We knew who was being mistreated on the block. After we begged her, she even went down the street and tried to talk with our friend's mother about her drinking and the beatings that came with her drinking. I remember how we nervously listened outside the front door while Miz Moore calmly spoke with her. I don't recall whether it helped in the long run, but I think he got a few days' reprieve from the beatings.

Miz Moore knew how to relate to the young. I still remember the day when we were practicing one of the latest dances—the Four Corners. She came in and watched for a while, much to our embarrassment. Back then, this dance was deemed risqué.

We expected disapproval, but she just remarked, "That doesn't look much different than the 'snake hip' we used to do when we were young."

We asked her what that was and without warning, she broke out into a hip-swinging, gyrating move that brought howls of surprise from all of us. Miz Moore could dance! She not only knew how to do the snake hip, she could cha-cha, bop, swing and waltz. And she taught us all of them.

As poor as the family was, she always managed to have

a meal on the table at dinnertime. You could tell when funds and food were low. If it was the middle of the week and there was yellow puddin' cake with a creamy, warm, chocolate sauce or a blackberry cobbler, you knew she was trying to make up for having served whatever she'd concocted for dinner, which was always somehow extra tasty to us.

If we asked her to repeat a dish from the week before, she'd say, "I'm not sure what I put in it; I just used whatever I could find in the freezer."

The old freezer in the basement was magical: There was always something in there, even when there seemed to be nothing. Miz Moore could see past the surface; she was a little magical herself. I believed she could make lemonade without lemons. She always found a way.

Recently, we sat around her house in the afterglow of a tremendous Thanksgiving feast with childhood friends and relatives streaming in from their own family dinners. I reflected upon the results of all the caring, the tears, the sharing, the fears that came with the journey she had taken to this point in her life. It was especially touching to see grown men from the old neighborhood, sitting around laughing about old times and paying Miz Moore the respect and the love she had earned from the days long ago—while they relayed stories about their adventures they thought she didn't know.

It was even more wonderful to consider that with her courage, her innovation, her strength, creativity and tenacity, she managed to bring up six children, none of whom are in jail or on drugs. Being poor was not an acceptable excuse for not being the best you could be— whatever you decided to become. And those who decided to marry brought up their children with the same style and class. All of her grandchildren completed college; one is pursuing a Ph.D. All of them see some connection between their success and Miz Moore, also known as Grammy, Gram, Grandmother, even Mom by adults who tend to adopt her as their own.

I find myself smiling sometimes, when I am seeking a solution to a seemingly impossible task or when I have been victorious in a given situation. My creativity and tenacity were often the only things I brought to the table. I recall what Miz Moore always told me, "Nothin' beats a failure but a try."

In my own way I'm hoping I become a Miz Moore, passing on the same strong wisdom, love and life example to the generations to come. Since Miz Moore is *my* momma, I know I'm off to a good start!

Edwina Joyce Moore

Living History

I made up my mind not to move.

Rosa Parks

Working at the Greensboro Health Care Center was rewarding. Especially knowing David.

David came to the nursing home after I had been there but a short time. Possessed of a quiet countenance and mild demeanor, David worked as a custodian. He was color-blind. I don't mean literally, but rather David didn't see black or white when he looked at people. He saw what he called "gray." Observing his daily contact both with the elderly residents and the staff of the home, I discovered David treated all with dignity and respect.

He was a nature lover and often took his lunch outside, where I would find him reading Thoreau. I would frequently "brown-bag" as an excuse to join him and listen to his wisdom on the beauty of God's gifts to be found in nature. Our friendship grew, yet remained casual (work-related), so I was quite surprised when one day in late January 1983, David asked me to join him for breakfast on

February 1 at the downtown Woolworth's lunch counter. The date and occasion of our breakfast didn't register in my mind as significant. That would change forever.

You can imagine my shock when I walked into the Woolworth's on February 1 to find the lunch counter packed and reporters with cameramen from all the national television networks focusing on David and three other African American gentlemen.

What in the world . . . ? I asked myself. David caught my eye, smiled and motioned me through the throng of onlookers and the media to take a stool beside him.

"David," I whispered. "What is all this about?"

"Gary, I wanted you to join me for an anniversary breakfast."

"Anniversary? Whose anniversary?" I asked dumbly.

"Today is the twenty-third anniversary of the Woolworth sit-ins."

"You mean . . . you?"

David just shyly smiled and nodded. I quickly learned that "David," the same man who would take the time out of his busy day to read to an elderly nursing home resident or spend his lunch hour watching the birds and flowers, was David Richmond, one of the four students from A&T University in Greensboro, North Carolina, who took a seat at the once "whites only" lunch counter at Woolworth's and thus began the nationwide movement known as "sit-ins" to desegregate restaurants. I was in the presence of living history.

It was cold on February 1, 1960. The icy winds sweeping down North Elm Street in downtown Greensboro were second only to the icy reception that David Richmond and his three fellow students received at the Woolworth's. Taking stools at the counter, they endured the dagger stares from the secretaries, bankers, clerks and lawyers having lunch.

"Fear?" David remembered. "Sure we were afraid. We were four scared college kids challenging the status quo. Separate but equal was being defied. Jim Crow, nearly one hundred years after our emancipation, was on his deathbed.

"We were four very frightened young men, but our quest for recognition as equals allowed me and my fellow students to overcome that fear. We were only four, but we were not alone. The spirit of our fathers—their bondage, their blood, their tears and sweat from which this republic was built, their sacrifices made, both at home and on the battlefields overseas, to keep this nation free—their courage was in us."

It's true, there were only four, but on February 2 there would be ten; then fifty. Across this great land the numbers grew daily to merge into one voice, one message, one song: equality.

David Richmond passed away in 1991. His friendship, guidance and belief in a "gray society" will forever remain a part of my heart, mind and soul. His quiet wisdom, thoughtful perspective, rare insight and deep understanding of the human condition is something I shall always miss.

Gary K. Farlow

White Water

Life loves to be taken by the lapel and told: "I'm with you kid. Let's go."

Maya Angelou

The "For Whites Only" signs over the water fountains in H. L. Green's Store really bothered me. I'd seen the signs before, because I spent more time in Green's than any other place. They had cloth in the back, stacked as high as possible on tables, and more came in boxes each week. Momma loved picking through the piles, and when she got off work some evenings we headed to Broad Street. If there was a new shipment of fabric, I knew how to amuse myself while Momma searched for hidden treasures.

I knew where everything was in the store, and I liked walking up and down the aisles pretending I was the boss and I pretended it was up to me to keep the merchandise looking neat. It was also up to me to count all the money at the end of the day. I pretended I had a big box of money and got someone to carry it to the bank for me. Sometimes I even looked through the cloth myself with an eye for something that would look good on my Barbie doll. Grandma had been helping me make clothes for her. On late weekday afternoons, there weren't many people in the stores downtown. One day, Momma and I got off the bus in front of Green's. A clerk had told her there was going to be a new shipment of cloth coming in that morning, and Momma wanted to get into it before it was all picked over. I knew she was going to be busy for a while, so I decided to walk around the store. I walked up and down the aisles, but nothing looked special to me. Then I saw the water fountains. All three of them sat there looking back at me. A shiny large one with a big "White Only" sign over it. Next to it was a smaller fountain with a wooden step in front. And, a few feet away, a broken-down, sad fountain with the water running all the time. The handle on the faucet was broken, and the sign above it looked just as bad. A black sign with white letters read, "Colored." The whole thing was dingy, and somebody would have to be very thirsty to take a drink from it.

I'd seen the fountains many times, but this was the first time I'd been around them when no one was watching. No clerks or shoppers were anywhere near. It was a perfect time to finally see exactly what the white folks were hiding. I would finally get to drink some water from the "White Only" fountain. My knees shook. I knew I was taking a big step. Would white people's water kill me? Worst of all, maybe I'd turn white and colored people wouldn't like me anymore. I had to take the chance anyway. If anyone saw me, I would just say I was thirsty and made a mistake. Most of the clerks knew my face from being in the store so much. They would go to the cloth department and get Momma. She would probably just tell me not to try that again, I reasoned.

I quickly ran to the smaller fountain, climbed onto the wooden step and looked behind me to make sure I was still alone. The beige knob on the spigot turned easily. The water ran into the basin. It looked like regular water. My heart was pounding fast, and my hands were so sweaty I could hardly hold onto the knob. I took a deep breath and waited for my life to flash before my eyes. I knew the water could kill me, but the only thing I saw in my mind was me sitting at my piano recital, trying to remember my piece, "Turkey in the Straw." Maybe I hadn't been alive long enough and what should have been a flash was just a drop. I closed my eyes, leaned down and took a big mouthful. I hopped off the step and raced to the end of one of the aisles. My mouth was filled with water, but my throat wasn't working at all. Try as hard as I could, I couldn't swallow!

My cheeks puffed out, filled with water, and I figured I'd better go and get help. Momma was busy digging in a box of cloth pieces. I pulled at her skirt, and without turning around, she told me we would get a hot dog before we left the store. I couldn't talk with the water in my mouth, so I tugged again. I moaned through the mouthful of water. Thinking I was playing some kind of game, Momma turned away from the cloth long enough to place both hands on my face, smile and squeeze my cheeks. I fought the urge to spit because it would have sprayed all over Momma. I wouldn't have had to worry about the white people's water killing me because she would have finished me off, right on the spot! I gave one big gulp and felt the water go down my throat all at once. Momma went back to her cloth box, and I headed toward my favorite aisle in the toy department to die or turn white, whichever came first.

I carefully looked at my hands to see if I was changing color. I stopped and stared in a mirror on the cosmetics aisle. My eyes were as brown as ever. I felt the same as always, just a bit scared. Finally, Momma came to the toy department and said it was time to get a hot dog. I was happy she still recognized me.

The lunch counter at H. L. Green's was my favorite of all places downtown—the one in the back, of course, the one up front was for white people. The stools were uncomfortable, but the hot dogs, fries and drinks made up for everything.

I was afraid to tell Momma I'd taken a drink from the white fountain because I didn't want her to worry in case I didn't make it. I decided it was best not to say anything.

After we got home, I checked in the bathroom mirror all evening to see if I'd changed. My heart didn't feel weak, but I wasn't sure how a dying person was supposed to feel. No one had to argue with me to go to bed that night.

I put on my best nightgown and took my favorite pink teddy bear to bed with me. I thought maybe I would fall asleep and wake up the next morning white as snow. Granddad would wonder where the little white girl in my bed had come from. Grandma would fall down on her knees in prayer, and I didn't know what Momma would do. Maybe dying in my sleep would make things easier for everyone. I lay there waiting for something to happen. I was afraid to close my eyes.

The next morning, I was happy to hear the rooster crowing! I had all my parts and was still breathing. I rushed into the bathroom to look at myself. I was the same color as always and everything was in the right places. Colored people who drank from forbidden fountains didn't turn white or die!

The next time I went into H. L. Green's Store and saw the drinking fountains with the "For Whites Only" signs, I giggled, *That's what you think!*

Jayme Washington Smalley

Funtown

*Some people dream of great accomplishments,
while others stay awake and do them.*

Constance Newman

Since my mother taught me to read at the age of four,
she thought it best to enroll me in school to take advan-
tage of my eagerness to learn. I was not old enough for
public school, so it was necessary to enroll me in a private one.

Now, when I say private, I do not mean affluent. This
was the segregated South, back in the early 1960s. My
school was actually a house with the first, second and
third grades combined in one room. It was a bare-bones
classroom, but it truly was a home. My ability to read
earned me the respect of my teacher, and I had friends. I
was liked, I was comfortable and school was fun!

But what I really wanted to do was to go to Funtown.
I can remember seeing the commercials on television. I
didn't know exactly what an amusement park was, but it
looked like people had a good time going there, and I

couldn't wait to go there too! I remember bothering my parents about taking a trip there, and asking, "When can we go?" What I didn't know at the time was that Funtown was for whites only.

Daddy was always leaving, it seemed, to go somewhere and to help someone, and it was Mother who had the lion's share of taking care of the family. She was the one who tried to explain words like "racism" and "segregation" when I asked, again and again, why I couldn't go to Funtown. We took many trips to the airport as a family, to drop Daddy off, and we would drive right by Funtown going both ways. I could see Funtown. Why couldn't I go in?

I don't remember how Daddy finally explained to me I couldn't go. I know that he wrote and spoke about the fact that it was very difficult for him. Although he was a powerful orator, this time he was at a loss for words. How could he tell his beautiful little daughter that she could NOT go to Funtown, because she was a child of color? My father stated that event "caused the first dark cloud of inferiority to float over my little mental sky." I guess it did. But there was worse to come.

When I was in third grade, I was transferred into the local public school. Although this school was still segregated, the majority of students were the children of middle-class African Americans, or "Negroes," as we were called at that time. These parents were the doctors, lawyers, teachers and other professionals in the community. Many of the teachers at this school came with degrees earned from some of the best historically black colleges of the day.

Unfortunately, school there was no longer fun. I was taunted and teased unmercifully by the children of these middle-class professional families. I came home crying to my mother, and telling her the mean things the children said to me. They called my father a "jailbird"! Jailbirds were bad people. Only bad people went to jail. Why were they saying my daddy, the Rev. Dr. Martin Luther King Jr., was that kind of person?

Oh, I cried many tears over those comments. My mother spent hours talking to me and trying to explain my father's work. She tried to teach me about hatred, laws and equal access. She told me there were many people who didn't have enough food or proper housing, and how my daddy was working hard to help everyone. She told me about Africa and slavery, and how our people were forced to come over to America in slave ships, and after all of these years there was still much suffering and so much work that had to be done. Yes, my mother laid it all out for me, but I really didn't get it. I could not grasp what all that had to do with my daddy not being home and having to go to jail. What did that have to do with my world and what was happening to me?

I don't know if it was divine wisdom or sheer frustration over my tears, but finally Mother told me that the reason Daddy had to go to jail was so that I could go to Funtown. That was it! I got that. I thought, *If my daddy is going to jail so I can go to Funtown, well great! He can stay as long as he needs to.* After that, nobody could tell me my daddy was a bad man.

My daddy was a good man. A great man. A man who was not only helping the world, but knew the value of the little things that mattered to me, too.

My daddy finally did take me to Funtown. It was a big deal, with media and cameras everywhere, but do you know what? Funtown wasn't all that great after all. What was wonderful, and important, was the rare opportunity to spend time with my daddy.

Yolanda King, daughter of
Martin Luther King Jr., with Elodia Tate

The Day I Walked and Walked

The greatest inspiration is often born of desperation.

Comer Cotrell

I remember getting ready to go downtown with my mom. The day was really pretty. The sun was out, the flowers were in full bloom, and I was so happy. My mom and I were going shopping to buy me a new Sunday dress for church. We always wore our best clothes for church. Church was a very special place. It was the place that we went to say "thank you" to God. As I sat down on the bus and looked out of the window, I thought to myself how lucky I was. I felt good and special and loved. I had a lot to be thankful for.

When we got off the bus, my mom took my hand like she always did and we started walking toward the store. As we passed a giant building, we saw hundreds and hundreds of people. They didn't look happy at all. Some people were crying, some were talking in loud angry voices, and some were just staring. They all looked so sad.

We stopped and watched. All of the people were black and they were all grown-ups. I didn't see any children at all. To the side of us there was a really big group of people, and they were walking very slowly. My mom questioned a woman standing nearby. I couldn't hear what she said, but I felt her grip tighten on my hand as she led us into the group walking. After a short while I realized that we were actually walking around the big building. Because I was so little I could only see feet and legs and even those looked sad. Their dragging feet made a squishing sound as they walked.

Well, we walked and we walked, and it seemed like we walked around that building for a long time. And now I was feeling sad, too; something just wasn't right.

I tugged at my mom's hand, "Can we go now? I'm tired and I want to get my dress."

"In a little while we'll go."

And we walked some more. Then I got really tired and I had to go to the bathroom. "Can we go now? I wanna go."

I will never forget the look on my mother's face as she looked down at me. Her eyes filled with tears, and she gently pulled me out of the line and squatted to look me in the eyes. She put both her hands on my shoulders, and I could see the pain on her face as she searched for words to explain why we were walking—why, we weren't going to get my dress today, after all.

She wiped away her tears like she was trying to push her emotions out of the way so she could speak.

"Last Sunday, some very bad people set a bomb that blew up four little black girls just like you while they were at Sunday school. We are walking in this line because we want those bad people to know that it is not okay that they killed those little girls."

As I looked at my mom, I could see tears rolling down her face and hurt and sadness in her eyes. All I could think about was how much I loved my Sunday school class and my church. I thought about those little girls and how they probably loved their church, too. And then it hit me. It could have been me in that church. I stood frozen in time and space. When we moved back into the line I was completely changed. I was not just a little girl walking with her mother. I was a little girl walking for justice. I stood up as straight as I could, threw back my head, and I made a promise to myself. *I will walk and I will walk and I will not stop walking.* Everyone has to know that no more little girls will ever be blown up again. That day I walked and I never looked back. I never put my head down, and I never got tired. I felt good, and then I felt happy again.

I was walking to show the world those four little black girls mattered. They were more important than getting a new dress, they were more important than me getting tired. That day, they were the most important things in my world, and I was walking to show it.

Ahmon'dra (Brenda) McClendon

Ripples in the Pond

It's not what you take but what you leave behind that defines greatness.

Edward Gardner

There have been times in my life when I've felt insignificant. Sometimes it was because I felt stuck in unfulfilling jobs or empty relationships. Sometimes I felt as though I wasn't connecting with other people and that I didn't make much difference on the planet. Sometimes it seemed I had no real effect on the rest of the world, as though my coming and going didn't matter to anyone. When I start to buy into that feeling, I remember a story that was told to me by a stranger over a decade ago at a wake for my grandfather George.

As I stood in the center of the room, mourning his passing, I noticed someone who seemed out of place. He looked like an old weathered farmer, rumpled and wearing a suit coat that hadn't been in style for many years. His shoes were old and worn, but I could see that he had taken the time to polish them. His unkempt hair was as white as snow, and he had the bluest eyes I'd ever seen.

He noticed my stares and approached me and told me his name was Paul. He had met my grandfather more than sixty years ago, but never knew his name nor ever exchanged a word with him. Grinning at the curious expression on my face, and in a voice that sounded as worn and as old as he looked, Paul told me the most compelling story.

"I was just a little boy. Me and Momma and my little sister were on our way home from visiting my momma's people. It was a hot August morning. The Chevy broke down in the middle of nowhere. Momma tried to tinker with it, but she didn't know about cars. I was just a little boy and I knew even less. Me and my baby sister were hot and thirsty. Seems like we'd been there for days off on the side of the road.

"Finally around noontime, we heard a car. We felt great relief, believing that help was coming. 'Course that was until the car got closer and we could see it was a colored man in it, your granddaddy. See, in those days we didn't have much exchange with colored people. They stayed on their side and we stayed on ours, no mixing. He pulled his car right up to us and asked if he could help. I knew Momma didn't want any part of that, but God, it was so hot that day and she had her babies to think about. She had no choice but to accept help from him.

"As he approached our car I was so scared I memorized every line on his face. I figured the time would come when I'd have to identify him since I just knew he meant to do us harm. I wasn't sure exactly what I was going to do, but I was ready to fight to protect my momma and baby sister. I tried to keep my eyes on him while he was under our hood. It had to be 120 degrees under there. Well, he worked for what seemed like hours but he couldn't bring the old Chevy back to life.

"Finally he says, 'I'm sorry, I can't fix your car, ma'am, but why don't you let me ride you and your children home?'

"We were terrified at the thought of getting into that colored man's car. Momma agonized over it, but it was so hot and her babies so thirsty, she decided she had no better choice. She piled us all into the backseat of his car, trying to stay as far away from him as possible. It must have been a good forty miles out of his way, but he didn't even ask for money. He drove us all the way home, then just dropped us off as sure as you please. He never even tried nothing.

"Later that night when Daddy heard about it, he nearly beat Momma to death for getting into a car with a colored man. We were forbidden to ever talk about it again. Your granddaddy was an angel that day. Imagine, an angel that looked just like a colored man."

Paul smiled and continued, "You know, when you get to be my age, you start to read the obituaries 'cause that's where all your friends are. Just two days ago, I saw your granddaddy's face staring back at me after all those years. It came back to me all at once. I never even knew his name, but I'd never forgotten his face. The way he just smiled at us even when we never even thanked him for all he did that day. I had to come here to pay my respects because it turned out to be more than just a ride home on a hot August day. Something about that day changed the way I saw the world despite what my daddy said.

"Today, I got two grown boys I'm proud of. They're good boys. Both became civil rights lawyers. They work in Chicago, and they have a partner who's a black man. My daddy would turn over in his grave if he saw that. I'm old and sick. It won't be too long before I'm laying there just like your granddaddy. You know, when my time to cross comes, I'm gonna find your granddaddy and thank him for that ride, put my arms around him and tell him all about my boys."

Paul had a far-off look in his eyes as he turned and walked away.

By now, my tears streamed freely as I stood there frozen, filled with pride and love for the man in the coffin. Even now he was teaching me.

After all of these years I still become lost sometimes. When that happens I close my eyes and see my grandfather's face with that huge smile. I hear his voice reminding me how much I matter, how much we all matter.

Tyrone Dawkins

The Opening of a New World

When you know that you don't know, you've got to read.

Solomon B. Fuller

Many who today hear me somewhere in person, or on television, or those who read something I've said, will think I went to school far beyond the eighth grade. This impression is due entirely to my prison studies.

It began back in the Charlestown Prison, when Bimbi first made me feel envy of his stock of knowledge. Bimbi had always taken charge of any conversation he was in, and I had tried to emulate him. But each book I picked up had a few sentences which contained words I didn't understand. When I just skipped those words, of course, I really ended up with little idea of what the book said. So I had come to the Norfolk Prison Colony still going through only book-reading motions. Pretty soon, I would have quit even these motions, unless I had received the motivation that I did.

I saw that the best thing I could do was get hold of a

dictionary to study, to learn some words. I was lucky enough to reason also that I should try to improve my penmanship. It was sad. I couldn't even write in a straight line. It was both ideas together that moved me to request a dictionary along with some tablets and pencils from the Norfolk Prison Colony School.

I spent two days just riffling uncertainly through the dictionary's pages. I'd never realized so many words existed! I didn't know which words I needed to learn. Finally, just to start some kind of action, I began copying. In my slow, painstaking, ragged handwriting, I copied into my tablet everything printed on that first page, down to the punctuation marks.

I believe it took me a day. Then, aloud, I read back, to myself, everything I'd written on the tablet. Over and over, aloud, to myself, I read my own handwriting.

I woke up the next morning, thinking about those words—immensely proud to realize that not only had I written so much at one time, but I'd written words that I never knew were in the world. Moreover, with a little effort, I also could remember what many of these words meant. I reviewed the words whose meanings I didn't remember. Funny thing, from the dictionary first page right now, that "aardvark" springs to mind. The dictionary had a picture of it, a long-tailed, long-eared, burrowing African mammal, which lives off termites caught by sticking its tongue out as an anteater does for ants.

I was so fascinated that I went on—I copied the dictionary's next page. And the same experience came when I studied that. With every succeeding page, I also learned of people and places and events from history. Actually the dictionary is like a miniature encyclopedia. Finally, the dictionary's A section had filled a whole tablet—and I went on into the B's. That was the way I started copying what eventually became the entire dictionary. It went a lot faster after so much practice helped me to pick up hand-writing speed. Between what I wrote in my tablet, and writing letters, during the rest of my time in prison I would guess I wrote a million words.

I suppose it was inevitable that as my word-base broad-ened, I could for the first time pick up a book and read and now begin to understand what the book was saying. Anyone who has read a great deal can imagine the new world that opened. Let me tell you something: From then until I left that prison, in every free moment I had, if I was not reading in the library, I was reading on my bunk. You couldn't have gotten me out of books with a wedge. Between Mr. Muhammad's teachings, my correspon-dence, my visitors—usually Ella and Reginald—and my reading of books, months passed without my even think-ing about being imprisoned. In fact, up to then, I never had been so truly free in my life.

The Norfolk Prison Colony's library was in the school building. A variety of classes was taught there by instruc-tors who came from such places as Harvard and Boston Universities. The weekly debates between inmate teams were also held in the school building. You would be astonished to know how worked up convict debaters and audiences would get over subjects like "Should Babies Be Fed Milk?"

Available on the prison library's shelves were books on just about every general subject. Much of the big pri-vate collection that Parkhurst had willed to the prisons was still in crates and boxes in the back of the library—thousands of old books. Some of them looked ancient: covers faded, old-time parchment-looking binding. Parkhurst, I've mentioned, seemed to have been princi-pally interested in history and religion. He had the money and the special interest to have a lot of books that you wouldn't have in general circulation. Any college library would have been lucky to get that collection. As you can imagine, especially in a prison where there was heavy emphasis on rehabilitation, an inmate was smiled upon if he demonstrated an unusually intense interest in books. There was a sizable number of well-read inmates, especially the popular debaters. Some were said by many to be practically walking encyclopedias. They were almost celebrities. No university would ask any student to devour literature as I did when this new world opened to me, of being able to read and *understand*.

I read more in my room than in the library itself. An inmate who was known to read a lot could check out more than the permitted maximum number of books. I preferred reading in the total isolation of my own room.

When I had progressed to really serious reading, every night at about 10 p.m. I would be outraged with the "lights out." It always seemed to catch me right in the middle of something engrossing.

Fortunately, right outside my door was a corridor light that cast a glow into my room. The glow was enough to read by, once my eyes adjusted to it. So when "lights out" came, I would sit on the floor where I could continue reading in that glow.

At one-hour intervals the night guards paced past every room. Each time I heard the approaching footsteps, I jumped into bed and feigned sleep. And as soon as the guard passed, I got back out of bed onto the floor area of that light-glow, where I would read for another fifty-eight minutes—until the guard approached again. That went on until three or four every morning. Three or four hours of sleep a night was enough for me. Often in the years in the streets I had slept less than that.

Malcolm X
Submitted by Henry Smith

Black Children DO Read!

In order to change a people you must first change their literature.

Noble Drew Ali

Books had always been my refuge. As a young boy growing up in segregated Louisiana during the 1950s and 1960s, I turned to books to explore the world outside my small hometown. I read whatever I could get my hands on: newspaper articles, essays, poetry and novels. In all my reading, I rarely came across anything that reflected my own experiences as a black youngster. Black people were largely missing from the literature I read, and when we were included, negative images like that of Little Black Sambo often stared back at us. I felt left out.

When I became a parent years later, I was eager to provide my children with the things I had missed as a child. In 1976, when our first child was born, my wife Cheryl and I planned to decorate her room with vibrant and positive images of African American culture and history. We found just one poster of Dr. Martin Luther King Jr. Disappointed but not discouraged, Cheryl, an artist and graphic designer, decided to create her own illustrations of black children. The characters she created displayed a lot of the characteristics we saw in our daughter and her friends: bright eyes, curious minds, mahogany skin, energetic spirits. On decorative poster board, Cheryl made the adorable characters twist and turn to form the letters in our daughter's name. Friends with young children asked for custom-made nameplates, too. We named the lively young characters the AFRO-BETS® Kids. Response to her designs reinforced what we already knew: We weren't the only ones looking for learning material that featured positive images of black children.

Our search to give our children the very books I yearned for as a child turned up the same large void. The children in most picture books hardly ever had cornrows like our daughter, Katura, or chubby brown cheeks like our son, Stephan. And the few books that did reflect African American culture were scarcely available outside Black History Month. I instantly remembered what a challenge it was for me growing up to ignore the negative stereotypes, look past the intentional omissions, and see myself and my people as strong, smart and capable. I didn't want our children to face the same challenge.

Joining my background in marketing and writing with Cheryl's in art and design, we set out to publish the kind of books we felt our children needed. We developed an idea for a children's book that taught the alphabet using Afrocentric themes, and presented it to various publishing companies. "A is for Africa, B is for a brown baby, C is for cornrows." The idea was fun, innovative, even necessary, some editors agreed. But all we received were rejections. There was just "no viable market for black-interest books for children," some told us. Dismayed, we wondered how could this be? Were they implying that black kids don't read?

We were charged with a motivation that only an insult like that could spark. Cheryl and I used the dozens of rejection letters that filled our mailbox as a springboard. We decided to publish the *AFRO-BETS ABC Book* ourselves. Before the book was even printed, orders were pouring in from parents, teachers and black bookstores. In less than three months, we sold all five thousand copies of the books. We quickly went back to press, printing five thousand more. Those books sold even more quickly. It was clear we were on to something important.

With the publication of our second book a year later, we launched our own publishing company. It would specialize in positive, educational and entertaining black-interest books for children—the kind of book skeptics said no one would buy. Stepping out on faith, we withdrew all the money from our personal savings and set up shop in our home to start Just Us Books. And that's what it was: just us. Just two of us who were convinced about the importance of our mission, who were driven to fulfill this need, and who had no previous experience in how to do it.

In a few years, Just Us Books was an established leader in multicultural publishing, with a growing book list available throughout the country. It wasn't long before large publishing companies followed in our footsteps. The market that many said didn't even exist is today a thriving segment of the publishing industry. We welcomed the "competition," knowing this meant change: change in the way black children would be allowed to see themselves, which warmed our hearts.

In 2003, Just Us Books celebrated its fifteenth anniversary. But what's made all the hard work worthwhile isn't our success as a company, or the multicultural publishing industry's tremendous growth. Rather, it's the impact that books like ours have had on young readers.

Since we published our very first book, Cheryl and I

have been uplifted and encouraged by the positive feed-back from parents, grandparents and teachers who say that our books are exactly what they had been looking for. Some of the most touching feedback, however, comes from the children themselves.

One day, among the usual pile of bills and other mail that crowds my desk, I spotted an envelope that stood out from the rest. It was addressed to Mr. and Mrs. Hudson in big, bold letters written with bright red crayon. Already smiling, I carefully opened the envelope and pulled out its contents, which were written with the same colorful and carefully drawn letters. There was the unforgettable waxy smell of crayons. I could tell this was going to be good, so I sat down to enjoy it.

Dear Mr. and Mrs. Hudson,
    I love your Afro-Bets books. I read one every day. Please write more books.

Your friend, Angela

P.S. I love Glo. She is a dancer just like me and she is the best Afro-Bets kid.

I held that letter in my hand for several minutes, as my mind embraced the meaning of this simple but powerful message. Phrases like "just like me *and* she is the best . . ." that were foreign to my childhood now rolled easily from a crayon-filled little hand. I thanked God for giving us this mission, for ordering our direction and allowing us to help black children understand their value, their place and their belonging in the world through literature.

My mission was reinforced.

Wade Hudson

The Bionic Woman Is Black

I feel that the most important requirement in success is learning to overcome failure. You must learn to tolerate it, but never accept it.

Reggie Jackson

I can still remember my mother and father sitting my brother and me down one summer day and explaining the Educational Integration Program that was to be instituted in the fall. The program was designed to take inner-city kids—like us—and provide them the opportunity for a better education in the traditionally white suburban communities. I was not sure what "better education" meant, but I trusted my mom and dad when they said that this was something they had never had—a chance at receiving an equal and fair education.

On the first day of school, riding on the bus an eerie silence and thick tension in the air confirmed that the other kids on the bus were just as anxious, hopeful and frightened as me. When our bus arrived on the school grounds, I expected a big "Welcome" sign greeting us as the first class of integration students. After all, this was 1979 and we were in Los Angeles—right? To my surprise, however, we were greeted with eggs, tomatoes and rocks thrown at our bus. Fear and confusion overwhelmed me. I had seen this type of thing on TV. Tears of pain and anger stung my eyes when I witnessed water hoses hurting the people marching for equality, and I got chills when I heard Dr. King say, " . . . one day little black kids and little white kids can play together and go to school together . . . free at last, free at last." I realized that I was that little black girl he was talking about, and maybe staying in this scary school with these mean people was my way of contributing to what Dr. King had died for. If I ran back to safety, then we really weren't "free at last." So I convinced my parents to let me stay.

An athlete since the age of eight, I had just begun to run track when tryouts were announced for both a Charlie's Angels and a Bionic Woman competition. I was thrilled and sure I could win. At ten years old I ran the fastest in the entire school. I had mastered my roll . . . stop . . . point . . . and "Freeze, sucker!" to sheer perfection. In the days leading up to the big competition, which included over forty hopeful little girls and over seventy-five curious onlookers, I sharpened every skill to ensure my placement. I knew all the key lines of both the Angels and the Bionic Woman.

On the day of the big competition I was calm and assured.

"Ready. Set. Go!"

I was out in front instantly! When I finished the one-hundred-yard race, many of the girls were just approaching the seventy-five-yard mark. This gave me the additional boost of confidence I needed as the only African American in the competition. The judges were five very popular girls and a boy I guessed represented Charlie.

Only the first six of us who placed in the race advanced to the "Roll, Freeze and Pose" competition. I waited to be the last candidate, and my competitors did just as I thought: They giggled, fumbled and foiled the freeze. I, however, froze right on the mark—hot asphalt and all. My performance was so impressive that the audience gave a gasping "WOW." You would have thought I had been an Angel for years—at least since I had been six!

Finally, it was time to decide who would be Charlie's Angels and the Bionic Woman for the entire school year. I stood there as the judges huddled, periodically looking over their shoulders before their final selection. With six girls left, three would be Angels, one would be the Bionic Woman, and one would be alternate. This would leave only one person who would not be selected at all.

I looked to both sides to see who that could be. Maybe Cindy—she came in last in the race, or Kim—she couldn't coordinate herself enough to roll and freeze. Maybe it would be Michelle, who made a habit of calling everyone ugly names and just did not come across as an Angel. I felt sorry for whoever was not going to be chosen.

"The decision is made!" exclaimed Charlie's agent.

"The official Charlie's Angels will be Diane, Tiffany . . . ," I felt my heart sink, "and Cindy."

"The official Bionic Woman . . . ," the young judge went on to say.

My mind was racing, partly in disbelief and partly in hopefulness. *One chance, I know I will be chosen for this,* I thought, as I could feel my palms sweating and my chest getting tight to hold back the tears.

"Bionic Woman will be Michelle." He went on to announce, "Kim was chosen as the alternate."

Boos began to fly from the audience.

As each person approached me to protest the decision, I could see nothing but blur between my tears. My head spun, and my anger rose. I had been cheated and I didn't know why. I stood frozen on my mark. I replayed the entire chain of events in my head to see what I could have done better or should have done with more passion. After five horrifically long minutes of scanning my brain for answers, I concluded that I could not have produced better results. I had outperformed every other girl.

I deserved an answer, so I walked directly over to the judges, "Why was I not selected if I outperformed everyone in each competition?"

Suddenly, as if waiting for me to ask that question, the school ground fell silent. Everyone stopped and stared, and I wondered then if I had made a big mistake. *Nothing could embarrass me more than what just happened,* or so I thought.

The judges just looked at me with no sense of care or concern for my feelings and asked the question that would change my life forever, "What hero have you ever seen that was black?"

Another girl taunted, "We did not choose you, Lisa, because you don't look like any Angel or the Bionic Woman, but you can try out again next year if you happen to begin to look more like them in the future."

I walked away crying, as they laughed hysterically.

That day in September 1979, I became acquainted with some of the pain and hurt my grandparents and great ancestors endured. Since that year in fifth grade, I committed myself to being a hero for other little girls who needed one, and so I became a motivational speaker.

Twenty years later, during my keynote at a church in Los Angeles, I shared my commitment to change and the importance of empowerment. I emphasized that the cost of living this dream can never exceed the cost of throwing it away. I received a standing ovation from the audience and was elated and overjoyed.

As I made my way through the crowd stopping to acknowledge admiring guests, a hand touched my shoulder and the most familiar voice said, "You are so inspiring; you are a true heroine." I turned and nearly fainted. I stood amidst three thousand people and hugged Lindsay Wagner (television's Bionic Woman), scrambling to explain that she was my longtime favorite. She said clearly and with conviction, "Today, you became my favorite and the true Bionic Woman."

On that day, I forgave each of those judges from my childhood for judging my outside—and not seeing my inside. I also forgave myself for being angry for the dark skin I was born in and the pain that it brought. I knew in that moment that it didn't matter which heroine I looked like, because I now knew exactly which heroine I resembled: me.

Lisa Nichols

The Lady at the Bus Stop

*I was shackled by a heavy burden, beneath a
load of guilt and shame. And then the hand of
my mother, my godmother, my grandmother, my
sister, my sister-friend . . . touched me, and now
I am no longer the same.*

Monya Aletha Stubbs

Hot and humid was normal for Houston, Texas, in the
fall. I was seventeen years old, and one of a handful of
black students who attended a formerly all-white college.
On that day, in 1967, I was standing at a bus stop downtown at the interchange. At this transfer point, near the
Kress's store where a bag of Spanish peanuts cost a quarter, domestic workers changed busses from the "other side
of town," where their maid jobs were, to the side of town
where they lived in strictly segregated communities.
Dressed in uniforms of white or black and comfortable
shoes, these ladies met here twice daily. Their conversations were intimate—quiet and loud, by turn. Talk of hurting bunions, the meanest "Ms. Ann" or the most spoiled

white children were punctuated with "Amen" and "Yeah, girl." Most were middle-aged, but some were elderly— their fingers gnarled with arthritis, and a few were not much older than I was. Each carried a package or a shopping bag that no doubt held leftover food or a child's discarded dress or toy.

With my huge Afro, clunky shoes and bell-bottomed pants, I was obviously an outsider, but a lady standing near me struck up a conversation anyway.

"What yo' name, honey?"

"Evelyn."

"Where you from? You from 'round here?"

"No ma'am," I said, adding the title Mama and Grama had taught me to use when addressing my elders.

"Well, what you doing here, baby?"

"I'm a student at the college."

"College? You go to college? I'm *so proud* of you." And indeed a look of pride settled on her face.

"Yes, ma'am. But this is just my first year," I said self-consciously. Since I was the third generation in my family to attend college, I didn't feel that being only a freshman deserved her pride.

"That's alright, baby," she said, disregarding my reticence. "You got to finish that college. For us. I'mo hep you."

Help me? How could she help me? And who was "us"?

But when I met her eyes, I saw them. They were women of every hue, from blue-black to high yellow. I saw the women who had fervently prayed, to a black god or a white Jesus, for the end of slavery. I saw the women who had killed their children rather than allow them to live as slaves. I saw the women who had died, with their hands tied at the whipping post, because they had learned to read a few words. I saw the women who had given birth to their masters' children only to see them sold as chattel.

And I saw the women who, with heads held high, had stared Jim Crow in the eye. All of these women, who knew education was the key to unlocking the chains that bound them, were in her eyes. They stared back at me—asking me how I could take such a gift for granted.

The lady reached into her high pocket, and pulled from her full bosom a handkerchief tied with the knot that only grandmas and church mothers know. Deliberately and painstakingly, she untied the knot, dug out a crumpled dollar bill and pressed it into my hand.

Although I'd seen my own grandmother untie such a knot to give me a coin or a bill to put in the collection plate in Sunday school, I was embarrassed to receive this gift from a stranger.

"Thank you, ma'am, but I don't really need money. My parents saved up to send me to college. And I have a part-time job in an office." I knew she worked much harder for a dollar bill than I ever had, so I tried to give it back to her. But she folded my fingers over it, and patted my hand.

"I'm just doing my part, Sugar. This is all I can afford. I want you to keep it. And you remember me." Then her bus came, and she was gone.

I will always remember her. I cannot count the times I have regretted not getting her name and address, and that I didn't save her crumpled dollar bill.

At my graduation ceremony four years later, I was surrounded by friends and family who appreciated the milestone—but who had fully expected that I would graduate from college. I wished the lady at the bus stop was there. In a strange way, I think it would have meant more to her than it did to them.

Ten years later, I graduated from the University of Texas Law School. In the huge and ornate hall where the Sunflower Ceremony was held, again friends and family surrounded me. But my thoughts focused on the lady at the bus stop. A few months later, I opened an envelope, which held confirmation that I had passed the Bar exam. I smiled. The lady at the bus stop would *really* be proud.

On a cold January day several years later, I was sworn in as a judge. I am so grateful my father, who scrimped and saved for my education, and who died the next November, was able to attend the swearing-in ceremony. I am so grateful that my uncle, who had tied perfect bows in my sashes when I was a little girl, and who never had a little girl of his own, came too—against the advice of his heart doctor. One of my girlfriends took off work and drove two hundred miles to be with me. Even surrounded by friends and family, I wished that the lady at the bus stop could have been there. I know that she—and those women I saw in her eyes—would have been proud.

I have been a lawyer for over twenty years now and I have written three best-selling novels. At every milestone in my life, I have remembered the lady at the bus stop. I wish that she could know that I have tried to earn that crumpled dollar bill she worked so hard for and the pride on her face that hot and humid day. I wish she could know how I strive to emulate her by taking every opportunity to *be* the lady at the bus stop for another generation of descendants of slaves. I pray that forty years from now, another woman will remember me, and remember seeing the lady at the bus stop—and all those other women—in *my* eyes.

Evelyn Palfrey

Over the Wall

Don't be afraid to go out on a limb. That's where the fruit is.

Janie Mines

I would not have been there except they had lowered the height requirement in the late 1970s to recruit more minorities and women—and I was both a "minority" and a "woman." Their goal was to recruit Asian and Latino men, but it also opened the door for a "little" woman like me to get through. This was my chance—me, Linda Coleman— to become a deputy sheriff.

The day was young and overcast when I arrived at the police academy. But as far as I was concerned, the sun was shining. I'd made it.

It had been a long, grueling year getting to this point. I had taken a written test, a psychological exam and an oral interview, and I had passed all three. Then the background investigation began. They investigated everyone, from my grandmother in Texas, to my next-door neighbors, to the babysitter of my two small children. They knew everything about me from the day I was born. As part of my qualification process I spent a day at a sheriff station with the captain. I was scrutinized, chastised and downright ostracized. It was no secret how he felt; he never missed an opportunity to tell me. "Women don't belong on the department, all gays should be taken out and shot, where do 'you people' get off thinking you can do whatever you want nowadays?" If I heard one more story about the "good ole days" when women were women and men were men and "you people" knew your place, I think I would have puked.

But all that was behind me now. I was at the academy, and I was going to be a deputy sheriff. My excitement didn't last long.

My first encounter was with a twenty-year career officer, a sergeant nicknamed "Goliath." He was six-feet-four-inches tall, and 300 pounds of solid muscle, to my five-feet-three-inches and 118 pounds of woman. "Sgt. Goliath" let me know in no uncertain terms he was not happy I was there. Like others in the department, he believed this was a "men only" profession. And it would suit many of them just fine if it were "white men only."

The sergeant never called me by name. It was always "little lady" or "little girl." When he looked at me, he would stare as if he were looking right through me. It was apparent he was not going to make it easy. In fact, his job was to make it as difficult as possible for me to pass the physical agility test, and he did a darn good job.

I had to run the mile, climb through one window and out another, walk a balance beam five feet off the ground, pull a 150-pound mannequin thirty yards and push a police car twenty feet, all in record time. And as the sergeant said before I began, "Look here, Little Lady, if you can't do all of these activities including pushing that police car over here until it touches my kneecaps, I'm

gonna have the pleasure of sending you home."
I completed each task, but every bone, muscle and fiber
of my body ached. I could hardly catch my breath. Some
of the recruits passed out and had to be carried off the
course. My vision was blurred, my heart beat a mile a
minute, and my ears hummed, but I didn't pass out. In
fact, I walked off the course on my own and felt pride
welling up inside. I had completed that obstacle course,
and I was going to be a deputy sheriff.

But the smirk on the sergeant's face told me I was
wrong. That's when I discovered yet another challenge
waiting for me. This time even I didn't know if I would be
able to make it. My head ached, my legs were as heavy as
lead, and my arms felt as if someone had yanked them
from their sockets.

The ultimate challenge? Climbing a six-foot, solid concrete wall. If somehow you were able to get through the
physical agility test, this would separate the boys from the
men—or girls from the women, as it were. Recruit after
recruit, both men and women, tackled the six-foot wall
only to fall to the ground in defeat. Most of them were
taller and bigger than me. I could feel my heart sink and
my confidence fade. I saw my career with the sheriff's
department slipping away.

Two more recruits, and then it would be my turn. I
closed my eyes and tried to envision myself going over
the wall. Suddenly, I remembered a song my grandmother
used to sing in church, an old Negro spiritual. *"I shall, I
shall, I shall not be moved."* My nerves calmed. I heard my
father's voice, *"You have to be twice as good and do twice as
much just to compete."* And I thought, *I have been twice as good
and I have done twice as much and I have given it my all and now
this. . . .*

And then I swear I heard the words of my high school
track coach. *"A lady's strength is in her legs, not in her arms."* I

had watched the women try to tackle the wall by jumping up like the men and grabbing hold of the wall with their arms in an attempt to pull themselves atop the wall, straddle it and drop to the other side. It hadn't worked for them, and I knew it wouldn't work for me. *I shall not be moved. Be twice as good and do twice as much. A lady's strength is in her legs.* It was my turn. The six-foot, solid concrete wall loomed bigger than life—the only thing standing between me and my dream. I closed my eyes and imagined it was a track field.

I took off running as fast as I could, and when my feet hit the concrete I looked up to the heavens. And I ran up that wall! *I shall not be moved. Twice as good. A lady's strength.* I straddled the top and dropped to the other side.

The whole camp was cheering—everyone, that is, except the sergeant. He never said a word. He turned his back and walked away. Several men made it over that day, but I was the *only* woman.

Since then, I have gone over a lot of walls, but I learned some valuable lessons at the academy that have helped me. What the Goliaths think is not nearly as important as what I think about myself. The Goliaths despise change and progress, but there are some things even they can't control.

Linda Coleman-Willis

On Becoming a Farmer

I may not be responsible for getting knocked down, but I am responsible for getting back up.

Jesse Jackson

I sat with dreaded anticipation and a feeling of impending doom. I was sitting two rows from the front in a crowded college amphitheater filled with more than one hundred pre-med science majors. We were all waiting for our chemistry professor to return the year's first exam.

I had started my freshman year in a Southern California university filled with anticipation. I had a full scholarship. I graduated valedictorian of a small black Christian school of seventy-four students and had all the earmarks for a bright future. However, after arriving on a campus where the student body was 96 percent white and 90 percent pre-med, I was filled with doubt. It quickly became evident that many of the other students' level of college preparation far exceeded mine.

The professor, Dr. Kraig,* wore black horn-rimmed glasses, was extremely sarcastic and spit when he talked. What made it even more dreadful was that he made comments loud enough for others to hear as he passed back the exams. I held my head down and began to sink lower into my seat as I watched his stack of exams grow smaller. I had done poorly, and I knew it.

Having been born and reared in Compton, California, I came from a family with a rich heritage but very little formal education. I had decided in the third grade that I wanted to become a doctor. Yet now that the time had come, I was afraid I wasn't smart enough and afraid I couldn't measure up. I was fearful that the reality of my goal was available to everyone but me. Many of my peers' parents were either doctors or professionals. My mother was the only college graduate in our family, and she had just graduated the year before.

I was snapped back to reality as Dr. Kraig stood looking down on me, waving his horn-rimmed glasses, smirking and spitting as he spoke. "If you think you are going to become a doctor, that is a joke! If you want to help people, you should become a farmer and grow food . . . you will never be a doctor!"

He then crumpled up my exam like a piece of trash and dropped it on my lap. I blinked back the tears as I opened it up and read scrawled across the top—36 percent. *Oh no! I knew I had done poorly—but this!* I wished I could evaporate and disappear into thin air. I was humiliated.

I held my head down during the remainder of the lecture, unable to listen or take notes. Every negative thought, every self-doubt that I'd ever had reared its ugly head. *Maybe Dr. Kraig was right; maybe I should just give up and change my major and*—but no.

---

*Name has been changed

While I did not have role models with higher degrees of formal education, I had a family who had taught me the value of integrity, perseverance and tenacity in the most difficult of situations. Though my father had little formal education, he was the smartest man I ever knew; he had a keen sense of wisdom and business foresight. He would always smile and say he had a Ph.D. from the school of hard knocks. Though he ran a junkyard and used-car lot, he wore a suit and tie to work every day of his life.

Sitting in that university amphitheater, I began to envision my father dressed in his suit, standing in the pouring rain with his feet sinking in the dirt and grease, attempting to get those old junk cars started. I began to hear my mother's typewriter clatter at 6:00 a.m. as I awakened for high school. She had been up all night finishing a paper toward the completion of her college degree. She would then head to work at my father's junkyard where she was the secretary. I began to hear my father saying, "Do not be shaken by what others say or think of you. Cover the ground you are standing on, and who you are and what you are will show up anyway."

I felt my life flow return as I unconsciously clenched my fist and dug my heels into the floor. I had always been taught by word and example that God is in control and that all things are possible through God's power.

I sat straighter in my seat, wiped away any remaining tears, gathered my books and waited for the amphitheater to clear. I quietly made my way to Dr. Kraig's office and stood outside his door praying for strength and courage.

I tapped on his door, walked in and began to speak from my heart: "Whether I become a doctor or not is immaterial. Your comments were demeaning, disrespectful and hurtful. Furthermore, one day I *will* come back and place my M.D. degree on your desk!"

With that, I turned around and marched out of his office. I went on to graduate with honors with a degree in biology and was accepted into five different medical schools. I also had the privilege of being elected class president and giving the baccalaureate address during my senior class graduation. I wish I could report that life was easy from that point, devoid of drama and trauma. The truth is that the journey through medical school and residency tested my core sense of self and survival at every level. At different times, I had to fight back the demons of doubt and negative voices that prompted feelings of inadequacy.

It has been through God's grace that I was able to complete a residency and a fellowship in child and adolescent psychiatry. I am board certified in two different areas of psychiatry. In my specialty, there are no more exams to be taken. I can say from personal experience that out of adversity come many blessings.

Fifteen years ago I received an alumni newsletter that reported Dr. Kraig had died of cancer. Pity—he died before I could share the valuable life lessons about the merit and value of belief and determination that began in his chemistry class.

"A farmer"? Perhaps. Today, I plant seeds of hope and courage in lives lost in barren fields, shrouded in darkness. By warmth and nurturing, I help these dormant seeds blossom and grow into hope-filled lives. Dr. Kraig, you will never know the impact your words had upon my life, but others have reaped the results. It takes rain as well as sun and good seed that is resistant against drought and disease, for prolific growth. Perhaps God sent you my way to propagate seed resistant to doubt and discouragement, to quicken dormant desires to help others. I am proud to fertilize and farm these fields.

Jenée Walker

Buffalo Soldiers

A Letter from Then-Chairman of the Joint Chiefs of Staff General Colin L. Powell to Senator Nancy Kassebaum

March 12, 1991

Dear Senator Kassebaum:

I am very grateful you invited me to provide a letter expressing my thoughts about the Buffalo Soldiers. I'm also thankful for your efforts on behalf of those soldiers and especially for introducing in the U.S. Senate the Joint Resolution to designate July 28, 1992, as "Buffalo Soldier Day."

When I was a brigadier general and assigned to Fort Leavenworth in 1982, I was jogging around the post one day and noticed a couple of gravel alleys that were named "Ninth and Tenth Cavalry Streets." I wondered if that were all there was to commemorate those great soldiers. I wondered if on one of America's most historic Army posts, a post where the Tenth Cavalry spent so much of its garrison life, a post in the center of the region where both the Ninth and Tenth Cavalry spent so much of their blood, I wondered if those gravel alleyways were all there was to signify their presence, all there was to commemorate their incredible contribution to the settlement of the American West. And so I looked around some more. And on the entire post all I could find to commemorate two of the greatest regiments in the Army were those two alleys. That was a situation that I believed had to be changed. So a few of us set in motion a project to honor the Buffalo Soldiers. You, Senator, now co-chair the committee that grew from that project. Your committee oversees the construction of a proper monument to those great soldiers—a monument not simply to honor Buffalo Soldiers: instead, to honor all black soldiers who have served this nation over its long history.

Since 1641 there has never been a time in this country when blacks were unwilling to serve and sacrifice for America. From pre-Revolutionary times through the Revolutionary War, through every one of our wars and on up to the present, black men and women have willingly served and died. But it is also a part of our history that for most of that time blacks served without recognition or reward for the contribution they made for our freedom—for the freedom they did not enjoy here in their own beloved native land. The Buffalo Soldiers are a symbol of one chapter in a proud and glorious history.

To remind me of that history I have a painting that hangs on a wall in my office directly across from my desk. From that painting, Colonel Benjamin H. Grierson, Tenth Cavalry Regimental Commander, Lieutenant Henry O. Flipper, the first black graduate of West Point, and a troop of Buffalo Soldiers constantly look at me. They remind me of my heritage and of the thousands of African Americans who went before me and who shed their blood and made their sacrifices so that I could be Chairman of the Joint Chiefs of Staff. They look at me and make sure that I will never forget the courage and the determination of African Americans who defied all odds to fight for their country, and who wore the uniform of the U.S. Army as proudly and as courageously as any other American who ever wore it.

The legacy of that pride and courage motivates every black soldier, sailor, airman, marine and Coast Guardsman taking part today in Operation Desert Storm, and every black man and woman who helps man the ramparts of freedom around the world from Japan to Panama to Germany. It's as if a full century had passed in the blink of an eye and Frederick Douglass's words were suddenly and vividly fulfilled, "Once let the black man get upon his person the brass letters, 'U.S.', let him get an eagle on his button, and a musket on his shoulder and bullets in his pocket, and there is no power on earth which can deny that he has earned the right to citizenship in the United States." Amen.

Joint Chiefs of Staff General Colin L. Powell

What Black History Means to Me

The first interpretation of African history is the responsibility of scholars of African descent.

John Henrik Clarke

What black history means to me:

We are the children and descendants of the great African empires of Mali, Songhay and Old Ghana.

We are Estevanico, an African who accompanied Spanish explorers through the Arizona and New Mexico territories in 1538.

We are the slave Phillis Wheatley, who in the 1770s wrote poetry that has been read throughout the world.

We are Jean Point du Sable, a Negro trader who founded and helped settle Chicago.

We are five thousand slaves and free blacks who served in the Continental Army and Navy between 1776 and 1781.

What black history means to me:

We are black abolitionists Frederick Douglass, Harriet

Tubman and Sojourner Truth, and rebel slaves Denmark Vesey, Gabriel Prosser and Nat Turner.

We are the black scout George W. Bush, who led white settlers into the Oregon Territory in 1844.

We are James Beckwourth and Nat Love and countless other black cowboys and Buffalo Soldiers who helped to pioneer and settle the Old West during the mid- and late 1800s.

We are the many countless and faceless blacks who served with distinction and honor for the Union Army during the Civil War.

What black history means to me:

We are Jan Matzelinger, who in 1883 invented the first machine that manufactured an entire shoe.

We are Dr. Daniel Hale Williams, who in 1893 was the first licensed physician to perform a successful open-heart operation.

We are John Arthur "Jack" Johnson, who pioneered the way for other blacks in modern sports by becoming the first black heavyweight-boxing champion of the world and holding that title from 1908 to 1915.

We are Mathew Henson, who accompanied Commander Robert E. Peary on his North Pole expedition in 1909.

What black history means to me:

We are the budding legends and giants of the Black Renaissance during the 1920s through the 1940s: James Weldon Johnson, Richard Wright, Paul Robeson, Louis Armstrong, Duke Ellington, Josephine Baker, Bessie Smith, Lena Horne, Bill "Bojangles" Robinson, Billie Holiday, Ella Fitzgerald, Mahalia Jackson, Marian Anderson and Hattie McDaniels, among others.

We are Carter G. Woodson, organizer of the first black

historical association and journal, and founder of Black History Week.

What black history means to me:
We are Mary McLeod Bethune, cofounder of Bethune-Cookman College, and a prominent advisor to President Franklin D. Roosevelt.
We are Army Brigadier General Benjamin O. Davis Sr., who became the first black person to attain that rank in 1940.
We are Dr. Charles Drew who in 1941 developed and laid the early groundwork for the blood transfusion process and the plasma blood bank.
We are Dorie Miller, Negro American hero of World War II, who shot down four Japanese planes at Pearl Harbor in 1941.

What black history means to me:
We are Ralph Bunche, first black to be awarded a doctorate in political science at Harvard University, and winner of the Nobel Peace Prize as a member of the U.S. delegation to the United Nations in 1950.
We are some of the black legends and superstars of the modern sports world: Jackie Robinson, Willie Mays, Hank Aaron, Sugar Ray Robinson, Joe Louis, Muhammad Ali, Jim Brown, Rafer Johnson, Bob Hayes, Wilma Rudolph, Bill Russell, Wilt Chamberlain, Oscar Robertson, Charles Sifford, Althea Gibson and Arthur Ashe, among others.

What black history means to me:
We are the black students of North Carolina A&T College, who introduced the revolutionary civil rights "sit-in" technique at W. T. Grant's and F. W. Woolworth's Department Stores in Greensboro, North Carolina, in 1960.
We are Edward Brooke, Massachusetts senator, elected

in 1966, and the first black person since Reconstruction to be elected to the U.S. Senate.

We are Robert Weaver, who became the first black Cabinet chief in 1966, when appointed the secretary of Housing and Urban Development.

What black history means to me:
We are Thurgood Marshall, former solicitor general of the United States, and in 1967 the first black to sit on the U.S. Supreme Court.

We are Shirley Chisholm, U.S. representative from Brooklyn, New York, the first black to formally run for president of the United States in 1972.

We are Lieutenant Colonel Guion S. Bluford Jr., USAF, American astronaut, the first black to fly into space, as a member of the space shuttle Challenger in 1983.

What black history means to me:
We are Booker T. Washington, W. E. B. DuBois, Marcus Garvey, Malcolm X, Martin Luther King Jr., Whitney Young Jr., Roy Wilkins, and other names forever enshrined in memory and history.

We are our ancestors and forefathers of times past; we are our men, women and children of today; we are our hopes and dreams for tomorrow.

We are a vehicle of heritage, culture and pride on a journey of love, understanding and acceptance. Yes, we are a beautiful and noble people. We are somebody special.

This is what black history means to me.

John Horton

2

CELEBRATING FAMILY

A river can't rise beyond its source. What's in the seed determines the fruit.

T. M. Alexander

Remembering Eric

You cannot do a kindness too soon, for you never know how soon it will be too late.

Ralph Waldo Emerson

I'm sure he never expected to see me there. He froze right in his tracks. His big green eyes looked like they might pop out of his head!

There he was—my eleven-year-old son Eric, standing among the crowd of children entering the cafeteria at his school. It was lunchtime. From a distance, I waved. I summoned him out of the lunch line, shaking the familiar fastfood bag I held in my hand. As he eagerly ran toward me with a huge grin on his face, I knew this would be a special time for us. As it turns out, it was one of the most rewarding experiences I remember with my son.

It was a Wednesday morning and probably one of the most hectic days in my office. The telephone was ringing off the hook; there were numerous reports due at the end of the day, and an important meeting to prepare for that afternoon. I had not yet had my first cup of coffee. As I reached into my pocket, searching for my favorite mint, I found a pink paper with a list of things I intended to buy at the grocery store during my lunch hour. There were several more items to add.

I turned it over and discovered it was actually a flyer inviting parents to come to the school and have lunch with their child. How could something like this have slipped my mind? I guess I hadn't paid much attention to the flyer because my son wasn't fond of things like that.

But for some reason, I couldn't seem to get that invitation off of my mind. Eric was a fifth-grader and would be graduating and going to middle school the next year. This would probably be my last opportunity to have lunch with my son. I checked my watch. There was time. I could still make it. Forty-five minutes before the scheduled lunch, I shut down my computer, locked the file cabinets and dashed out to fetch Eric's favorite double cheeseburger and fries.

The shock on Eric's face mirrored my own. This was not the same child I had sent to school that morning. The son I dropped off wore clean, starched, navy blue slacks and a spotless, button-up white cotton dress shirt. The child before me sported a white mesh football jersey (with no shirt underneath), navy blue fleece shorts (three sizes too big), and a very nice and rather large gold hoop earring. Around his neck was a fancy gold chain with the initial "A" dangling from it. (I only hoped that it was for the grades he intended to earn.) As it turned out, the necklace belonged to a little girl named Ashanti.

As we both recovered, we slowly made our way to the lunch benches to begin our midday meal. Prior to arriving, I feared he would be too embarrassed to have lunch with his mother. After all, it had only been three years earlier when he had adamantly refused to take a picture with me at school in front of his buddies. I prepared myself. I knew he wouldn't be rude to me, but I thought he might eat as quickly and quietly as possible, and then run off to play with his friends.

But Eric began to tell me what he did in class that day. He told me a story he had read in his social studies book and described in detail a film he watched about Indians. Funny, he didn't tell me how or when he had changed his clothes. I was enjoying his company so much that I chose not to bring it up.

As he talked, he became the little boy who always drew a picture in preschool to show me. He was the small child who wanted me to kneel at his bedside at night and pray with him. He was my young son yelling in triumph while I clapped my hands as he rode down the street for the first time on his two-wheeler.

As he spoke, ketchup ran down the side of his mouth and proceeded to drip onto his white mesh football jersey. He seemed to neither notice nor care. Young girls passed slowly, at first trying to get his attention, and then to whisper and giggle as they watched him talk at full speed, so unlike the cool jock they all adored.

Although I hated for the lunch to end, we began to gather our trash. He would go back to the playground to finish recess with his classmates. I would go back to my office, this time in much better spirits. Eric actually wanted me there. My son was enjoying my company as much as I was enjoying his. He began a joke but fell out laughing hysterically before he could finish it. His laughter was so contagious I, too, doubled over with giggles, and we laughed so long and so hard I thought we would both lose our lunch.

It really didn't matter whether or not he finished the joke or even if it was funny. All that mattered was that for twenty minutes, on a Wednesday afternoon, we tuned out the entire world, my son and I, and no one else existed but us. We had made magic memories on the elementary school lunch benches with a $2.99 burger special.

Two weeks after our luncheon together, the child I had prayed for, loved, treasured and adored died during the night, without warning, suddenly and silently of a massive seizure.

There are no more funny stories. There are no more opportunities for me to hug him tightly and kiss his forehead. There will be no new photographs.

Even as I watch his friends grow up, he will always remain that eleven-year-old boy. I still talk to him. I think of him constantly. I miss him terribly. His memory is so precious to me. We shared many things in the short time we had together. But I'll always be thankful I took the time for that schoolyard lunch we shared; it was one of the most rewarding experiences in my life.

Tracy Clausell-Alexander

My Father's Son

The measure of a man is how well he provides for his children.

Sidney Poitier

It was one of those excruciatingly cold New England mornings in 1964. A four-day-old snow had turned to ice as it pressed against my bedroom window. In my twelve-year-old sleepiness, I staggered through the dark hallway into the bathroom, hearing the truck's engine idling audibly outside.

Peering out, I saw his figure—a dark shadow moving against the white background, his breath clouding the air when he exhaled. I heard his work boots crunching the hard snow with his giant steps. I saw his dark face hidden beneath a knit cap, the upturned coat collar, the woolen scarf wrapped around his neck and chin. One gloved hand guided the ice scraper across the truck's windshield; the other brushed the shavings like a crystal beard from the truck's old weathered face.

Daddy. Moving with a quick purpose, driven by a

commitment and a responsibility taught him thirty-five years earlier in Depression-era Georgia. Daddy. A silent gladiator who was stepping once more into the hostile arena of the day's battle. Daddy. Awake while the rest of the world slept. And as he slid behind the steering wheel, driving carefully from the driveway onto the street, the truck was swallowed up by dawn's dimness. As I returned to the warmth of my blankets—in my own bed, in my own room—I knew I could go back to sleep, to dream, because Daddy was outside facing the cold.

Throughout the many junior- and senior-high mornings I watched my father go to work, I never told him how that vision affected me. I simply wondered at his ability to do what he did: keeping the kitchen filled with food, making the payments on my music lessons, covering the car insurance so I could drive during my senior year, piling the Christmas gifts beneath the tree, taking me to Boston to buy new clothes, dragging me to church on Sundays, driving me to visit college campuses on his day off, kissing and teasing my mother in the living room, and nodding off in his easy chair in the middle of a sentence. Perhaps it was because these scenes seemed so ordinary that I never spoke of them, never weighed them beyond my own selfish adolescent needs.

And then at college, away from him—when his presence became merely the voice over the phone during weekend calls or the name scribbled at the bottom of the weekly letter stuffed with a ten-dollar bill—I thought other men were more significant than Daddy. Those men who taught my classes in polysyllabic words, wrote articles in journals and explained complex theorems and philosophies. Daddy never did any of that—he couldn't with only a high school education. My hero worship made me a disciple to Ivy League scholars who ignited my dormant ideas and dead men whose names were printed on book covers, buildings and the currency I hungered to possess.

Then, as I traveled to Europe in my later college years, I realized I had seen more, had traveled farther and had achieved greater distinctions than Daddy ever had. I was filled with a sense of self-importance, puffed up with grad-school grants, deluded with degrees and accolades assigned to my name.

Then, I entered the formidable arena—the job, the relationships, the creditors, the pressures and the indignities of racial politics. As I reached my late twenties, I looked forward to returning home, talking with Daddy, sharing a ball game, watching an old Western on television, drinking a beer, listening to a story about his childhood days in Georgia and hearing his warm, fulfilling laughter. I rediscovered Daddy again—not as a boy in awe, but with respect as a man. And I realized a truth that I could not articulate as a child—Daddy was always there for me. Unlike the professors, the books, the celebrity heroes, the mentors, he was always there. He was my father, a man who committed himself to a thankless job in a society that had written him off with statistics and stereotypes.

When I reached my early thirties, when I became a father myself, I saw my own father with greater clarity. As I awoke in the early morning hours, compromised my wants, dealt with insults and worked overtime in order to give my son his own room—with his own bed and his own dreams—I realized I was able to do those things because my father had done them for me.

And now, at age forty-seven, when I spend precious moments with my own thirteen-year-old son, when we spend fleeting moments together at a movie, on a basketball court, in church or on the highway, I wonder what he thinks of me. At what point will I slip away from his world of important men, and will there be a point when he'll return to me with a nod of understanding? How will he measure my weaknesses and strengths, my flaws and distinctions, my nightmares and dreams? Will he claim me in the name of love and respect?

Sometimes the simple lessons are the most difficult to teach. Sometimes the most essential truths are the most difficult to learn. I hope my son will one day cherish all the lessons and truths that have flowed to him, through me, from his grandfather. And as my son grows older, I believe that he, too, will measure his steps by the strides I have made for him, just as I have achieved my goals because of the strides my father has made for me. When my son does this, perhaps he will feel the same pride and fulfillment that I do when I say, "I am my father's son."

Mel Donalson

Denied the Prize

Excellence is the best deterrent to racism.

Jesse Jackson

In the mid-seventies, a door of opportunity opened to those who had been asking for years to be let in. It didn't open for the asking; it opened because it was torn down by a mighty hand. For those of us who walked through there was no welcome mat outside nor a cordial welcome from inside. We became professional firefighters, and we had to prove ourselves, just as all new firefighters, but we had an extra mile to go—up a steeper hill, with a heavier load. The heavier load made us stronger.

At the time of my hire, I was father to a seven-year-old son and four-year-old daughter. In my third year I became father to my little buddy, Enson. By then the men and I had forged a professional respect for one another. I'd say friendship, of a sort. We just understood we wouldn't be buddies off the job.

My regular inner-city duty was Engine House Eighteen. It became necessary at times to send a firefighter to another station in our battalion to balance the manpower. Often it was Station Seven. This was one such day.

At about 2:00 A.M., we were returning from the local campus where we extinguished several Dumpsters that maladjusted college students had lit on fire for kicks. It was summer—warm with a light breeze. Head down and bobbing around, I anticipated finding my way back to my bunk. Instead, I heard the siren come on and the adrenaline rush caused me to snap to. The emergency lights spun, and we accelerated toward downtown.

The lieutenant slid the window back, "Prepare yourself. We've just been dispatched to an apartment fire in a high-rise downtown."

I began the exercise of breathing control as my heart raced and I pulled the straps on my air tank harness snug.

As the building came into view I could make out black smoke escaping from second-story windows. Normally, we were the second or third engine company on the scene downtown, but since we were already on the street we were going to be first. It was a classic fire with people pouring out of the building and calling with sobbing voices for loved ones.

A frantic man stormed us with an anguished plea, "Please hurry! My daughter is up there in the apartment that's on fire. Please . . . please get her out!"

The lieutenant radioed the situation to the command center, the driver put the pumper in operation, all eyes were on me because rescue was my job. With no time for thought or fear I entered the building against the current of people.

As I reached the second floor landing, I noticed a few tenants attempting entry into the apartment. They managed to knock one of the panels of the door out, which gave a view of the fire inside and provided an air source for the fire to breathe.

I hollered a choking command, "Get me that hose line up here now!"

It was already being hoisted. The flames were leaping through the hole with vengeance. Grabbing the line, I cracked the nozzle open and shoved it into the opening, knocking down the flames in the immediate area. Shouldering the door with a heave, I forced it open just enough to make entry.

I donned my mask and began systematically searching room to room. Ten years of experience had given me a sketchy mental picture of what my surroundings might look like. The practiced feel of furniture through my thick gloves added to my vision. I was going to have to remember in reverse every move I made, so I could get out, *when* I found the victim. There's no *if* because I wasn't leaving without her.

I heard moaning. I followed the sound to my left and felt a bedpost. There I found a young woman on the floor against the wall. She was stressed, full of fear and no doubt burned, but she was alive. I scooped her up as quickly and gently as possible.

"I'm gonna get you out of here," I told her.

Going through the front room, I passed other firefighters who had arrived and were now extinguishing the fire.

"Victim, victim!" I yelled to alert them.

Not wanting to risk a slip and fall on the stairs I handed the young woman to a medic who was on the landing.

I was about to go back in when another firefighter beckoned. "Come on down. You've done your job. We'll take care of the rest."

Once outside, I tugged away the face-piece to drink in a splendid stream of refreshing night air. "Nice job," a few of my brother firefighters slapped my shoulder. The lieutenant, a cigar in his hand, acknowledged me with just a nod.

A father had his daughter back alive. I didn't see him,

but it's my guess that he spoke a volume of appreciation to the chief. I'm told the chief entered the building and began asking the firefighters who made the forced entry, who had knocked down the fire and effected the rescue.

"It was Newman, sir. He did it all."

I was getting a drink of water when the chief approached. "Newman, fine job; we're all proud of what you've done here. You can expect a medal citation."

"Thank you, sir!"

My next duty day I was back at Station Eighteen. The guys had all heard about what had taken place, and I was collecting more slaps on the back.

"We heard you did us proud at Sevens. Way to go. Word is you'll be getting a medal for that."

I couldn't help but think, *Hmmm, a medal would be nice for my family, but it wouldn't lift me any higher than I was feeling after having been able to save a life and soothe a father's agonizing soul.* Any firefighter who receives such recognition shares it with all firefighters, and it would bode well for the black firefighters who were being passed over for these awards while whites were getting them for lesser accomplishments. *Yes, a medal would be nice.*

The problem was the lieutenant didn't believe in medals for firefighters, especially the Johnny-come-latelys. "Firefighters are sworn to do their duty and they get paid. That's enough." Cigar smoke carried the words from his gruff voice to the ceiling.

The captain, my supervising officer, spoke to the lieutenant and told me.

"Well, fellas, I spoke with the lieutenant. I even offered to do the write-up for him, so all he'd have to do is sign it, but he wouldn't budge. Newman, you deserve it, but there's nothing more I can do."

An extra mile . . . up a steeper hill . . . carrying a heavier load. Lord, give me strength!

It is good to appreciate the inherent rewards of doing a job to the best of your ability. All else is icing on the cake. I remember the variety of faces that said, "Fine job." There is some sweet to the bitter. I retired in 1999 with twenty-five years' service credit. I have a good measure of health and a grandson.

In March 2002, my little buddy Enson turned twenty-one. He came to me and told me, "Dad, I've been thinking, and I've decided I want to become a firefighter. I'm going to take the civil service exam next go-round."

Up until then I had only considered what I was protecting. I hadn't even considered that I'd been an example for a little boy.

Life surely has its rewards, if not its awards. In that moment God Himself pinned on my Medal of Honor.

Herchel E. Newman

In Sickness and in Health

It's not the load that breaks you down. It's the way you carry it.

Lena Horne

When Herman and I took our wedding vows over fifteen years ago, we were committed to our relationship. We became best friends, sharing everything, holding hands, laughing at our mistakes and failures, as well as our triumphs and successes. We liked to go on mini-vacations and often would get away for rest and relaxation. Our honeymoon never ended.

Yet little did we know how much our love for each other would be tested through those five little words we proclaimed in our vows, "In sickness and in health."

It was January 1990. Herman had just come from a routine visit to his doctor—a trip he had taken for over two decades since his kidney transplant in 1967.

Herman was only seventeen years old when his father unselfishly gave his son the gift of life: one of his kidneys. At the time, Herman was well known on the Centennial

High School campus in Compton, California, where he excelled in sports. Baseball was his life, but the transplant ended his dreams of professional success. Even during those trying times, Herman kept his smile.

But on that day in 1990, Herman—whose broad smile and heartfelt laughter always bred celebration—showed terror, hurt and despair, mirroring the feelings in my heart. Without warning, the transplanted kidney had stopped functioning.

Herman began dialysis treatments two months later. A machine substituted for his kidney by purifying his blood three days a week, three to four hours at a time. His smooth muscular arms soon knotted with bulges from the constant needle pricks. His exhausted veins collapsed.

No more unplanned vacations; the dialysis treatments came first. Often passionate lovemaking became cuddling each other to sleep. We found solace in our love and made laughter the key to our survival.

And we prayed for another kidney.

Eleven years later, an unexpected phone call from UCLA Medical Center answered those prayers: "We have a donor."

Together, we rejoiced and offered more prayers, this time in thanksgiving. But, would it be a match? We waited to hear . . . one hour, two hours, then three. The phone rang again, this time with disappointing news.

Oh, well, we consoled ourselves, *we've waited this long. Surely we can keep waiting.*

One week to the day later, we received another call. It was a perfect match! We anxiously rushed down to UCLA. As we drove, we reflected on all the years of dialysis and how we had prayed for this miracle, and then we cried— happy tears and tears of sorrow. For the other side of our joy was the reality that someone had lost their life to give Herman this opportunity to live.

It was a nineteen-year-old man who had died of head trauma. He had only been eight years old when Herman's kidney failed. For eleven years we prayed for a perfect match. For that same eleven years this young man had grown up, graduated from elementary, junior high and high school. He was probably in college. It never occurred to us that someone so young would give life to a fifty-one-year-old man. We never thought that the answer to our prayers would be the devastation of someone else's. How unselfish of his family. Now, instead of praying for a kidney, we pray for this young man's family.

Throughout the process, I remained at Herman's side. I learned every medication and followed the prescribed routine for his recovery. Everything else in my life faded. His care was my primary concern.

While he was in the hospital, one nurse remarked on my commitment to my husband. "You have no idea how many people separate and divorce because of the strain on the relationship when dealing with dialysis and transplants," she told me.

Leave my husband during a time of sickness? Never. I was committed to our vows. More importantly, I could never leave the love of my life!

It's been a year since the surgery, and Herman is doing well. His body is still recovering, but he is the same happy and joyful person he was when we met. And now we both truly understand that life is precious. We travel again, and we still hold hands and take long walks. We laugh a lot, even when Herman's recovering body is not up to making love. Our marriage has been sustained by our commitment to love and to cherish each other in sickness and in health.

Dorothy C. Randle

The Letter

To send a letter is a good way to go somewhere without moving anything but your heart.

Phyllis Theroux

I sat at my dining-room table, signing my name to the most difficult letter I'd ever penned. The letter was to my son Luke's birth mom. This was not the first time I had reached out to the woman whose name I didn't know. I'd sent several letters over the years with photos of Luke, which the adoption agency had agreed to forward, but had never received a single reply. I didn't know if Luke's birth mom had even received my letters.

Please read this letter, I prayed as I folded the paper and slipped it into its envelope. Luke's life may depend on it.

With four teenagers of our own, my husband Mark and I still felt we had more love to give. And so we adopted Luke, now six.

When Luke was one year old the pediatrician ran a routine blood test: "Your son has sickle-cell disease," the doctor grimly informed us.

"People die from that!" I gasped.

A gene inherited from both of his birth parents had caused Luke to be born with defective red blood cells, the doctor explained.

"As he grows older Luke will probably suffer anemia and extremely painful swelling in his joints," the doctor said. "But we can give Luke monthly transfusions of healthy blood to help keep up his strength."

I thanked God for every healthy day Luke enjoyed. But when Luke was three, he caught a cold and was having trouble breathing. We admitted Luke to the hospital immediately for IV antibiotics.

Luke had acute chest syndrome. Large clumps of sickle-shaped red blood cells were clogging the vessels in his lungs. The blockage was preventing Luke's blood from getting enough oxygen. This caused further sickling, which led to even more blockage in a vicious cycle that was spiraling dangerously out of control.

I held Luke's tiny hand while a heart-lung bypass machine struggled to raise his blood-oxygen levels.

Finally, Luke began to rally.

"Luke has been through quite an ordeal, but he is feeling much better now," I wrote to my son's birth mom, who, I had learned from the adoption agency, was a single mother of three with little money, struggling to finish her education.

After his crisis Luke's doctor increased his transfusions from monthly to every third week, but this only forestalled the inevitable. Soon Luke was back in the hospital, fighting once again for his life.

Luke recovered from the second crisis, but I knew it was only a matter of time before my son succumbed to his illness. "Isn't there anything more we can do?" I begged the doctors.

Then Luke's hematologist related some exciting news.

"There's a chance Luke's sickle-cell disease could be cured with a bone-marrow transplant," he told us. "The new marrow would produce healthy blood cells that wouldn't carry the sickle-cell disease."

My heart soared, but it landed with a thud when the doctor inquired, "Do you know if Luke has any siblings?" To perform a transplant, they would have to locate a matching donor. "A blood brother or sister would offer the best hope for a successful antigen match," the doctor explained.

I anguished over what to do. "Do I even have the right to ask Luke's birth mother for help?" I asked an adoption agency counselor.

"Luke is your child. You have a right to do whatever it takes to save his life," the counselor replied without hesitation.

And so I penned a letter describing the situation to Luke's birth mom. "Would you consider having your other children tested as possible marrow donors?" I wrote. I dropped the letter into the mailbox and then waited and prayed.

Two weeks later the hematologist called. "Luke's birth mom had her children tested, and I just got the results from her doctor," he said, excited. "One of them is a 100 percent match, and he can't wait to become his brother's marrow donor."

"She brought him into this world, and now he'll have a second chance to live a long and happy life," I told Mark.

The cutting-edge transplant was performed at the University of Michigan Medical Center in Ann Arbor. Luke received eight days of strong chemotherapy to kill off his diseased bone marrow. Meanwhile, many hundreds of miles away, one of Luke's older brothers visited a local hospital where doctors extracted a few ounces of his healthy bone marrow. The precious cargo was rushed to

Michigan, where the doctor used a simple IV line to infuse the life-giving marrow cells into Luke's bloodstream. Within weeks, tests revealed that Luke's new bone marrow was taking hold and already producing healthy red blood cells. Two weeks later Luke was ready to go home, his sickle-cell disease gone forever.

In a letter I shared the happy news with Luke's birth mom, who this time wrote back:

"I've written many letters but never had the courage to mail them. Many times I've felt like I did the wrong thing, but now I know it was right. I never could have given Luke the medical attention he needed. Now I know he's right where God needed him to be. Luke has two families who love him. He's a very lucky little boy."

I think I'm the lucky one. I get to watch Luke grow up healthy and strong.

Julane DeBoer
As told to Bill Holton

We of One Blood

I savor the memory of that last good day. Can still hear the slapping sounds of red-back Tally Ho's as they slid across the Formica tabletop in a blizzard of colorful quadrilaterals. Can feel the energy radiating from his eyes as he studied his hand with analytical intensity. And then I saw it. The telltale tucking of his bottom lip, snagged between his teeth in anticipation. Man. He had our butts. It was all over but the shouting.

"Seven," he said. "No trump."

He was a Whistologist, of that there was no doubt, but today he was going for broke, playing with a particular fury, risking all wrath and coming *this close* to going out the dreaded back door. Bidding high and taking his partner out, letting skill and genius rule. He would lead with the big joker today. Today, he would play to win. Play like it was the last game of his life.

He was feeling much better, he said on that last good day. After spending torturous days glued to the bed, soaking his pajamas, soiling his sheets, and retching up his future, he felt like being in the kitchen where all the action was. He wanted to play cards. After all, The Bid was in our blood. Spades was for scrubs, and he was a big dog who never even looked at the porch.

As his eyes scanned the cards, greedily counting books, wagering set-cards, calculating which suits to keep and which to toss back into the kitty, I examined his faded youth. Deep lines creased his brows where mischievous vigor had once dwelled. His flesh hung limply about his cheeks, listless and sagging, its plumpness now all gone. Never one who would pass a paper bag test, his caramel skin had darkened to mocha. And his hair. What could I say? In the beginning, before we'd known, we'd marveled that our kinky-haired brother had suddenly sprouted the baby-fine tresses gently framing his deepening cowlicks. Junior! Boy, how'd your hair get so good? And then we rationalized. Good hair runs on our grandmother's side, doesn't it?

What disturbed me most on that last good day, though, were his eyes. Luminous beacons in the sunken recesses of his skull, they had never been more lively, more determined. More accepting, more at peace. More beautiful.

Roaming the surface of the cards, they'd shone with something that had been sorely missing in our lives during the past year. Something the monster that was AIDS had stolen from us. Something the ever-haunting specter of death had kept us from sharing as we counted down the days and kept a watchful vigil over our cherished, only boy-child. And as he raised his eyes in triumph, filled with confidence that the power he held in his hand would shut my partner and me out and take him and his straight to Boston, the thing I saw shining in my big brother's eyes, reaching out to touch me and bring comfort to my heart, was given a name.

And its name was hope.

We were both due to leave Brooklyn in two days' time. Me back to Virginia to deploy further south with my military unit, him back to the city and his rented room on Riverside Drive.

"There's something I think you should know," he'd told me a few days earlier, his voice quiet and devoid of its usual humor. This cat never tiptoed anywhere. After all, he was who he was: simple, sweet, unassuming, honest, black and gay. He plunged straight to the bottom line with a single sentence. "There was this guy."

Whoaa! Not gonna get deep on me, are you?

"I think he might have been married," he continued, the words falling from his lips straight, no chaser. "He always denied it, so when I found out I was positive I told him to get tested, but he wouldn't." He sighed, and for the first time I saw sorrow and remorse creep into his eyes and nearly defeat him. "I don't know what happened to him. He disappeared. I did everything I knew to contact him. . . . I just thought I should tell somebody about this."

I know we're tight and all, but like, isn't this just waaay too much information?

He repeated. "I just thought somebody should know."

And it was clear that that somebody was me. He knew my love was strong enough to bear the weight of his guilt. Knew I'd love him regardless. Knew I'd respect him. Regardless.

"I understand," I answered, and swallowed my share of his pain. Why should he carry that burden by his lonesome? Why should he drag it with him to his grave? I was his sister, and we were bonded. We were of one blood, and nothing he shared with me could have ever changed that. Besides, he was an innocent victim too, refusing to blame or even name his executioner.

But he told everybody about his condition. Embarrassed me to no end at times, but there was absolutely no shame in his game. It was shame, he said, that kept black folks from getting education and treatment. From learning how to protect themselves. Kept them in a state of blissful ignorance, which further perpetuated the problem and gave the disease the upper hand. No, he wanted folks to *know* what it was that had landed him in that wheelchair. To know exactly what it was that had thinned his hair and loosened his teeth. To know what had stripped the flesh from his bones and produced that sickening stench of decay that seemed to slough off with his dying skin. He wanted the world to know the proper name of the beast that had left him wearing diapers at the age of thirty-four, and would, in three weeks time, send him to a lonely, early grave.

"I've got AIDS, you know," he'd tell family and friends alike, spreading his arms to allow them a good look at the once-muscular, athletic body that was now nothing but bone and large puddles of skin beneath his clothing. Then he'd wait a moment or two for his declaration to sink in, calmly accepting first the blank stare, then the silent judgment and the subtle shifting of the feet into backward gear, as though his very words were contagious. He'd call out loudly, often at retreating backs, "If you're not careful, you can get it too! Protect yourself, you hear? We know how this thing is spread now. No reason for you to end up the same way as me."

I was called home again in early May.

"He's asking for you," my sister Michelle said, surprising me with a telephone call to North Carolina where my military unit had deployed to an Army airfield. "He opened his eyes and said, 'Get Tracy.'"

I was off that base on the first thing smoking.

At his bedside, I smiled. Yes, he was emaciated and struggling for his life, but he was my brother and I was happy to be in his presence. Even if he didn't know I was there. My parents looked lost, helpless. After a lifetime of looking to them as my source of stability and solidity, it was frightening to see them so withered by pain. So beat down by this haunting thing called death.

In the bed, Bland struggled. I approached him and kissed his forehead. He opened his eyes and wiggled his eyebrows, our special signal that he was aware of my presence. We stood around his bed and formed a barrier with our love, touching his arms, rubbing his legs and feet, and hoping the power of our family bond was strong enough to keep death at bay, somehow make it all better. You see, he was the only one we had. Our only boy. And that he chose an alternative lifestyle was unimportant to us. We wanted to keep him. We'd deal with our biases and prejudices later. Right now, we wanted our boy-child. Our brother. Our son.

I wanted to stay with him. To be with him throughout the night just in case he met up with something he couldn't handle alone. To let him know I had his back.

They took me home.

The call came in the predawn hours. He'd slipped away in much the same way he'd come into this world, gently and during the night. I cried mightily for him. For what AIDS had stolen from us, from him. I cried for all he would never be, all he would never do, and I cried some selfish tears as well. Tears for my children and my nieces and nephews who would grow up without knowing the love, the humor and the beauty of their uncle. "Don't let them forget me," he'd begged. I cried so that I would remember.

It hit me at the funeral home in Brooklyn. His name was spelled out in neat, white block letters on a large black felt board, BLAND JENTRY CARR, JR, so it must be true. I stared down into the casket and tried my best to understand. What did this shell lying before me have to do with my beautiful, vibrant brother?

But I still felt a link. A bond that death had not been able to sever. Did death know my brother played a mean game of Bid Whist? That he had been a champion chess player? That he'd played and won tournaments all over New York City? Did death care that my brother had been blessed with the gift of prose? A prolific poet who kept journals filled to the brim, and who wrote because it was as natural to him as breathing. You see, it was difficult for me to concede victory to death, because I still felt so *bonded*. Hah! I laughed right in death's face. You didn't get all of him! We cheated you after all. You've done nothing by taking his body. The part of him that really matters lives right here in my heart.

We'd removed Bland's personal belongings from his rented room several days earlier. There wasn't much in the way of material things to leave his mark on the world, to say he'd even come this way. A few items of clothing, countless books and leather-bound journals, two marble chess sets, boxes of letters I'd sent from far corners of the world.

Walking past his coffin, I pulled a folded square of paper from my pocket and faced a room filled with kinfolks and friends and read from a page in my brother's journal:

Sister
Close to me as my own
heartbeat
We wordlessly say
I know your feelings
You know mine
Of one mind, We
Of one blood, Us
I love you
Sister

And as I stood in that crowded room with wails flying from my mouth, gazing into the finality of my brother's face and feeling his blood running through my veins, I had but one thought.

Brother, did you get enough love?

Tracy Price-Thompson

My Sister, Myself

Afro-American history cannot be honestly taught without some reference to its African background and the black American search for the meaning of that background and its relevance to their present-day lives.

W. E. B. DuBois

The first time I visit his bungalow at the University of Nigeria, I perch on a vinyl settee in the parlor and drink milky tea while my father rambles on about the student riots, the military government's Structural Adjustment Program, his college years with my mother, what he recalls her saying about her family's farm in Washington State—never a pause for me or anyone else to speak.

Meanwhile my stepmother, another stranger, flits about the room, dipping forward with black-market sugar and tins of Danish biscuits, slipping coasters under our cups the instant we lift to sip. From the darkened hallway come giggles and the slap of flip-flops.

"You have children?" I ask politely, as if this were a

question for a daughter to ask her father, as if it were not the question I traveled halfway around the globe to ask.

When I was not quite two, my father, a graduate student from Nigeria, returned home, leaving clothes and books scattered across the floor of his rented room. He was to attend to family business, scout out job prospects and come back. Though my parents had split, and my mother was raising me alone in Seattle, she maintained relations with my father for my sake.

"I want you to know that this is not a good-bye," he wrote to us from a ship in the middle of the Atlantic, nervous about reports of ethnic and religious tensions awaiting him. "I shall look forward to our meeting so long as we are all alive." My mother never saw him again.

Now, more than two decades later, my stepmother nods at my question, glances at my father. She is light-skinned and solicitous, with a wide nose and a voice like the breeze of the fans she angles at me.

"Yes, yes, there are children." My father waves his hands. "You'll meet them later." He is short like me, his weathered skin dark as plums. A strip of wiry black hair encircles the back of his head. There's a space in his mouth where a tooth should be. I don't see the broad-shouldered rugby player who stared out from my wall all those years. The only feature I recognize is that round nose.

A blur flashes tan and red in the hallway. I glance up to see a velvety-brown girl in a scarlet school uniform receding into the dimness, familiar eyes stunned wide in a face I could swear is mine.

It's not possible, I tell myself. Even if the girl in the hall is my sister, we have different mothers of different races. *How can we look so alike?* For twenty-six years I have been an only child, the only black member of our family, our town.

My father explains that during Christmas we'll travel to our ancestral village, where I will be formally presented to the extended family and clan elders. I do not mention that for me Christmas has always been white.

After my mother moved from Seattle to my grandparents' farm, I grew up hearing Finnish spoken, with a wreath of candles in my curls on St. Lucia Day. Mummi, my Finnish grandmother, and I spent all December at the kitchen table cutting out *nissu,* cookies in the shape of pigs, and six-pointed stars from the almond-scented dough. Before baking, we painted them with tiny brushes, like the ones Mummi used for tinting family photographs. Sheet after sheet of cookies emerged transformed from the oven, the egg paint set in a deep satiny glaze.

Old Pappa, my Swedish grandfather, and I built snow lanterns in the yard for the *tonttu,* farm sprites, and I imagined that we were conductors on the Underground Railroad, lighting the way for runaway slaves.

I spent my childhood at the window waiting for Anansi the Spider and Loki the Half-Giant, tricksters from my African folktales and Norse legends, to come scuttling over the purple mountains that ringed the farm. They would say, "Welcome, sister!" in a special language that only we understood. But no one ever came. No one has ever looked like me. Until now.

In true African fashion, my new parents and I move slowly, circuitously, as if conversation were a tribal praise song with instrumental flourishes and digressive harmonies. Eventually my father calls, "Emekachukwu, Okechukwu, Adanna! Come and greet your sister!"

Even before the words leave his mouth, the three are quivering in the center of the parlor. Grins split their faces. The eldest boy, Emekachukwu, is already languid with teenage charisma. Behind him stoops a lanky boy with yellow skin and glittering, feverish eyes: Okechukwu. Pressed close to his side is twelve-year-old Adanna. She is me, fourteen years ago.

"Okay," our father says, the Igbo chieftain making clan policy, "this is your older sister from America. She's come to visit. You love her." With one sentence, I go from being the sole daughter, niece, grandchild to being the eldest of four, the one with the responsibility for love. Adanna reaches me first. She is exquisite—luminous skin the color of Dutch cocoa; heart-shaped face with high, rounded cheekbones, slimmer than mine; a mouth that flowers above a delicate pointed chin. We come face-to-face, and the rest of the family gasps, steps back. I can see myself for the first time—we are exquisite.

"I've missed you," I tell her. She gleams.

Later, during the brief calm before the arrival of relatives, she will lie with her head in my lap and stare at me: Elder sister. One who spoils. Exotic American. Passport to what lies ahead, whom she will become. And I will stare back at her: Younger sister. One who adores. Exotic African. Passport back home, to what I have always been.

Faith Adiele

Where's Your Notebook?

Being a black man in America is like having another job.

Arthur Ashe

I was thirteen years old when Dad called my two younger brothers and me into the game room of our house. I was excited! I thought we were going to play pool or pinball or maybe even watch movies together, just us guys! "Bring a notebook and something to write with," my dad bellowed before we reached the game room. My brothers and I stopped dead in our tracks and stared at each other in horror! His request was unusual, and our excitement turned to dread as we became well aware that games or movies were not the reason we were pulled away from watching *Fat Albert*. This felt more official and tedious, like schoolwork, chores or worse, a family meeting.

As we each retrieved a notebook and pencil we continued to ponder the reason for this summons. We ruled out a family meeting because Mom was still out shopping. We entered the game room to find three metal folding chairs facing a huge blackboard. Dad instructed us to sit in the chairs and NOT on the cushioned sofa just inches from us.

"I want your full attention. That is why I have you sitting in these chairs," he stated, businesslike.

Immediately we began to pout and whine.

"Where's Mom, aren't we gonna wait for Mom?" my youngest brother asked.

"Is this gonna take long?" my other brother sighed.

I silently squirmed in the uncomfortable metal chair.

"Your mother won't be back for hours, and if you must know, she has nothing to do with this," he said calmly. "And how long this takes depends entirely upon each of you. The more you participate, the more you'll learn, and the faster we can move on and be done. Understood?"

"Yes, sir," we responded unenthusiastically.

"Now," my father began, "we are going to have a weekly meeting with just us guys. We will have these meetings every Saturday morning, but if you have school or sports activities on Saturday morning, we'll reschedule for Sundays after church. I'm going to teach you what I have learned about life. It is my responsibility, before God, to prepare you to be strong, proud, African American men who will be assets to the community and to the world at large. It is a responsibility I take very seriously."

I just had to jump in, "You're going to teach us *everything* about life?"

"Everything I can."

"But that will take forever."

"Maybe." He turned to begin writing on the blackboard. "Maybe."

For the next five years, rain or shine, in sickness or in health, Dad taught us about life once a week. He instructed us on a wide variety of subjects—personal hygiene, puberty, etiquette, the importance of education, racism, dating, respect for women, respect for those in authority, respect for our elders, Christian salvation, a good work ethic, what it means to be an adult, what to look for in a wife, landscaping, minor home repairs, auto repairs, budgeting, investing, civic duties and the list goes on. We begrudgingly filled notebook after notebook after notebook.

As I approached my eighteenth birthday, the weekly lessons became monthly lessons and then every other month, until they slowly drifted away. My brothers and I were older, we had girlfriends, school activities, sports activities and job responsibilities that became extremely difficult to schedule around. I'm not sure when it happened, but the importance of our weekly lessons and notebooks began to pale in comparison to our busy teenage lives. Soon the classes and the notebooks were mere memories.

It's been years now since we had those classes with Dad in the game room. We are grown with careers and wives of our own. At every challenge in life, my brothers and I have frantically looked in attics, basements and storage sheds for our notebooks. We can't find them anywhere.

At least once a month one of us has a situation where we need to call home and ask Dad for his advice or guidance. We hesitantly pick up the phone to call him, knowing good and well he's going to laugh and say, "Where's your notebook?"

John W. Stewart Jr.

It Runs in the Family

How far you go in life depends on your being tender with the young, compassionate with the aged, sympathetic with the striving, and tolerant of the weak and strong. Because someday in life you will have been all these.

George Washington Carver

My childhood had its ups and downs but included my momma, Karen, who was so supportive that I was destined to succeed in life.

She never missed any of my school events, poetry contests, honor roll assemblies, student government elections or the countless football and basketball games spanning six years of cheerleading. When I graduated from college, I was selected to give the commencement address. Just like old times, my mother sat in a chair in my dorm room and listened to my speech over and over again.

That reminded me of a time when I used to be embarrassed by my mother. She always laughed just a little too loud. She never dressed the way I wanted her to dress.

She had very few outfits that weren't gold or red, and you'd be hard pressed to find something in her closet without a sequin sewn on it. I respected my mother for her talents, but I just wanted her to be a little more like other mothers and a lot less crazy.

When I entered a statewide speech contest, I prayed for my mother to magically transform into the normal mother everyone else seemed to have. The whole time I gave my speech she moved her lips as if she was coaching me. Instead of feeling grateful for her involvement, I worried other people would think she was talking to herself.

It felt impossible to pass for normal when our craziness was as obvious as the frilly Easter-looking dress I had to wear. By the time I made it to the finals, I had given my mother strict conditions. First, even though we couldn't afford it, I demanded a blue suit, like the other girls. I instructed her not to mouth the words to my speech. Finally, I warned, under no circumstances should she jump up and down and make whooping noises if I won. This wasn't a Dunbar High School pep rally; it was the suburban Optimist Club speech contest, and we had to look the part.

When I took to the stage, one of ten finalists remaining of the thousands of girls in the competition, I looked around the room. There was only one other brown face that looked like mine. Momma's. The opinion of the other contestants, the crowd and the judges became increasingly less important to me.

As I delivered my presentation, possibly one of the most flawless performances of my fourteen years on Earth, I realized my mother was sitting in her seat with her face turned toward the door rather than the stage—obeying my strict directives. I had thought that if she didn't look at me, she wouldn't be tempted to do any of those crazy things that distracted me.

I realized now that the only way she knew all the words to my speech was because she had obviously memorized it, too—just to show her support for me. I knew then that I had no desire to win without my mother seeing it and celebrating in whatever way she chose to.

Near the end of my speech, I stepped from behind the podium, walked down the stage and onto the main floor. I wanted Momma's attention. My mother sat still in her contorted position gripping the side of the white linen tablecloth, desperately trying to do what I had asked her to do: Be someone else. She never moved. I finished with a dramatic close, but she never looked up. While the rest of the crowd rose to their feet in a standing ovation, Momma was still. When they handed me the plaque and the scholarship money, Momma allowed herself to simply smile.

Without our traditional 'cutting up' and 'act a fool' celebration, my victory felt empty. In that moment, with my future looking bright, I realized you can't enjoy where you are going if you deny where you are from.

I let her know from that moment on she could whoop and holler and be herself. I wouldn't want her any other way. After all, she was my momma, and if she was crazy, then call me crazy, too.

Jarralynne Agee

Fried Chicken and Collard Greens

*For every one of us that succeeds, it's because
there's somebody there to show you the way out.*

Oprah Winfrey

It was eight months since Momma had prepared fried chicken and collard greens. I distinctly remember standing beside her as she cracked some eggs, added Carnation milk, sprinkled her secret seasonings, beat the mixture and then carefully dipped a piece of chicken for a full coating. This precision seemed wasted as she dropped each piece in a brown grocery store bag filled with flour. Once all the pieces were in, the shakedown began until the entire chicken skin was covered in flour. I'll never figure how each piece got so evenly coated, but when the shaking was over, the chicken was entirely white.

The finale was placing each piece in a skillet of hot grease. The crackle and sizzle meant we'd be "grubbing down" soon and always drew my four brothers.

"Do I smell chicken and collard greens?" one would ask warmly.

And they would be correct. Boiling next to the chicken was always a big pot of collard greens—handpicked from our garden and cleaned by the women in the house (including any kinfolk who might have dropped by).

The preparation was as much a part of dinner as the cooking. We would gather in a circle around a table—as if we were going to play cards—with greens spread atop. Then the real pickin' began as we inspected one leaf at a time, examining it for worms or unfamiliars. We also picked over topics of discussion, usually ranging from boys to men. However, as "young 'uns" my three sisters and I dared not talk too much for fear of getting a "pop in the mouth" for being "fast."

This ritual was known as Soul Food Sunday by some, but we just called it Dinner at Momma's, until I renamed it The Last Supper when Momma died.

It was mid-November when she left us. My siblings and I, fully grown, were planning our usual visit home for Thanksgiving. I believe Momma timed her passing so we'd be together without an added trip home. We arrived during Thanksgiving just to become eight motherless children. There was nothing to be thankful for that year.

My oldest sister insisted we still have Thanksgiving dinner and so we womenfolk gathered in the kitchen while the men pretended to help but really watched football. It was just like all the other Thanksgivings—except Momma wasn't there.

"You should fry the chicken and do the collard greens," my youngest sister said. I was stunned and angry. "You watched Momma all the time, and you cook the most like her," she finished.

Although intended as a compliment, I knew she was really saying, "Momma's gone so you help us move on." I refused.

"There will be no fried chicken or collard greens," I stated.

My sisters glared at me, and my brothers seemed to gain bionic hearing, darting into the kitchen as if it were on fire. "What's dinner without fried chicken and collard greens?" they all sang out in unison.

"It's the same as dinner without Momma," I shouted back—hitting a nerve in every one of their bodies.

The rest of Thanksgiving passed solemnly as we ate turkey, string beans, mashed potatoes and desserts. Nothing tasted quite right, and by the end of the meal, we agreed we'd never eat collard greens and chicken as good as Momma's ever again; therefore, we'd never have them again. Sadly, we surrendered the two foods we remembered Momma for most.

Six months later the family gathered for a grand celebration of Momma's first (and favored) grandchild's graduation. After the graduation, my friend invited us to her family reunion cookout later in the day.

When we arrived, Mrs. Spark, the family matriarch, grabbed my sisters and I, leading us to the kitchen while jabbering about "needing more hands to work." My brothers settled in front of the living room's big screen television and ball game.

I stopped dead in my tracks when I saw card table setups. On each were vegetables—snap peas, green beans and yes, collard greens.

"Y'all know how to pick greens and all?" Mrs. Spark asked shortly.

"Yes, ma'am," we stuttered uneasily.

She chuckled and said, "Well, pull up a chair. What you standin' there for? Hmmph, young folk act like they ain't never seen fresh greens and such."

The other women started in chiding about the state of the world and how bagged greens were an abomination to how God intended us to cook.

We took our seats and began the familiar process of

cleaning greens. My sisters jumped into the conversation and the laughter, but I was still dazed. Then, as if reading my mind, Mrs. Spark tapped me on the shoulder and asked me to join her at the stove.

"I'm gonna teach you my secret fried chicken recipe," she whispered. "Now pay attention."

I couldn't believe as I watched Mrs. Spark mix eggs with Carnation milk, sprinkle her secret seasoning, beat the mixture, precisely dip each piece and drop it in a bag—filled with flour.

"There ain't nothing to soothe the soul like fried chicken and collard greens," she chuckled. "You try."

With each piece I felt a weight lift from my hands, to my arms and all the way through my body. As I finished, I looked at my brothers howling about game scores, and my sisters laughing like schoolgirls with strangers around a table.

I suddenly realized the truth in Mrs. Spark's words, and my heart felt lighter.

Our souls were healing from our loss. The balm was simple and well-loved: fried chicken and collard greens.

Thyonne Gordon

Rusty Feet

That best portion of a good man's life: his little, nameless, unremembered acts of kindness and love.

William Wordsworth

Kneeling here on my forty-one-year-old knees holding a crusty, dry, rusty unkempt foot in my towel-draped lap. Slowly and gently rubbing off the foot scrapings and thinking how gross all this is. Trying not to get any of the stuff I'm scraping off on my new sweater. Feet turning colors from lack of circulation and swollen because his kidneys aren't properly functioning. I look up at the teakwood face covered with wiry silver hair, and he grimaces at me.

"A little more gently, okay, but that feels good."

"Can you lift up your foot a little?" I watch him strain fruitlessly, until I finally just shift and pull his foot higher and try not to hurt him any more than he must be hurting. A little moan. He cuts off.

"Your feet look awful," I whine, but keep scraping

because somewhere under the crud I see the strong, supple toes and arches that leapt and lumbered on the cement in the backyard, schooling me in how to play basketball, and running up the hill to shoot me down the toboggan run just one more time on frigid, snow-covered slopes.

These are the feet that trudged through woods for the ultimate camping experience (in spite of his snake phobia) and through countless museums for the ultimate cultural experience. The feet that jumped the fence to catch the stupid dog that kept leaping it and running away. The feet that chased the mouse out of the house so I could get down off the counter. The feet that chased the ice cream man for a block to stop—so I could get that Strawberry Shortcake bar—and then took me to the supermarket to get a whole pack of Strawberry Shortcakes where they were cheaper.

I see the feet connected to the legs connected to the hips, chest and shoulders that carried me to my first Jackson Five concert. And let me sit there and jump up and down and scream onto the connected head that holds the ears that listened to all of my deepest fears and hopes and prayers and tried to make the most important ones come true.

The feet that walked into my room when I started my period and stamped impatiently for me to get up out of bed and get on with life because every other woman has a period, too. The feet that taught me how to bop, foxtrot, waltz and square dance, and then learned all the latest dances so they wouldn't shame me at the dance I forced him to attend with me. The feet that stampeded in panic into the hospital and skidded to the gurney in relief when I stopped a Cadillac with my body.

I put the foot on my lap into the waiting soapy hot water, to soak off the most recalcitrant gunk, and take out the other foot. I massage each toe individually as he pants with discomfort.

"Don't rub there. It hurts," he breathes when I get to his instep.

"There?" I touch the spot.

"There," he grits, and rolls his eyes at me. I keep scrubbing away.

"You have to take better care of yourself, you know."

He gives me a long look and sighs, "Yeah, you're right. I talked to the Lord and told him that I will do right from now on."

My eyes mist over and I lower them to the foot in my lap because that mouth has never said anything about talking to the Lord before in my hearing. *He must be feeling worse than I know.* I quash the thought. *No negative thinking,* I tell myself sternly and rub a spot on his sole with a little more vigor.

"You need to see a podiatrist. What happened to this toe?" I point to the blackened big toe with my pumice stone. He opens his mouth to tell me but I don't pause, "This is nasty. You have to take better care of your feet. You have to walk on them for the rest of your life, you know."

I'm fussing and I know I'm nagging, but I keep scraping and wiping and rubbing.

"Got that playing basketball," he smiles, reminiscing. "Some kid stepped on it when she came down from a rebound."

I finish the second foot and take the first one out of the water.

"I'm tired now." Weariness is on his face, so I dry off both feet and coat them in Vaseline because they are so dry from medication and neglect.

"They feel much better," he smiles. "Thanks."

I rise from the floor, knees creaking. He's cold so I

wrestle him into a fleece sweater because he is too weak to do it himself. I help him lay on the bed and pick up his swollen feet and elevate them on some pillows.

I cover him up and he says, "It's interesting."

"What?"

"How the circle continues." He eyes me wistfully. "I used to take care of you, and now you're taking care of me. It was kind of fun, you know?"

I look down at the foot tub brimming with cloudy water, filled with the layers of our life together. I look back at his face.

"Yes, Dad," I smile for the first time. "It was." I lean down and kiss his face as his eyes drift closed for a nap.

Landis Mayers Lain

Walking to Wisdom

Grammy woke me with unfortunate news. Her speedometer was broken, and she needed to take the car to a nearby repair shop—understandable. She wanted me to accompany her—unforgivable. It meant the ruin of a precious carefree summer day. As I hurried to get ready I thought, *No fourteen-year-old should be subjected to such cruel and unsuspecting punishment.* I knew that resistance was futile, and my only hope was for a speedy on-site repair so I could resume my sleep.

While Grammy inched along New Orleans' streets, she played her favorite oldies on the AM radio dial. Sweat beaded my body in the sauna of the car. No one spoke. At the shop, Grammy spoke to a mechanic while I slouched at the entrance, attempting to neutralize my irritation.

Everything about this place was filthy, most notably the stench of toxic liquids and a handful of greasy mechanics. The atmosphere was more akin to demolition than repair. More good news: the car would not be ready until tomorrow so we would have to rely on public transportation to return home. My day was deteriorating by the minute.

We made our way to the nearest bus stop. The area was

void of shade. Once a mosquito entourage flew our way it was impossible to remain still. My intuition told me that the longer we wait for a bus to arrive, the longer it will take for a bus to arrive. Minutes later, Grammy announced, "Let's walk home."

It was roughly a three-mile journey, up a one-way road, back home. En route were a handful of bus stops at various intervals, meaning that if a bus appeared and we were, by chance, near a bus stop, we could hop onboard. I didn't have much hope.

In typical teenage fashion, all of my upsetting thoughts were directed inward. *How could Grammy sucker me into this? Why had she decided to go so early? As slow as she drives, surely she didn't need a functioning speedometer in the first place. She could have arranged for someone to give us a ride home. Why is it so hot, why is Grammy walking so slow?*

I was drenched in sweat after five minutes of walking. I'd made a conscious effort to slow the pace of my stride to walk side-by-side with Grammy. A few cars passed, and I noticed some passengers stared. *What a pathetic scene,* I thought, *a young black male in the prime of his teenage years slow-trotting with his Grandmother along a road to nowhere.* Embarrassed, I looked down and examined each step I took. The heat, the sweat and my irritation grew. There was complete silence between the two of us.

As we continued, a brief conversation started. She asked what I was doing later that day. I asked what she was cooking for dinner. I told her a funny story about a friend and we both laughed. Other insignificant conversations came about and soon I became engrossed in the simple uniqueness of the moment. Each summer I'd stay at Grammy's house, and each year I'd spend less time with her and more time eating, sleeping and playing with my friends, but now we were together again, enduring the same circumstances.

Frequently I would turn my head, take a close look at Grammy and detail her entire profile. I gulped. Despite my private concern for her, she held steadfast through the heat and journey. The sun shined bright on her, illuminating the course of her life. I saw the lady born in New Orleans, 1931, in the heart of poverty and the height of Jim Crow laws. Undoubtedly the effects of the Great Depression reverberated in the city through her childhood. There were times she reminisced about the advent of television, the civil rights movement, the assassination of international and national leaders, wars, hurricanes, man's first step on the moon, and the changing phases of music and dress style. At home she endured to keep the family and house in one piece, and had lived long enough to tell many tales of birth, coming of age and death.

I remembered the times I'd seen her laugh and smile and the times I'd seen her break down and cry. Every step of the way, I could remember Grammy being there, and now, walking with her, each step she took reminded me of an important moment she had shared. Through all the events and circumstances that formed her life, she retained her unmistakable vitality and brightness and a rich inner beauty that was priceless.

By the time we neared home, I had completely lost touch of the heat, my irritation and selfish shame. The moment had been wholly transformed into something of unequaled profoundness. The struggle against the adverse conditions was now a promenade down memory lane and back home, and Grammy appeared no more exhausted than I. Our chitchat continued as I walked with great pride and joy with Grammy by my side.

Miiky Cola

Not Gone Yet

Life is short, and it's up to you to make it sweet.

Sadie Delaney

Good grandmothers are the commodities of great child-hoods. My Grandma Versie, mother of seventeen children and grandmother to more than fifty, was the center of our universe.

During my visits "home," I would keep Grandma Versie company as she made breakfast for the twenty folks sleeping there. I pulled up a stool and watched as she rolled out dough for biscuits, stoked the fireplace for cooking and traipsed to the well for water for our coffee. She took her coffee black with a hint of milk. I took my milk with a hint of coffee. She moved carefully around the kitchen, dropping pearls of wisdom that fell on my preoccupied five-year-old ears. Instead, I wanted so badly to tell her everything I knew, to teach her as much as she was teaching me.

As we both grew older, our together time switched to early afternoon. We slept in later and she was forced out of the kitchen to "rest." We sat by the fireplace in the living room of her new, less spacious, ranch-style home. With my head cradled in her lap, the same hands that kneaded dough now kneaded through my worries. She listened as I tried to explain to her what no grown-up could ever understand: what it is like to be thirteen.

During college, my trips to Grandma were more infrequent. We sat together in her garden. More discerning and considerate, I talked less and listened more. I asked her questions about her life, searching for a window into mine. Taking her hand, I examined her fire-red polish, while she asked me about the boys in college. I told her how beautiful and flavorful they were.

Grandma said, "You know I was only thirteen when I married your grandfather. He was so handsome." After an hour or two of her funny stories, I hit the clubs to hang out with my cousins.

Once I began my career, trips back to Mississippi were event motivated. Most of the time, they coincided with the loss of aunts, uncles and cousins. Before the family left for my Aunt Grace's funeral, I made my way to Grandma. Her polish needed touching up, so I searched out some red and I painted her nails.

"Baby girl, you know it's not right for a mother to bury her child."

Until that moment it had never occurred to me to think of what Grandma was feeling. She didn't have anything else to say about the topic so we went on to something else. I told her about my job and the places it sent me. She shared with me how she ran away to the big city once before she got married.

"I wanted to be a professional and work in the factories in Memphis," Grandma said.

Before she could get settled, her brother came for her and a little while later she married my grandfather. Her professional life consisted of helping him run his 800-acre farm. In her eyes, I could see that somehow she was living her dreams through me, through all of us, and she was proud.

When my father called and told me not to wait too long to go home and visit Grandma, I almost shrugged it off. In my mind, Grandma was immortal. After all, she was in her nineties and looked as beautiful as she did in my childhood memories of her. Weeks led into months, and it wasn't until she was bedridden that I felt the urgency to go see her. My cousin Demetria, who loved Grandma as much as I did, accompanied me. Upon my arrival, my youngest aunt tried to prepare me for how she looked physically: Her once 95-pound frame had dwindled to 70. Her strong facial features emerged skeletal under her thinning skin. Her voice was failing. Her eyes slowly opened after every blink.

My grandmother was dying. Without seeing her, I ran outside wailing tears of pain, loss, regret and sorrow. All I thought was, *It's over.*

All of our talks, our private conversations, are over. Never again will I hear her comments on life. My procrastination cost me life lessons that only she could provide. Her absence will leave a void at reunions and during the holidays.

Demetria followed me. "She's not dead yet." I listened intently as she continued, "Michelle, you are mourning her before she is gone. Don't waste this time mourning her as if death has already come."

Her softly spoken truth resonated with me. With regained composure, I went into my grandmother's room. I sat beside her.

"I am going to get married, Grandma," I chatted, trying to assure her—and me. "And I am going to have seventeen children, too."

She frowned with disapproval and held up three fingers

and whispered, "Three is a good number. You don't have any land for all those kids to work."

I was there for a few hours before my aunt brought me a can of Ensure and a baby spoon for me to feed my grandmother. I fought back tears, recalling all the times that she had made me breakfast. *She is still here,* I kept saying to myself. *She is still here.* As I put the spoon to her mouth, she beckoned me closer. I leaned toward her. "Where's the beef?" she murmured.

"What, Grandma?" I asked.

"Where is the beef? I want some meat!" she said definitively.

I fell back in my chair laughing and watched her chest bounce in silent laughter, too. Demetria was right. Grandma was still here!

My aunt ran in the room at the noise, and I repeated the phrase Wendy's Restaurant had made famous. My aunt looked puzzled, but when I looked at Grandma, I knew she was serious.

"Y'all better get my grandma some beef!"

I fed her crumbled hamburger meat and afterwards polished her nails. There was no longer anything to mourn, only a life to celebrate.

Michelle Gipson

3

TRIUMPH AND RESILIENCE

*It doesn't matter how many times you fall
   down.
What matters is how many times you get up.*

Marian Wright Edelman

Winners Never Quit

*It's not a question of can you succeed; a better
question is will you succeed.*

George Johnson

I had been swimming competitively for about five years
and was ready to quit, not because I had satisfied my
desire to swim, but because I felt I was horrible at it. I was
often the only African American at a swim competition,
and our team could not afford anything close to the great
uniforms the other teams were wearing. Worst of all
though, and my number-one reason for wanting to quit,
was that I kept receiving "Honorable Mentions" at each
competition, which simply means, "Thank you for coming.
You did not even rank first, second or third, but we don't
want you to go home with nothing, so here is something
to hide later." Any athlete knows that you don't want to
have a bookshelf or a photo album full of "Honorable
Mentions." They call that the "show-up ribbon"; you get
one just because you showed up.

One hot summer day, the very day before a big swim

meet, I decided to break the news to my grandma that I was quitting the swim team. On the one hand I thought it was a big deal because I was the only athlete in the family, but on the other hand, because no one ever came to see me compete, I didn't think it would be a major issue. You have to know my grandma—she stood on tiptoe to five-feet-two-inches and weighed a maximum ninety-five pounds, but could run the entire operation of her house without ever leaving her sofa or raising her voice. As I sat next to my grandma, I assumed my usual position of laying my big head on her tiny little lap so that she could rub it.

When I told her of my desire to quit swimming, she abruptly pushed my head off of her lap, sat me straight up facing her and said, "Baby, remember these words: 'A quitter never wins and a winner never quits.' Your grandmother didn't raise no losers or quitters. You go to that swim meet tomorrow, and you swim like you are a grandchild of mine, you hear?"

I was too afraid to say anything but, "Yes, ma'am."

The next day we arrived at the swim meet late, missing my group of swimmers in the fifteen/sixteen age group. My coach insisted I be allowed to swim with the next group, the next age older. I could have just as easily crawled out of the gym. I knew she was including me in the race so our long drive would not be wasted, and she had no expectations whatsoever that I would come in anything but eighth—and only that because there were not nine lanes.

As I mounted the board, I quickly noticed that these girls with their skintight caps, goggles and Speedo suits were here to do one thing—kick my chocolate butt!

All of a sudden my grandma's words rang in my head, *Quitters never win and winners never quit, quitters never win and winners never quit.*

SPLASH!

Quitters never win and winners never quit, quitters never win and winners never quit.

I was swimming harder than I'd ever swum before. As I drew my right arm back, I noticed I was tied with one person. I assumed we were battling for eighth place and I refused to finish dead last, so I added more kick on the last two hundred yards.

Quitters never win and winners never quit, quitters never win and winners never quit.

I hit the wall and looked to the left and to the right for the swimmers who had beat me, but no one was there. They must have gotten out of the water already.

I raised my head to see my coach screaming hysterically. My eyes followed her pointing finger and I couldn't believe what I saw. The other swimmers had just reached the halfway point of the pool! That day, at age fifteen, I broke the national seventeen/eighteen-year-old 400-freestyle record. I hung up my honorable mentions and replaced them with a huge trophy.

Back at Grandma's, I laid my head on her lap and told her about our great race.

Lisa Nichols

Hand-Me-Down Love

Character is what you know you are, not what others think you have.

Marva Collins

It was a typical spring day in my local high school science class. Each student was to show proficiency in anatomy by dissecting a frog. We were called up in alphabetical order. My day was today, and I was ready for the task.

I wore my favorite power shirt—the one I knew I looked good in, the one everyone told me I looked good in. I had studied and was ready for the assignment. When my name was called I walked confidently to the front of the room, smiled to the class and grabbed the scalpel to begin the task.

A voice from the back of the room said, "Nice shirt."

I beamed from ear to ear, when suddenly another voice from the back of the room said, "That shirt belonged to my Dad. Greg's mother is our maid and she took that shirt out of a bag headed for the Salvation Army."

My heart sank. I was speechless. It was probably one minute, but it felt like ten minutes of total emptiness and embarrassment in front of my peers. Vice President of Student Government, born with a gift of gab, I stood for the first time in my life speechless with nothing to say. As I looked to the left, another African American whose mother was also a maid, looked down; to my right, the only other African American in the class laughed out loud. I wanted to crawl into a hole.

My biology teacher asked me to begin the dissection. I stood speechless; he repeated the question. After total silence, he said, "Mr. Franklin, you may be seated. Your grade, a D."

I don't know which was more embarrassing, receiving the low mark or being found out. At home, I stuck the shirt in the back of the closet. My mom found the shirt and brought it to the front. This time I put it in the middle of the closet. Again, she moved it to the front.

A few weeks passed and my mom asked why had I not worn the shirt. I responded, "I just don't like it anymore."

She pressed with more questions. I didn't want to hurt her, but I had been raised to tell the truth. I explained what had happened in front of the whole class.

Mom sat in total silence while tears fell from her eyes. Then she stood and called her employer, "I will no longer work for your family," she told him, and asked for an apology for the incident at school. My mom was quiet for the rest of the day. At dinner, where she was typically the life of the family, Mom was totally quiet. After the kids were down for the night, I stood outside my mom and dad's door to hear what was going on.

In tears, Mom shared her humiliation with my dad— how she had quit her job and how embarrassed she felt for me. She said she couldn't clean anymore; she knew her life's purpose was something greater.

"What do you want to do?" Dad asked.

"Teach children," she answered with sudden clarity.

"You have no education." Dad pointed out.

With conviction she said, "Well, that's what I want to do, and I am going to find a way to make it happen."

The next morning she met with the personnel manager at the Board of Education, who thanked her for her interest but told her without an education she could not teach school. That evening Mom, a mother of seven children and a high school graduate far removed from school, shared with us her new plans to attend the university.

Mom started her studies by taking nine hours. She spread her books at the dining room table, studying right along with the rest of us.

After her first semester, she immediately went back to the personnel manager and asked for a teaching assignment. Again she was told, "Not without an education."

Mom went back to school the second semester, took six more hours and again went back to the personnel manager.

He said, "You are serious, aren't you? I think I have a position for you as a teacher's assistant. This opportunity is dealing with children who are mentally challenged, slow learners with, in many cases, little to no chance of learning. This is the highest area of teacher turnover due to sheer frustration."

Mom leaped at the opportunity.

She got us kids ready for school in the morning, went to work and came home and fixed dinner. I knew it was tough, but it is what she wanted to do and she did it with so much love. For almost five years my Mom was a teacher's assistant at the Starkey Special Education Center. Then, after three teacher changes during that five-year period, the personnel manager and the principal showed up in her classroom one day.

The principal said, "We have watched you and admired your diligence over the last five years. We have watched how you interact with the children and how they interact with you. We've talked to the other teachers, and we are all in agreement that you should be the teacher of this class."

My mom spent twenty-plus years with the Wichita Public School System. Through her career, she was voted Teacher of the Year for both her work with the Special Olympics and the special education center. All of this came about because of the thoughtless comment made in the classroom that day.

It has been said children learn not from what you say, but what you do. Mom showed me how to look challenging situations in the face and never give up.

As for me, my biology teacher approached me as I gathered my books to leave the classroom that day. He said, "I know this was a tough day for you, but I will give you a second chance on the assignment tomorrow."

I showed up, dissected the frog, and he changed my grade from a D to a B. I challenged him for an A, but he said, "You should have gotten it right the first time. It would be unfair to others."

As I grabbed my books and walked toward the door, he said, "Do you think you are the only one who has had to wear used clothes? Do you think you are the only one who has grown up poor?"

I responded with an assured, "Yes!"

My teacher put his arm around me and shared his story of growing up during the depression, and how on his graduation day he was laughed at because he did not have enough money for a cap and gown. He showed up with the same pants and shirt he wore to school every day.

He said, "I know how you felt; my heart went out to you. But you know something, kid? I have faith in you. I think you are going to be something special. I can feel it in my heart."

I was speechless again. Both of us were fighting back the tears, but I felt the love from him—a white man reaching out to a young black student who had been bussed across town.

I went on to become President of the Student Body, and my teacher was my mentor. Before I opened assembly, I would always look for him and he would give me a thumbs up—a secret only he and I shared.

It was at that point I realized that we are all the same—different colors, different backgrounds, but many of our experiences are the same. We all want to be happy; we all want great things in life. My teacher and my mother showed me that it's not what you wear, your education or your money, but what's in your heart that counts.

Greg Franklin

The Fragile Eight

Hold a true friend with both hands.

African Proverb

"Please," appealed the principal. "Nobody can handle him. Please take him."

It was the fall of 1987, in Albuquerque, New Mexico. She stood in the spacious hall with Brad Earlewine, the new D-Level special education teacher, discussing eight-year-old Roscoe Williams. This child's aggressive behavior seemed devoid of sensitivity and reason, yet he was so likable. The veteran principal couldn't understand the boy.

Roscoe was a hyperactive, severely learning-disabled child with a communication disorder. He couldn't walk down a hall without causing trouble. He was a whirl of motion; a tiny, black-bespectacled tempest in a teapot. A spindly-legged catastrophe dressed in a Superman cape. There was talk about a behavior disorder condition to add to the baggage he was already carrying.

After batteries of tests, Roscoe was placed in Earlewine's class. The minute the pair looked at each other, there was

a certain magic, like two elements combining, both stimu-
lating and challenging each other. Single, caring and gentle, Earlewine held a degree in special education and even
trained for the priesthood.

A maverick to tradition, he looked for ways to get inside
his kids' heads, trying to find a key. His eight "Fragile Ds"
as he soon called them, provided his first experience at
this level. The bunch had it all. Some were orphans, some
sexually abused. Some were full of rage, some immeasur-
able sorrow. Some possessed every kind of handicap, even
genius imprisoned by mixed-up neurology. Like human
pincushions stuck with dozens of fluttering labels, they
were often the butt of cruel jokes.

"We just don't stand being called names!" he instructed
his kids hotly. "Face up to them! Be brave. Don't take it!"

But they took it.

He taught the three Rs, placing each child on an indi-
vidualized program of studies, but after weeks he couldn't
find the spark. One day he thought of his beloved, crusty
old uncle who'd taught him chess.

Unorthodox? he mused. *Yeah. Why not! It's worth a shot.*

He brought a children's chess book to class and began
reading the fairytale-like myths that explained the basics.
Within a week, the Fragiles, especially Roscoe, gobbled up
everything. Earlewine purchased boards for school and
sent one home with each kid. While they all showed real
promise with the game, Roscoe was the bold, tactical
player.

A few weeks later, Earlewine, an adept player, realized
that the boy was thinking five to seven moves ahead after
only the barest of instruction. Roscoe started studying his
teacher's moves and beat him five times in a row.

Something else began to happen in that portable classroom as well. The Fragiles were changing. As they grasped
more and more chess, a newfound courage began to

emerge. They were absorbed, more confident, purposeful and even proud.

Earlewine began a before-school chess club. Dozens of kids flocked in, to be taught and played by the Fragiles. It was only a matter of time before the little team began beating junior- and senior-high chess clubs. Boldly, Earlewine entered the whole team in the chess nationals to be held in Albuquerque where eight hundred top U.S. kids would assemble for the challenge.

Tiny Roscoe Williams became America's newest junior chess champion. Sitting atop four telephone books, he beat a large junior-high boy who never knew what happened until the checkmate. Newspaper reporters stared incredulously when Earlewine explained that his Fragiles, dressed in hand-decorated school Ts instead of classy wool blazers with team crests, were D-level special education students.

Saturday, February 11, 1989, dawned sunny after many days of snow and rain. Roscoe, full of starch and vinegar, hopped onto his bike, to deliver candy for the chess club's recent fund-raiser. Laughing at a friend, he looked back over his shoulder, and sailed right through the stop sign. There was a screech of brakes and a horrible thud.

Roscoe hit the side of the automobile, rolled over the hood, flew thirty feet through the air, and struck the median with the right side of his head.

A week later Earlewine was finally allowed to see his young student. Roscoe's face was unrecognizable. His body was there, but it was a hollow shell more dead than alive. Earlewine joined the ancient practice of the laying-on of hands by adding his white hands to a dozen black ones, all members of the Pilgrim's Rest Church, who touched the bandaged broken lump under the covers. Voices sang old spirituals that rose and floated softly into the beautiful Southwest's burgeoning spring evenings.

Roscoe was transferred to the Carrie Tingley Hospital for Crippled Children, unable to move or talk. He was tube-fed because of mouth sutures and fractured teeth. It looked as if he was going to keep his eyes, but mental functioning was almost zero.

At school, Earlewine set up a tape recording station where the Fragiles could make daily personal messages to their friend.

"Please come back, we miss you," they'd record. "Do you remember me?"

The teacher asked that the videotapes of past chess matches be played twenty-four hours a day. He sneaked kids to the bedside. One day, Earlewine brought a chessboard and set it up in front of the zombie that was Roscoe. By now, Roscoe's eyes were open, but no recognition, no spark, no life was living within.

"Okay, Buddy," the teacher began, "when I hold my hand over a piece, and you see a move you want to make, blink your eyes."

Earlewine touched pieces one at a time, pointing to all the possible moves, looking up and waiting. On the last choice, he detected the barest twitch.

"He's awake!" the teacher ran hollering down the hall.

Nobody believed him, but Earlewine didn't give up.

Finally released home, one day Roscoe said, "Uh-huh," his old stock phrase. But he made little progress past that. When authorities wanted to put him in a training school for the mentally handicapped, Earlewine demanded his student back.

"*I can do this!* My kids can do this," he beseeched. "Give us two weeks. Please."

The Fragiles cut Roscoe's food. They fed him, toileted him. They never left his side, nor did they stop talking to him or wrapping him in their arms. Earlewine told the kids they had to believe Roscoe was in there, and he would return. Every one of them surrounded their friend with such patient compassion and such unending tenderness that one day there was a spark in his eyes—just the barest flash of memory.

"You remember!" they cheered.

"Uh-huh," he chuckled.

And the remembering continued. Things flooded back in torrents. Through the days, their old Roscoe came back for longer and longer periods, and so did the sparkle and even the two-step. The kids supplied missing pieces anytime he needed them. The little group of barrio kids and their very special teacher never broke the circle of kind and gentle caring, praise and celebrations. They simply willed him, loved him back to life.

In the spring of 1990, the Fragiles, including Roscoe, went to the Kansas City Nationals, a chess tournament that attracted one thousand players. The boy who was loved back to health won a gold medal and placed tenth in the nation.

Isabel Bearman Bucher

[AUTHOR'S NOTE: *Roscoe and Brad Earlewine are still close. Every couple of months, they meet and set up the board. Roscoe volunteers time teaching chess to kids in after school programs, and Brad still dazzles his students with the game of Kings.*]

A Hardworking Man's Hand

A dream doesn't become a reality through magic; it takes sweat, determination and hard work.

Colin L. Powell

When I was eight years old, I started UNEEC (Urban Neighborhood Economic Enterprise Club), an investment club designed to help kids in the neighborhood turn our ideas and hobbies into bona fide businesses. We didn't have much—we lived in one of Chicago's poorest neighborhoods, the kind with more trash than trees and where people are so poor, hurt and frustrated that they begin to hurt themselves and others. I dreamed at night of getting my momma out of this place. I decided that, even if I had to work day and night, I would do whatever it took—my momma wouldn't grow old waiting to get out of this neighborhood. I had a dream to make it out one day, and I knew that all a kid needed, even an inner-city kid, was a dream.

I had been selling products door to door since I was

four. I'd accompanied my mother to business meetings since I was five. At six, I made my own business cards that said, "Farrah Gray, Future 21st Century CEO." By eight, I knew that it takes hard work to create a business, but I didn't yet know quite how much hard work.

My first job as leader of UNEEC was to find a place to meet. I spent days calling just about every hotel in Chicago before a local Ramada Inn owner gave us a small room to meet in every Saturday for two hours, with free pizza and soda. We were on our way—now all I needed was to find us all a ride.

All the members lived in the same neighborhood, but most of our parents didn't own cars. Mostly they used public transportation. I let my fingers do the walking in the phone book to find a taxicab company that could help us out with the free rides to and from the Ramada Inn. Nobody would help; lots of people laughed at me. It was a great lesson in business, because I was learning never to give up.

Then someone suggested the airport shuttles, which were even better than taxis because you could fit all eleven or twelve of us kids in one van. After a lot of rejections, I finally reached an owner-driver who listened to my story very attentively. He recognized my age from my voice; I recognized his general age range because his voice and speech were similar to my "old school" relatives.

"Little fella," he said, "I'll see what I can do. Let me speak to a parent because I want to come and meet you."

My mother gave me the okay and I gave him the address, but I reminded him that our club meeting was for young people not old people. He told me that, "Old people can teach you a thing or two, but that's all right. Always speak your mind. You don't waste folks' time and they won't waste yours."

An hour later, I was dressed in my Sunday best and

waiting outside my apartment for his van to drive up. People in my neighborhood rarely called airport shuttles unless they had to travel to fly out for a funeral, so I knew I wouldn't have a hard time spotting my welcomed visitor. Soon a yellow and brown passenger van came slowly down my street as if it were driving in a school zone. I met the driver as soon as his door opened.

"I'm Mr. Perry, the owner of this company," he said. He held out his hand. My eyes bugged out of my head from the pain when that gentle giant closed his hand around mine. He apologized for his strong shuttle-bus driver handshake grip.

"Little fella," he said. "There are two types of firm handshakes—the white collar handshake and the hardworking man's handshake. You're gonna have to have both to make it in this world with the competition that is out there now. None of the big boys are going to give you shelf space." He seemed to like the way I was listening to his advice. After a few minutes of discussion, he agreed to personally pick up the members of UNEEC every Saturday morning and return us home after the meeting.

"I wish my boys had listened to me when they were younger," he said with a sad look on his face. "We could have a fleet of vans by now." Then he asked me, "Farrah, can this old man sit in to see what goes on with your club?"

I remembered what he said earlier about older people knowing a thing or two. "Sure, Mr. Perry," I said. "You can come and speak to us about your life as a businessman."

"Little fella," he said, "you may scare off your club members if you tell them about something they don't know anything about."

"What's that, sir?"

Mr. Perry said, in a tone as strong as his handshake, "Hard work."

Mr. Perry received a pick-up call on his walkie-talkie. He said he'd be back Saturday morning to pick the club members up, then opened the driver's side door and hopped in with lightning speed. I thought to myself, *He moves fast, just like my grandmother.* Old people moving faster than young kids—wow! I was impressed!

UNEEC's first meeting was a great success; the second week I invited Mr. Perry to speak. No one was surprised to see him since he picked all of us up, but we were surprised to see two grown men in the back of the room.

When Mr. Perry stood up to speak, he needed no introduction. "I've been working hard all my life," he began, "and I like what I see in you all. Since I was your age I've been working. I've been my own boss since I moved away from home in Baltimore and caught a train, living like a hobo until I arrived here in Chicago." We hung on his every word. Mr. Perry was not reading from a book but telling us the amazing experiences in his own life. He touched our minds and hearts with his triumphs over trials and tribulations, and how he reared himself up to be a good man, a good father and a hardworking business person.

There wasn't a dry eye, including the two men in the back of the room, who turned out to be Mr. Perry's grown sons. They told me their father had asked them to come and hear the stories of his life, because he had always worked so hard that he never had time to tell them before. Now, at last, they finally understood their father and what he had gone through to give them a better life. That day, Mr. Perry was no longer an airport shuttle driver; he was no longer just a dad to these two men. Mr. Perry became our hero; he became our possibility. Mr. Perry became our way out of the ghetto. His story of hard work, dedication, sacrifice, integrity, and a strong handshake moved each one of us to the point of tears and inspired us. We never saw him the same from that day forward; we knew his ride to the Ramada was really a ride to our dreams come true. The only person not crying was Mr. Perry. He closed by humbly thanking us for the opportunity to speak publicly before an audience for the first time in his life. With his first handshake, Mr. Perry had reached down and pulled me up. His words lifted me to an even higher plane. His strength made me strong. I knew that with an example like Mr. Perry in my life, I couldn't go wrong.

Some would be amazed that I made my first million by the age of fourteen and that now, at the age of nineteen, I am the majority owner and publisher of *InnerCity* magazine in partnership with the oldest African-American owned media conglomerate in America. Yes, some would be amazed, but I'm not. After all, I learned to do three things very well in my young life: work really, really hard, know when I'm being blessed with a lesson and how to maintain a strong and confident handshake.

Farrah Gray

Consider This

My mother taught me very early to believe I could achieve any accomplishment I wanted to. The first was to walk without braces.

Wilma Rudolph

- Basketball superstar Michael Jordan was cut from his high school basketball team.
- Rafer Johnson, the decathlon champion, was born with a clubfoot.
- Early in her career, Whoopi Goldberg worked in a funeral parlor and as a bricklayer while taking small parts on Broadway.
- Sidney Poitier was told at his first acting audition that he should stick with dishwashing.
- Beyoncé Knowles says she was the really shy, quiet kid in school.
- Eddie Murphy was once paid one dollar per minute as a stand-up comedian.

- Wesley Snipes installed telephones before getting his first movie role.
- It was not until he reached his fifties that Morgan Freeman become a movie star.
- Alex Haley received a rejection letter once a week for four years as a budding writer. Later in his career, he was ready to give up on the book *Roots*. After nine years on the project, he felt inadequate to the task and was ready to throw himself off a freighter in the middle of the Pacific Ocean. As he was standing at the back of the freighter, looking at the wake, he heard the voices of his ancestors saying, "You go do what you got to do because they are all up there watching. Don't give up. You can do it. We're counting on you!" In subsequent weeks, the final draft of *Roots* poured out of him.
- Wilma Rudolph was the twentieth of twenty-two children. She was born prematurely and wasn't expected to survive. When she was four years old, Wilma contracted double pneumonia and scarlet fever, which left her with a paralyzed left leg. At age nine, she removed the metal leg brace and began to walk without it. By thirteen, she had developed a rhythmic walk, which doctors claimed as a miracle. That same year, she decided to become a runner. She entered a race and came in last. For the next few years, every race she entered, she came in last. Everyone told her to quit, but Wilma kept on running. One day, she actually won. From then on she won every race she entered. Eventually this little girl, who was told she would never walk again, went on to win three Olympic gold medals.
- In 1962, four young women started a professional singing career. They began performing in their church and doing small concerts. Then they cut a record. It

was a flop. Later, another record was recorded. The sales were a fiasco. The third, fourth, fifth and on through their ninth recordings were all failures. Early in 1964, they were booked for Dick Clark's show, *American Bandstand*. He barely paid enough to meet expenses, and no great contracts resulted from their national exposure. Later that summer, they recorded "Where Did Our Love Go?" This song raced to the top of the charts, and Diana Ross and the Supremes gained national recognition and prominence as a musical sensation.

- Scottie Pippen, who won four NBA championship rings and two Olympic gold medals, received no athletic scholarship from any university and originally made his small college basketball team only as the equipment manager.
- Renowned photographer Howard Bingham flunked his college photography class and was fired from his first job as staff photographer at a Los Angeles newspaper. He went on to become one of the top photographers in the world, working with such notables as Bill Cosby and Dr. Martin Luther King Jr., and circling the globe with Muhammad Ali.
- One of the most beautiful speaking voices on stage and screen belongs to James Earl Jones. Did you know that Jones has long battled a severe stuttering problem? From age nine until his mid-teens, he had to communicate with teachers and classmates by handwritten notes. A high school English teacher gave him the help he needed, but he still struggles. Yet there is no finer speaking voice than his.

Divine Diva

The greatest education in the world is watching the masters at work.

Michael Jackson

My wife and I arrived at the auditorium in New York in a limousine provided by the music company. We were amazed by the many celebrities hovering around the entrance, eliciting screams of recognition and flashes of cameras from the fans and reporters. When our driver opened the door for us and we made our way out of the limo, I panicked because I figured that none of the fans surrounding the barricaded premises would recognize us. Most looked at us, trying to figure out what sitcom they had seen us on or what news show we anchored, until finally they realized that they didn't know us at all; therefore we must not be that important. But a few ladies over in the corner took our picture and one of them shouted out my name. I was so happy I almost gave them all a twenty-dollar bill—I didn't mind not being famous; I just didn't want them to boo us or throw tomatoes at us for wasting their film. I will always believe that God planted those ladies, obviously from someone's church, to spare us the embarrassment of coming into the Grammy Awards without the traditional greeting of fans and flashbulbs.

The city was abuzz as usual, but this night was even more electrifying than normal. It was the night of the much-revered Grammy Awards, one of the most prestigious events in the music and recording industry. People were dressed in tuxedos and fabulous gowns, smiling and milling through the auditorium to find their seats. Tickets were difficult to obtain but had been given to us by our own record label, and so we were making an evening of it. I could not believe that our work with "Woman Thou Art Loosed" had been nominated. So my wife and I put on our Sunday best to attend that evening's ceremony, although by then we knew that the actual Grammy in our category had gone to another nominee. No matter, it was still such an honor to attend the event. I will never forget watching Bill Gates as he walked right past me, dressed in his distinguished suit and looking quite successful. Then I saw Danny DeVito, an actor I have enjoyed watching on television and in many motion pictures. Boy, I had come a long way from where I grew up in the hills of West Virginia!

As my wife, Serita, and I sat in the auditorium and watched the numerous celebrities around us make their way down the aisle to present or receive an award, I was so awed by each act and presentation made. But the life lesson I was to learn that night far exceeded the excitement I experienced over these celebrity sightings. You see, that was the night that I learned what versatility and creativity can do in the life of a real lady who has mastered her craft.

Well into the ceremony, a hush went through the crowded, star-studded auditorium. Evidently, there was a problem

backstage. One of the world-renowned performers scheduled to sing had suddenly taken ill halfway through the
live, televised awards program. The producer could simply cut the scheduled highlight of the show, but then the
timing of the entire broadcast would be thrown off course.
No, someone was needed to fill in for the ailing superstar.
But it would be an impossible job—the world's greatest
tenor, Luciano Pavarotti, had planned to sing the famous
aria "Nessun dorma" from Puccini's opera *Turandot*, complete with a seventy-two-piece symphony orchestra. And
if the selection didn't intimidate anyone willing to stand
in, then the glamour and grandeur of the event would: the
1998 Grammy Awards. Anyone willing to substitute for
the great Pavarotti would be performing unrehearsed
before hundreds of music-industry insiders, producers
and executives, not to mention the countless professional
musicians and singers. Of course, then there was the matter of the 25 million television viewers, and that was just
U.S. viewers and didn't include the millions watching
overseas!

When a bright star suddenly dims, where do you turn
to find another source of illumination? Another superstar,
of course. One firmly planted in the skies of success in her
own right. Informed of the situation with Pavarotti's illness, Aretha Franklin agreed to the producer's desperate
request to sing the aria. With only eight minutes to prepare backstage, the Queen of Soul took the stage as the
lights went down and the beautiful operatic melody was
ushered in by the strings of violins. All of us held our collective breath.

Certainly, this extraordinary lady was a living legend in
her own right, with more than fifteen Grammys of her
own—more than any other woman. She was the first
female ever admitted to the Rock and Roll Hall of Fame. In
1968, the R&B sensation graced the cover of *Time*

magazine, the first African American woman to appear on its venerable cover. But an operatic aria was a far cry from the glorious soul tunes this legend was accustomed to singing. Was she setting herself up for embarrassment? From the moment the powerful yet delicate instrument of her voice hit the first note—still in Pavarotti's key, three steps lower than her own—no one could believe their ears. The heart-wrenching emotion, the Italian lyrics, the exquisite synthesis of voice and virtuoso melted the audience and laid to rest any doubts about the simply amazing talent, courage and giftedness of the amazing Aretha Franklin. As difficult as it might have been to believe, the Soul Lady performed with the trained operatic professionalism of a Jessye Norman or Beverly Sills. Stunned and delighted, the cheering crowd gave her a standing ovation and begged for an encore from this genre-crossing superstar. She bowed demurely and thanked the applauding throng for their gracious reception of her offering.

What a class act! Long before she stepped in to fill the shoes of a male Italian opera singer, Miss Aretha had established herself as the premiere artist of countless R&B, soul, gospel and pop classics. Throughout the course of a career now spanning into its fourth decade and showing no signs of letting up, this woman has become the epitome of what every leading lady aspires to be. In one word, a diva . . . a woman who has earned her place of prominence on life's stage through her faithfulness to her unique calling and to her Lord.

Bishop T. D. Jakes
Submitted by Don Dible

Light at the End of the Tunnel

There is no paycheck that can equal the feeling of contentment that comes from being the person you are meant to be.

Oprah Winfrey

It was the telephone call that every mother dreads: "Something's happened—there's been an accident." In one instant, life as I knew it changed. I stood in my office cubicle clutching the phone while my entire world plunged into a long tunnel of darkness.

The woman running the in-home day care center had been ironing clothes. She had gone to the bathroom for just a second. My precocious six-month-old baby had crawled away from the play area, and pulled on the dangling cord. The iron fell, missing her infant skull by a millimeter. But the hot water . . . They told me to brace myself for what I'd see when I got to the hospital.

There was no time for tears or hysteria. Adrenaline shot through my system as I grabbed my purse with shaky hands, dropped the telephone and dashed out the door—ignoring the pleas from coworkers to let them drive. Before they could catch up to me, I'd reached my car, jumped in and screeched out of the company parking lot. During the interminable drive to the hospital, my thoughts ricocheted between cold logic and bargaining with God.

It was just an iron. How bad could it be? Okay, she might have a dark patch on her skin when she grows up, but if it really bothers her, we'll have it removed with plastic surgery. Lord, please don't let it be worse than that.

I saw her innocent, doe-brown eyes first. Eyes that had cried so much there was a nurse applying drops to keep them from drying out. My baby looked up at me, too worn out to even whimper. But her eyes said it all, "Mommy save me. Make it stop hurting."

In that moment I realized how powerless I was. There was nothing in my upbringing to prepare me for this. Nothing in my formal Ivy League education offered answers. Nothing I'd ever experienced caused the level of helplessness and pain that seeing my infant in this condition created.

I fought against the immediate instinct to sweep her into my arms as my eyes raked my child's body, searching for the wound. This took milliseconds, but it felt like it was happening in slow motion. Then I saw it. The doctor was talking in the background, but the ringing in my ears drowned out his words. Everything he was saying sounded like the parents in the Charlie Brown cartoons: "Blah, blah, blah, waah, waah, waah."

My beautiful, perfect baby, born just six months ago, looked like a cherry bomb had exploded in her hand. The water had run out of the iron, and her fleece outfit had held in the heat. The veins beneath her butter-soft skin had fused and imploded internally. The doctor was saying something about amputations . . . *God and I had talked—He could not be allowing this!* All that was left of the tiny, perfect, beautiful long fingers that used to touch my face when I nursed her was a bloody stump. That's when the room went black.

In the minutes I spent on my knees, my entire life flashed before me—every act of vanity, everything I'd ever done wrong, came back to haunt me with the question, was this why? Then I began questioning my career as a six-figure-salary sales executive for high-tech firms. As I knelt on the dirty hospital floor in designer hose, a stunning Ellen Tracy navy-blue suit, pearls, silk blouse by Liz Claiborne and shoes by Fendi, but with a marriage that was teetering on the edge, I blamed myself for every conceivable aspect of failing as a mother. I would have traded every accomplishment in the world to have my child in one piece. That's when the tears became blended with wails so piteous that I was sure they weren't coming from me. The people talking to me just didn't understand that I was having an out-of-body experience.

All I could envision was a young girl, a teenager, hiding her body beneath clothes, unable to freely go to the beach, unable to find someone who would look beyond the scars to see her beauty. My mind tortured itself until I shut down all thought of the future. I sat in a chair by the window, too numb to even cry.

Then came the lawyers. Eventually, I found out there was no legal case to be had, no settlement to insulate my family from financial burden while we suffered. The day care center had no substantial assets to claim in a civil case. Eighty percent of the medical costs would be paid for, but that left a whopping 20 percent that was my responsibility to pay—which wiped out ten years of stocks, bonds, 401(k) plans and everything I'd so-called put away for a rainy day. This was beyond a rainy day; this was a biblical flood. The difference was that Noah was prepared; God had at least warned him. I was caught off-guard in the downpour.

Next came the corporation's executives. Their voices were consoling, but their message was chilling: They couldn't leave my territory fallow. It wasn't personal—just business. I could either choose to be laid off, so that I'd have some monies coming in, or I could take parental leave for a year without pay. I took door number one, the lesser of two evils.

My survival instinct kicked in while I sat in the hospital, living like a quiet ghost for endless days . . . months. It was clear—I had to get my child home. But I knew I couldn't leave her in the care of anyone ever again. I just wasn't ready for that. So I consolidated and reorganized all my debt. I remembered what my mother used to say, "Pride goeth before a fall." I fell on my sword before every place that I owed money—utility companies, the mortgagor, the credit lenders—and I made arrangements. But soon, I knew my unemployment would run out, and I wouldn't even have those revenues to fall back on.

What could I do from home? How could I make money and watch my baby at the same time? I knew how to write good business proposals, and I realized that small non-profit agencies needed to raise money through grants. What I quickly began to see emerging within my life was a pattern of skills and support groups that I'd taken for granted. I started a home-based business as a grant-writing freelancer. My struggling marriage had finally collapsed, and divorce was imminent. Child support was spotty, at best. But after a few years I could take small adult-education teaching assignments, as my daughter's wounds had healed and she could now tie her shoes.

Meanwhile, I scoured my dwindling magazine subscriptions, knowing that each issue would probably be the last since I hadn't paid the bills. Then I saw a short story contest in *Essence* magazine. My goal was to write ten pages of drama in hopes of getting the twenty-five-hundred-dollar prize money. That effort turned into seventy-five seemingly useless pages of action adventure that I gave to my friends to edit down. We laughed at my foolishness, and they implored me to finish the story that they'd copied and passed around the office, even if for nothing more than my own therapy and theirs. Six weeks later I had 780 pages of a steamy romance with a dashing, Latino James Bond and a daring, strong African American heroine. Then I threw the story in the bottom of my closet and forgot about it for a year.

My friends, however, refused to believe this wasn't a book, and they insisted that I go to New York City to attend a writer's conference. That's when my life changed again. I found an editor and an agent at the same conference over lunch. The conversation ultimately turned into a two-book deal for Kensington Publishing's new Arabesque line, and the rest is history.

Ten years later, I have a solid reputation as an economic development consultant and sixteen novels and four novellas under my belt. I've remarried my high school sweetheart. My daughter is a laughing, happy twelve-year-old with a busy social schedule. No one would ever know what we'd gone through, except to glimpse her hand . . . and I'm at home, full-time, doing what I love: writing.

Mercifully, the light at the end of this tunnel wasn't an oncoming train. It was daylight. Pure, joyous daylight.

Leslie Banks

And He Looks Just Like Me

There should be no "Negro History Corner" or "Negro History Week." There should be an integration of African American culture in all of its diversity throughout the curriculum.

Janice Hale Benson

Every cell of my body quivered. I was about to step into unknown territory; I was terrified and alone. On the outside I looked great. My mom had made sure I was dressed superbly, but on the inside I was shaking. As I sat on the bus that early drizzly morning, I looked at the faces of the people around me. No one seemed to notice I was gripped with fear.

Today was "Youth in Government Day" in San Francisco, and I had been chosen to represent my high school. I had never been to City Hall, and now I was going to be a politician for one whole day. Everyone told me how lucky I was and that this was a great opportunity, but none of this soothed me.

We didn't have a car, so I was on my own during the

morning rush hour. As I boarded the second bus that would deliver me to City Hall, I had a panic attack. My knees started to shake, and I felt sick.

Clutching my umbrella, I approached City Hall determined to be okay. There was a steady line of cars dropping off other kids. My heart sank because no one looked like me. I walked into the reception room desperately looking for a familiar face. I was disappointed again. Out of two hundred high school kids, approximately ten were African American. We acknowledged each other with that *Oh, I am so happy to see another black face* nod. We were all feeling displaced, and I knew that we all held the same wish inside. We were hoping that Judge Kennedy was our city government official. He was the only African American in city government at that time, and we would feel safe with him.

No luck.

I was escorted down the hall to meet Mr. Tax Assessor. When his secretary called to him that his student replacement had arrived, he came out of his office with a big smile that vanished when he saw me. He exchanged glances with his aide, while I read disappointment in his eyes. He was cordial to me—for all of five minutes before he dismissed me to his aide. I never saw Mr. Tax Assessor again.

Around mid-morning I was taken across the street for coffee and donuts with four local politicians. When we walked into the coffee shop, everything stopped. The people stopped talking, the waiters stopped waiting, even the coffee being poured stopped in midair. All eyes were fixed on this little black girl surrounded by four white politicians. I squared my shoulders, locked my knees, pushed my head up and glided across the floor with the biggest smile on my face. When we reached our table, the coffee started pouring, they started talking, and the waiters went back to serving.

"Well, Brenda, what do you want to do when you finish

high school?" The conversation at the table turned toward me.

"I really like psychology, and I love to work with children. I want to be a child psychologist," I declared.

They turned beet red and looked quickly at each other. After they recovered, someone cleared his throat and said, "Oh, my son is a child psychologist."

Then another said, "Brenda, you seem to be a very bright girl. You will probably make a good secretary."

The words in my head screamed, *A good* what? *How dare you! Your son can be a child psychologist, but I can't? How dare you try to dissuade me from my dream!* But the words coming out of my mouth were said, calmly and with conviction, "Oh yes, I *would* make a good secretary. But I am going to be a child psychologist."

They started to play the invisible game with me after that. You know—talking like you are not there. But I didn't care. I had made my stand.

As the day rolled on, I longed for something to validate my existence. On several occasions I wanted to scream, *"I am here and I matter! I am somebody!"*

When lunch finally rolled around, I was grateful. Only one more hour and I would be free from this alien land. I sat at a table with two other students who looked more bored than me. The keynote address was going to be from the student mayor, but I wasn't really interested in who was speaking or what was going to be said. I felt like I had been in a fight all day to defend my existence. All I wanted to do was leave City Hall and put this whole day behind me.

The "mayor's" introduction was made, and everyone started to applaud. As I swung my chair around and looked toward the stage, my mouth fell open, my eyes widened, and my whole body swelled with pride. I was looking at the student mayor-for-a-day and he looked just like me!

His skin was mocha chocolate, and with his full lips and his parted afro he represented us, he represented me. He was the most articulate, well-versed young man in the place, and I loved him for that—for with him, on this day, we would be counted. I sat in my seat smiling and thought to myself, *Look out, world, because here I come!*

That day, I decided I was going to be successful no matter what anyone said or felt. I was just as good as anyone else, and I could be anything I desired to be—even if my skin was black, maybe even *because* my skin was black!

Forty years later, a black man chose to become mayor of San Francisco—and he did. A black woman chose to become the city's tax assessor—and she did.

I did not decide to become a politician, nor did I decide to become a child psychologist, and no, I did not decide to become a secretary. I chose to become a child protective worker, and the most important part is that *I* chose—and I did!

Ahmon'dra (Brenda) McClendon

At the End of My Block

Both tears and sweat are salty, but they render a different result. Tears will get you sympathy; sweat will get you change.

Jesse Jackson

My beautiful sisters, frying their brains, going insane,
   right at the end of *my* block.
My exquisite brothers, exterminating, terminating and
   self-assassinating, all for the sake of the rock,
   at the end of *my* block.
Mommas being robbed on *my* back doorstep;
   babies being killed at *my* feet; brothers executing
   brothers on *my* front lawn; someone's grandfather is
   dying from not enough to eat, right at the end of *my*
   block.
What is this bizarre, demented, deranged and insane
   occurrence? This is life, breath and existence in *my*
   world, at the end of *my* block?
Huh, no this ain't no day in hell.
No, this ain't no day in jail.

No this isn't even a day down skid row.
This is a day on *my* block.
Should I run? Should I hide?
Should I leave? I want to cry.
Should I become a part of the problem?
Lord, how do I become a part of the solution?
Alls I know is that on *my* block, I am a part of, and I will
    stand strong and tall, not to buckle and not to fall, for
    I am a quilt sewn from the backbones of *my* great
    mothers. For I am not just a descendent of . . . I am a
    descendent of greatness, manifested from the pain,
    suffering, tears and lives of my great ancestors. For
    I am an all-purpose cleaner, working day and night
    to scrub away the spot, to eliminate the stain and
    remove the pain that sits at the end of *my* block.

Lisa Nichols

Excuse Me, Who's Just Another Statistic?

As a man thinketh in his heart, so is he.

Proverbs 23:7

"Are you pregnant?" asked my eighth-grade teacher.

"Yes." My answer was barely audible.

The full broomstick skirt I had made in my home economics class no longer concealed my protruding belly. At the tender age of thirteen, I was six months pregnant and had gotten that way the same day I lost my virginity. My teacher marched me to the principal's office.

It's been forty-nine years and I don't think I'll ever forget the expressions on my teacher's and principal's faces: a combination of sorrow and disgust. But, even more so, I will never forget their penetrating words.

"What a tragedy. She's an honor roll student," my teacher said, with tears in her eyes.

"And now all she will ever be is just another welfare statistic," the principal responded.

Their words pierced my heart like arrows and echoed in my head, adding judgments and anger to my already overburdened load of emotions, *". . . just another welfare statistic."*

When Mama suspected I might be pregnant, she took me to the doctor for an examination. A single parent herself with five children and two jobs, all she needed was another mouth to feed. When the doctor suggested that because of my age I should have an abortion, my mother asked me what I wanted to do. What a dilemma! I didn't want to be a mother, but the alternative seemed even worse.

My childhood hadn't been easy and motherhood would be even harder, but I made my choice. In spite of her deep and understandable disappointment, Mother said, "Well, we are going to have a baby!" She supported me—no matter what!

This year I celebrated my sixtieth birthday. My son is forty-seven. Today, I am an ordained minister married to a wonderful man of God who is highly respected throughout the country. I have established numerous ministries throughout the city of Detroit and authored five books. We have received a Point of Light Award from former President George Bush for our community service work. I have mentored many single mothers and young girls over the past twenty-five years, emphasizing that they don't have to be just another statistic.

If you're going to count me among your statistics, consider this: that I graduated from high school with honors at the age of sixteen, have never been on welfare and this year was voted "One of the Most Influential African American Women in Metropolitan Detroit."

Minister Mary Edwards

My Mother's Gift

Diptheria swept through my neighborhood when I was a small boy and it took many lives, including that of my little buddy, a boy everyone called "Gramps." He and I contracted it about the same time and we became backyard buddies; we played together because no one else would for fear of contracting what we had.

When Gramps's condition worsened, his mother got enough money together so that she could afford to take him to the hospital. He died there. It was my first exposure to the death of someone my own age. I had thought only old people died. I could not understand why Gramps would die, especially since, at the wake, he looked to be just asleep.

With the death of Gramps and several other neighborhood children, my mother became extremely protective of me. She was determined not to lose me. She refused to put me in the hospital because Gramps had died there. She talked the doctors into giving her the expensive medicine so that she could administer it herself. I can still envision how her hands shook when she gave it to me because she was so fearful of wasting any of it.

Mama did not sleep much during my illness but one night when she had gone to her own room to get some rest, I awoke to see a figure at the end of my bed. I recognized Miss Henry, an elderly neighbor whom I had often visited before her death several months earlier. Miss Henry loved me. I would sit by her bedside for hours and talk to her.

When I saw that it was Miss Henry who had come to my bedside, I yelled for my mama. "Mama! Miss Henry is in my room!" Mama came running. She was angry. My mama believed in stories of dead people who come back to try to take loved ones with them. After nursing me along, she surely was not going to let Miss Henry get me.

Mama came storming into the room cursing, "If she ain't dead yet, she soon will be!"

I had NO idea how Mama was going to kill Miss Henry AGAIN! But Mama didn't get the chance. When she came into the room and turned the light on, Miss Henry disappeared.

Mama kept cursing just in case she was hanging around somewhere. "Don't you come in here ever again messin' with my boy!" Mama said. "Stay outta this house!"

After her cursing wore down, Mama went to praying at my bedside and apparently the prayers did their work. In the next few days, the diptheria began to release its hold on me.

Then, just as it appeared that I was recovering, I came to her one morning after awakening and my voice was gone. Mama was devastated. After all she had gone through in dealing with my illness, she feared it had sneaked back in and robbed me of my voice forever.

That night, she set to praying again, "Lord, give the child my voice. I've talked enough in my life. I don't need my voice no more."

In the morning, I awakened and I called to my mother.

My voice had returned. My mama said, "Thank God!"

Or she tried to say that. Her voice was nothing but a squeak. I swear it is true.

She went to the medicine cabinet and took some of my diptheria medicine herself, and in a few hours her voice returned. But always after that, if I sassed my mother or she heard me curse, she reminded me of that time.

She would say, "You talk like that again, I'll take my voice back. I asked Jesus to give you my voice and he did. You use it like that, I'll take it back.

"You know Jesus does what I ask of him!"

I intend to use my mama's voice for good, lest I lose it for good. I urge you to use your talents and gifts to their fullest, too.

Les Brown

4

ACCEPTING ME, LOVING YOU

I find in being black, a thing of beauty: a joy, a strength; a secret cup of gladness, a native land in neither time nor space, a native land in every Negro face! Be loyal to yourselves: your skin, your hair, your lips, your Southern speech, your laughing kindness, your Negro kingdoms, vast as any other.

Ossie Davis

Who's That Calling My Name?

Go home and tell your daughters they're beautiful!

Stokely Carmichael

My real name is Vici, pronounced Veeshee. But most people call me Vicki or Vic.

In my younger days, when I wasn't as bright as I knew I should have been, I was in a relationship with a real fool, and everyone knew it but me. This guy was so beautiful, prettier than handsome, kind of like Prince. He had long eyelashes, smooth tan skin and a rock-hard body. He was yummy and he knew it; he was also cruel and he knew that, too.

But I was in love despite his shortcomings, and I was going to be the one woman who would change him into the loving, kind man I desperately wanted him to be. He had his own ideas, one of which was to change me into a Halle Berry look-alike. We all know the only sistah who looks like Halle Berry is Halle Berry. But I gladly obliged because after my miraculous transformation, he was really going to love me.

"Vic, you got potential, you can look like a movie star, all you have to do is . . . ," he began to convince me.

My mind told me to run for my life, but I loved him so I stayed with him.

He wanted me to lose about thirty pounds from my 150-pound, five-foot-five-inches frame, tone up my flabby midsection and get rid of my unsightly cellulite by starving myself and working out seven days a week.

Armed with prescription diet pills given to me by a quack doctor, a no-carb, high-protein diet, six days of hard cardio and four days of strength training, I was well on my way. The only thing that kept me from passing out was my fantasy of him being swept away by my beauty and grace after I lost the weight. I imagined the look on his face as he would take me in his arms and declare his everlasting love. All I had to do is get through about thirty step classes and fifty pounds of grilled chicken.

I lost seventeen pounds and I looked great.

"Damn, baby, you got it going on. All you gotta do is lose fifteen more pounds, and you'll be a knockout. I can't wait to show you off," he said.

The fact that I was hungry didn't matter because my man was looking at me like he never looked at me before. I had given up all my favorite foods, including bacon cheeseburgers from my favorite fast-food restaurant.

But one day when he wasn't around I figured I could spare one nine-hundred-calorie meal. I decided to indulge my taste buds and just work it off with an extra workout. I went to the fast-food restaurant and ordered a bacon cheeseburger combo. It was hot and juicy; the melted cheese stuck to my fingers and the smell of onions overwhelming my breath—and the hot crispy fries were delicious! It was so good, I wanted to call on Jesus!

After I ate the burger I cried at the table. I tried to hide my tears from a group of elderly people drinking coffee across from me. If I gained another ounce my man wouldn't want me, so I rushed to the bathroom and did what I had accused only white girls of doing: I stuck my fingers down my throat and gagged, but nothing came up. So many thoughts ran through my mind. *Black girls shouldn't be bulimic. I'm supposed to have a round, full figure.*

Once again, I plunged my fingers down my throat; it was painful. It was really irritating me that I wasn't being successful, but on the third attempt I finally released the contents of my belly. It was disgusting. I had a terrible headache from the gagging, my throat was burning from the stomach acid, I began to tear from the strain, and I peed on myself, not to mention the bad breath. *Why would anyone do something like this?*

When I saw my boyfriend that night, I told him that I had made myself throw up, hoping that it would play on his sympathy. Instead of loving me and telling me that I was okay being a size nine, he congratulated me on making a wise choice.

"Better in the toilet than on your thighs," he said. But the worst part was, I was happy he was finally pleased with me, so the bingeing and purging continued for the next few months.

I always had a good relationship with the Lord. I was cool with Him and He was cool with me. But during this time I didn't pray much because I didn't need Him all up in my business and dropping hints about the low-down-dirty-no-good-dog I had on my hands. In other words, I was running away from the truth.

Now, I knew deep down inside that I was destroying myself and that I probably wouldn't get the guy anyway. But see, growing up I was never the pretty girl. I was the dork with glasses, and at last a beautiful man was interested in me and I didn't care at what price. So the Lord could do all the whispering in my ear he wanted; I wasn't listening because I needed to win this time.

One night at the neighborhood café, he said matter-of-factly, "I met this girl. She's awesome, and she's beautiful and she's thin. . . ."

His cruelty felt like a dull knife gnawing a wound into my soul. I held my peace. *Never let them see you cry; never let them know they got to you,* the words of my sister's advice echoed in my mind.

The next day, numbed by stupidity and pain and tight exercise shorts, I went to the gym to get in an extra workout; it was supposed to be my day off, but I wasn't going to lose to the skinny girls.

While on the treadmill, I heard someone call me by my real name. "Vici."

"Vici!" I heard the voice a second time. I looked all around but didn't see anyone even vaguely familiar.

"Vici, leave it alone and give it to Me!"

It was the voice of God. Instantly I could feel my anxiety, my sadness and problems release from my body as if someone had pulled a plug from a drain. I realized I hadn't been listening to the still voice of God for the two years I was with my boyfriend. I had pushed God aside. Now He came to my rescue to give me my life back and to claim me once again. I knew it was God who spoke to me that day because he called me by my name, he didn't say "Vic" or "Vicki," he said "Vici." He spoke truth and reminded me who I really am and who I always should be: myself.

One year later, I met the man who would become my husband. He loves every ounce of my 156-pound, five-foot-five-inches frame. And we have eaten plenty of bacon cheeseburgers with our two children during our twelve-year marriage.

Vici Howard-Prayitno

Mother-and-Son Moment

We know that we are beautiful.

Langston Hughes

I can remember the look that he had on his face. So young, cute, innocent and a creation from me with God's help, of course—a true miracle indeed. A blessing that is worth more than anything. I'm talking about my son. I'm talking about raising this little guy as a single mother into a responsible black man.

One day my son caught me by surprise when he came to me and asked me a question. It was a Saturday morning, and I was busy typing away on my computer as I always do. I could hear the Saturday morning cartoons on in his room, which was right across from my bedroom. And here this little guy comes. Face still needs to be washed, eyes big and alive, with his black and gray Batman pajamas on, one pant leg higher than the other.

He says with his arms folded, "Mommy, why am I black?"

I could still hear myself clicking away at my keyboard,

when what this little four-year-old boy had just asked me caught my complete attention. My eyebrows raised and I stopped what I was doing. I looked at him. And we were both looking at each other.

I sat straight up in my chair and said, "Baby, why do you ask me that?"

"Well, Mommy, my friend at day care said white is better than black. He said his daddy told him so. So I wanna know why God made me black?"

At this moment I could feel the anger slowly overcoming me. However, I stopped it in its tracks. I looked at my son, and I just shook my head as I took hold of his little hands.

"Baby, white is not better than black, and black is not better than white. We all are the same, just with different colors. Like your box of crayons, there are a lot of different colors but they are all in the same box. God wanted to make different colors of people. So he did. He didn't want to make everybody the same color because that would be boring. Don't listen to everything everybody says. Some people may not like others because they are a different color, but that's mean and that's not right. God loves us all. Nobody is better than anybody else. Even our hands, we all have different colors. This is a good thing, not a bad thing."

I stopped there, just to see what his reaction was.

He looked at me with his eyes still big, and he said, "Okay, Mommy, nobody's better than anybody else. God likes black people and God likes me. Okay, Mommy." He started to leave, then he came back. "So is that why Elmo is red, and the Cookie Monster is blue and Kermit the Frog is green?"

I smiled at him, "Yes, that is why." What could I say to that sort of reasoning?

Hours later that same day, I went into my son's room to

see what he was doing. He was very quiet, which was not usual at all. What I found left me speechless, to say the least. My emotions were mixed between, should I get mad? or should I compliment him on getting the point? My son had drawn different colored hands all over his wall—red, blue, green, brown, orange. . . . I looked at the wall, keeping my emotions balanced, because I knew it had to be cleaned sooner or later. My son had never drawn on his wall before. Okay, on his dresser drawer, but not his wall.

As I stood there looking at these little small hands all over his bedroom, he tapped me on my side. From behind his back my son pulled out two pieces of paper. One was black construction paper with a lot of little white hands on it, and another sheet of paper was white with a lot of little black hands on it.

My son said, "Look, Mommy! Look what I drew. Look at my two papers. I wanna take them to my day care tomorrow and show my teacher and friend."

"That's good, baby, you do that. I like your two papers," I answered, leaving the wall out of it, still in shock and not yet sure how to handle it.

"I like them, too. I have to teach my friend and his daddy the truth."

I watched him as he went over to his little backpack and proudly stuffed the two papers inside.

I shook my head laughing to myself as I walked back into my bedroom thinking, *Kids are so smart. My baby is so smart. Why not, I'll let those hands sit on his wall, just a few days longer.*

I thought about what happened for the rest of the day. *Another job well done as a single black mother,* I thought.

Tinisha Nicole Johnson

Black 'n' White Snapshots

Every day of my life I walk with the idea I am black, no matter how successful I am.

Danny Glover

A few years ago, I was listening to a radio talk show hosted by one of those irritating conservative "shock jocks." The subject was race relations. Everyone had an opinion, especially a white caller named Sam from San Jose. His complaint was that blacks were too preoccupied with race. His advice: Try not thinking about race for twenty-four hours. He was convinced that if blacks could experience a day without worrying about race, we would all be the happier for it.

I laughed to myself, thinking, *Is that what white folks really believe? That we just sit around thinking about race?*

What that caller didn't understand is that for folks of color, living with race isn't a choice; it just is. The fact is, I would give anything for the chance to go through twenty-four hours without being *reminded* of my skin color and all the assumptions and misconceptions that go with it.

Sometimes those assumptions are of my own doing. After years of expecting the worst, and often getting it, I see racist ghosts where there are only innocent shadows. More often, though, race comes roaring into my daily life uninvited like a heat-seeking missile. Some days I am amazed at my swiftness in dodging its impact. Other days I'm slow to respond and find myself bruised and knocked off balance. The blows are rarely fatal, but the built-up scar tissue becomes painful over time. But then there are the funny moments when we get a glimpse of our own ever-ready shields and are forced to set them down and laugh.

It was one of those lazy Sunday afternoons: I had dozed off on the sofa under a pile of unread Sunday papers. Suddenly I hear the kids' voices getting louder and angrier.

Oh, I moan to myself. *They're at it again.* For weeks my thirteen-year-old son and eight-year-old daughter have been fighting constantly. I push down deeper in the sofa, deciding to ignore this spat hoping, if I stall long enough, my husband will intervene.

My ears jump to attention when I hear my daughter wailing, "I am light. I am very light."

My heart starts pounding after I hear my son shoot back, "You are not light. I don't know where you got that impression. You're anything but light."

I immediately go into my whack attack mode. I jump off the sofa, newspapers flying, rush past my husband who is standing in a nearby hallway, and burst like a bull into the TV room, pointing my hands at two very startled children.

"In this house, we do not make judgments about skin color. It doesn't matter whether you're light or dark. We are all beautiful African American people." By this time I am practically hyperventilating.

My two children look at me like I truly am a crazed woman.

My son speaks first . . . slowly, as if he is talking to someone who has lost her mind. "Mommmm, I am just telling her to get her heavy behind off my foot."

My daughter chimes in, "And I told him that I'm not heavy. I'm light. I am light, right, Mom?"

But my thirteen-year-old son isn't going to let me off the hook so easily. After all, how many times do you get to make your mom squirm?

"So, Mom, you want to tell us why you're lecturing us on what it means to be good African Americans?"

As I am trying to find a graceful retreat, sounds of my husband's snickering in the adjacent room quickly evolve into huge, bellowing laughter.

I manage a weak apology and mumble something about "You shouldn't tease your sister about her behind," and make a hasty exit right to my husband who is now doubled over laughing.

"You could have stopped me, you know."

"And miss you make a fool out of yourself?" he says. "Are you kidding? It was one of your better performances."

Judy Belk

I'm Coming Out

To think that I denied hip-hop so that I wouldn't lose my status as a member of the "popular" crowd in a high school full of gun-toting, dip-chewing, blue-eyeliner wearing children makes me sad. At the time, I was a die-hard U2 fan (still am today) and made bold declarations that hip-hop, this new music that was drawing attention to my blackness, would die. I thought that by rejecting the beats that I secretly danced to as I heard them seeping from my brother's bedroom, I could prove that I was just as good as all the white kids that I went to school with in Marietta.

The problem was that my skin color (light and questionable as it is) and ability to follow an eight count better than most were stereotypes that they used to measure my suspected blackness. The more stereotypes they could check off their lists, the closer I would move from eating with the "in crowd" to moving to the "colored" table in the lunch room.

This music had to die. It was ruining my social life. It was 1985, and I was hoping and praying that it would all be over by the time I was a senior.

Things didn't look good. In 1986, DJs started scratching my favorite Tears for Fears song, "Shout," into the mix of popular hip-hop songs. I was doomed. I couldn't hide the fact that this music started to move me. It started to excite me. I wanted to come out. I loved hip-hop! Should I out myself and show the world that I was a black girl posing in a white girl get-up, usually in the uniform of a cheer-leading outfit? If I came out, I could lose everything: my white boyfriend, my popularity as "A team" cheerleader and my elusive position as "weird-looking" girl.

I wasn't ready to come out yet, even though I was diggin' the Salt and Pepa remix of "Push-It." I knew every word.

Then, on top of everything, my younger brother became a huge break-dancer. He was in the papers and everything. We had the same last name. It was okay to ignore him in the halls at school, but I couldn't ignore the headlines he was getting. High fives in the hall. Newspaper articles. People started to ask questions. Our "head cheerleader" asked me point blank, "Is that break-dancer your brother?" I sheepishly replied, "Maybe."

Cut to 1987. I am a senior in high school and have been named "dance choreographer" with none other than the two other black girls on the cheerleading squad. I made sure to keep my contact with them to a minimum because otherwise everyone would look at me as, well . . . black. But the music of Dougie Fresh's "The Show," Run DMC's "Walk This Way" and The Beastie Boys' "Brass Monkey" brought me closer to these women. We "snaked" and "wopped" our way to being one of the best cheerleading teams that year.

I bonded with these girls. We shared cultural traditions like dancing our dances, braiding one another's hair and talking about things in our community that only a young black girl would know. I never confessed my "blackness" but hid behind "mixed" identity labels that kept me feel-ing safe. I will never forget the knowing looks in their eyes that told me if I wanted to come over to their side, they would be there with open arms. I loved them for that. They offered true friendship despite my self-denial. I refused them, hip-hop and blackness once again.

After high school I went to Europe and took a long look at myself. How I had passed throughout high school is still a mystery to me. I found that hip-hop was all over the world. I met Africans in Paris who encouraged me to love myself and the hip-hop inside of me. My grandfather was Algerian, and I connected with African people for the first time in my life. The "real" me was a black me. If people didn't like me because I was African American, then they weren't my friends. I released all of the images projected on me about how to measure blackness. I accepted the fact that as a black woman, I had more to offer my community and the world by being myself, than I had if I pretended I was someone else.

In Paris, I came out. I was a black American woman and a hip-hop fan. I would support my brother in his music tastes and embrace the beauty of my family and community. I would never answer a question about my race or ethnicity with uncertainty. I was part of a legacy that was rich and beautiful. I would never hide from that again.

Nicole Hodges Persley

The Skin We're In

"His skin looks like charcoal," said my friend Nellie, when the new boy entered our fourth-grade classroom made up entirely of African American students. *Charcoal,* I thought, as I studied this newcomer with interest. He was taller than a lot of the other boys in the room. Tall and handsome. And he wasn't skinny. See, 'cuz most of the fourth-grade boys were skinny. Their knees looked like their bones were trying to escape from bein' suffocated by their skin, and their arms were frail and wobbly-like. But he wasn't skinny. Uh-uh. His bones were growin' strong, like he was a dedicated milk-drinker. And his skin, dark as the space behind my closed eyelids, was greeting our noisy classroom with a voice of its own. It spoke to us, and we all halted to attention, giving it our complete focus.

"Ha ha! Choco Bliss!" spunky little Wynton shouted to the room, and we erupted with laughter. I laughed too, not because it was very funny, but because I wanted Mr. "Choco Bliss" to catch me smiling.

"Michael, you may have a seat over there," pointed Mrs. McMorley, focusing Michael, aka Choco Bliss, toward the boys' side of the room. Michael looked at her and nodded confidently. He shoul' was confident. Um hmm. And did I mention he was tall? And handsome?

My eyes were on Michael as he took an empty desk across the room. I wondered how comfortable he was, sitting over there next to all of the silly boys. I wanted to make sure they weren't gonna be makin' him feel uncomfortable or nuthin'. 'Cuz sometimes they made me feel real uncomfortable. Always makin' jokes and laughing with each other. But you know, that's just how silly boys are.

The whole class musta been thinkin' what I was thinkin', 'cuz they wouldn't stop staring in Michael's direction. In fact, we were so engaged in the richness of him that Mrs. McMorley had to raise her voice a couple of octaves higher just to get our attention back.

"You all are supposed to be focusing on your logic problems, not our newcomer," she fussed.

Immediately the whole class shifted our eyeballs back to the class work laid out in front of us. I continued with my logic questions: *If Jesse is Johnny's cousin, and Johnny is the boy in the yellow sweater, and the boy in the yellow sweater is friends with Josie, then who is Josie's friend?*

There was no sense in me trying to make sense out of Josie, Johnny and Jesse. Michael made a lot more sense to me. I strayed from my work again and drove my eyes back over to his side of the room. I wondered how well he understood his logic questions. He had entered our class kind of late and Mrs. McMorley had already finished explaining the lesson. You would think she would've considered that before makin' him do it. Maybe I could volunteer to help him. Then I would be able to sit by him. Then we could talk and become friends and maybe even trade friendship rings or something. Then maybe . . .

RING! The school bell interrupted my concerns for Michael, and we were given free time. The class got up and began to move around the room, searching for books, games, etc. The giggling goofy girls circled the reading section (surely to gossip rather than to read). I got up and moved closer to Michael. He was headed for the game section with all of the other boys, of course. I preferred to be slow and calculating so that no one would notice my preoccupation with befriending this dark stranger.

I moved leisurely toward the reading section, keeping my eyes on Michael the entire time. That's when it happened.

Not paying attention to the shelf in front of me, I reached for the book at the same time as Natalie. She eyed me carefully and followed my gaze to Michael's whereabouts. A flame of dawning comprehension immediately ignited in her eyes. She giggled and squealed audibly, "Oooooo. . . . Dominique likes Michael. Dominique likes the charcoal boy!"

"I do not," I mumbled in annoyance, trying to maintain enough composure not to slap her face and push her into the bookshelf.

My calmed embarrassment must've been a sort of spinach to her, because suddenly her voice got stronger. Louder. "Dominique likes Charcoal!!!"

The other girls started laughing, singing along with her, "Ewwww . . . Dominique likes Michael!" or worse, "Dominique likes the black boy!!!" (Weren't we all black?!)

Now, I was always one for attention . . . but certainly not when the joke was on me! The boys looked toward me and snickered. Suddenly they joined in, sneering and chortling, pointing at me like I was on display. Michael looked on too, snorting and jeering with the rest of them. I was so confused my head began to pierce with pain. Didn't he know that they were laughing at him, too? My buttery skin was turning orange from flush, and I felt my eyebrows scowl in disgust. Suddenly, without thought, my defenses activated and went to work on my honor.

As loud as I could, I spattered, "I don't like ugly charcoal boy!"

The pointing stopped. The class turned to Michael and immediately erupted with laughter.

Michael smiled shyly in spite of himself. He shifted uncomfortably back and forth on his heels and dropped his head in shame. There. I had done it. I had now taken the attention off of myself and put it on him. He was embarrassed. Almost as embarrassed as me.

Mrs. McMorley found our laughter and ridicule annoying, and banished us to our desks. Free time was over. And so was my hope of ever coming to know Michael as a friend. I looked over to him as he followed his feet back to his desk. For the remainder of the day, his head never lifted from its bow.

I felt disgusted with myself. It was the easiest thing to do—just pass my embarrassment on to Michael, and they would leave me alone. But I felt worse than ever. I was never going to be his friend now. He would never like me after something so horrible as that. Never. I was sure that Michael hated me. But it didn't matter. At that point, I hated myself.

The next day at school, I was pulling my logic homework out of my bag at my locker. Both Michael and I had last names beginning with the letter M, so naturally, our lockers were close. He came up next to me and put his bag beside my feet. I watched him silently as he pulled his logic homework from his bag. It was incomplete.

"Did you know how to do your homework?" I inquired softly. I woulda spoke up a bit but, you know, I didn't want him to yell at me or nuthin'.

He shook his head apprehensively, "Uh . . . no . . . not really."

"Well . . . um . . . maybe I could . . . um . . . help you . . . if Mrs. McMorley'll let me," I stuttered. "She shouldna given you homework on your first day no way," I added. I hoped that he knew this was my way of apologizing.

"It's okay. She said she just wanted me to try. I'm not gonna get in trouble," he explained.

"Oh," I said disappointedly. I was really hoping to help. "But, uh . . . thanks," he finished, and smiled.

I blushed and smiled, too. He blushed back, and I swear I saw the most profound shade of red I had ever seen through his glowing skin.

It didn't take long after that before we were friends. And soon Michael became the most popular boy in the fourth grade. The other boys looked up to him because of his height and strength. Most of us little goofy giggling girls that were madly in love with him never quite learned how to express that, so instead we continued with bouts of "Choco Bliss" and "Charcoal" throughout our fourth-grade year. Michael would fight back, throwing out a "Mellow Yellow" or a "Banana Boat" in his defense. We would argue. We would laugh. We would continue to be insecure in the skin we were in.

Some fifteen years later, I fell in love and found my own "Choco Bliss." Dark skin glistening like the heavens, a familiar rouge glow in his skin when he blushes with passion, he is all I could ask for. When I look at him, I see a beauty I've always seen when I look at dark complexioned blackness. I tell him about Michael. He tells me about little girls just like me from his childhood that made loving his complexion a challenge. We laugh. We argue. We find comfort in the skin we're in.

Dominique Morisseau

Lord, When Will This Journey End?

Steep yourself in black history, but don't stop there. I love Duke Ellington and Count Basie, but I also listen to Bach and Beethoven. Do not allow yourself to be trapped and snared in limits set for you by someone else.

Gordon Parks

Who am I? I was born in 1929, the year of the Great Depression. My birth certificate defined me as colored and colored people were considered second-class citizens. To be more specific, we were considered nonentities.

I was born at a time in America when colored people entered through the back door, drank from separate water fountains, rode on the back of the bus or stood up if a white person needed the seat. In some Southern cities we couldn't walk on the same sidewalk when a white person approached. We attended schools for colored only, with worn-out, hand-me-down books.

I was born "colored." I reached my teens and was labeled "Negro." I looked the same, felt the same, so I didn't give it another thought. Some even labeled me "Nigrah." I reached adulthood and a twentieth-century prophet, Martin Luther King Jr., and his "I've Got a Dream" came along and labeled me "black"—black and proud. He said I was somebody. My mama had imprinted this on my brain since I was born; so I embraced this man and my blackness.

After Martin's assassination, Jesse Jackson, an idealist emerged. Just as I had become comfortable with my blackness, he labeled me "African-American." As soon as you could snap a finger the whole world took on this definition of me. It is true I have African ancestry. My great-great-grandmother, an African, was sold into slavery by her own people. A rape by her slave owner when she was only fifteen resulted in the birth of a baby girl. The baby grew into a woman, escaped slavery with her mother, was rescued by Native Americans, lived on the reservation, married and had six Native American children. One was my maternal grandmother, making me a mixture of African, Caucasian and Native American. I am not an immigrant in this country. I was born in America of American-born parents and grandparents, all of mixed heritage. Are we now expected to relinquish part of our heritage?

Who am I really? I have now reached the winter of my years. My feet are tired, and my body is worn. I have traveled a thousand miles, a dreamer. I have been called colored, nigrah, nigger, Negro, black, and now African American. I have been told to be peaceful, be a separatist, be militaristic, bear arms, be part of a rainbow, and all I want is to be recognized as a person, a person who has made significant accomplishments in a world that continues to try to define me. My life has been an instrument for good in a world filled with hate and divisiveness.

My time is running out, and all I want is to be me, a

woman who has made her mark in this world. I want to leave a legacy, to those who come behind me, the new seedling that will emerge come spring. I just want my gravestone to read, "Here lies a woman, a person, who walked a thousand miles in pursuit of her dream and made it."

Little seedling, keep on trucking, and never give up on your dream to be somebody in America, the land that all of your forebears had a hand in carving, and don't let nobody define who you are and what you should be, no matter what your race, religion or creed.

I've come to the end of my journey, folks, and I am going inside now to escape the cold of winter. And I want to leave you with this message: "Don't let nobody turn you 'round, turn you 'round, turn you 'round. No, don't let nobody turn you 'round. Glory hallelujah."

Myrtle Peterson

Lord, Why Did You Make Me Black?

Our flag is red, white and blue, but our nation is a rainbow—red, yellow, brown, black and white—and we're all precious in God's sight.

Jesse Jackson

Why did You make me black?
Why did You make me someone the world wants to hold back?

Black is the color of dirty clothes; the color of grimy hands and feet.
Black is the color of darkness; the color of tire-beaten streets.

Why did You give me thick lips, a broad nose and kinky hair?
Why did You make me someone who receives the hatred stare?

Black is the color of a bruised eye when somebody gets
   hurt.
Black is the color of darkness. Black is the color of dirt.

How come my bone structure's so thick; my hips and
   cheeks so high?
How come my eyes are brown and not the color of the
   daylight sky?

Why do people think I'm useless? How come I feel so
   used?
Why do some people see my skin and think I should be
   abused?

Lord, I just don't understand; What is it about my skin?
Why do some people want to hate me and not know the
   person within?

Black is what people are "listed," when others want to
   keep them away.
Black is the color of shadows cast. Black is the end of the
   day.

Lord, You know, my own people mistreat me; and I know
   this just isn't right. They don't like my hair or the way
   I look.
They say I'm too dark or too light.

Lord, don't You think it's time for You to make a change?
Why don't You re-do creation and make everyone the
   same?

God answered:

Why did I make you black? Why did I make you black?

Get off your knees and look around. Tell Me, what do
   you see?
I didn't make you in the image of darkness. I made you
   in the likeness of ME!

I made you the color of coal from which beautiful
   diamonds are formed.
I made you the color of oil, the black-gold that keeps
   people warm.

I made you from the rich, dark earth that can grow the
   food you need.
Your color's the same as the panther's, known for beauty
   and speed.

Your color's the same as the black stallion, a majestic
   animal is he.
I didn't make you in the image of darkness, I made you
   in the likeness of ME!

All the colors of a heavenly rainbow can be found
   throughout every nation;
And when all those colors were blended well, you
   became my greatest creation.

Your hair is the texture of lamb's wool, such a humble,
   little creature is he.
I am the Shepherd who watches them. I am the One who
   will watch over thee.

You are the color of midnight-sky, I put the stars' glitter
in your eyes.
There's a smile hidden behind your pain, that's the reason your cheeks are high.

You are the color of dark clouds formed when I send My
strongest weather.
I made your lips full so when you kiss the one you love
they will remember.

Your stature is strong; your bone structure thick to
withstand the burdens of time.
The reflection you see in the mirror . . . The image that
looks back at you is MINE!

RuNett Nia Ebo

Majority of One

My blackness has never been in my hair. Blackness is not a hairstyle.

Bertha Gilkey

I wanted to do it for so long—throw out my chemically relaxed hair for a natural. I had long admired sisters who sported braids, afros or locks and tossed their heads in defiance of mainstream-endorsed hair beauty regimens.

I want to be one of them, I often thought, but continually struggled with the idea of shedding the thick, dark brown, longer-than-shoulder-length hair I had been told I was blessed with.

It was so tied to my identity I could not bear to part with it. From my wide-eyed childhood to long-legged adolescence, each trip to the beauty parlor was marked by a beautician's friendly question.

"Chile, where in the world did you get all that hair?"

Not knowing exactly how to reply to the question, I would always look at the floor, and whisper "Thank you," while secretly harnessing the attention my hair brought.

Those precious times were a marked contrast to how I often felt about myself as a darker-skinned black adolescent, when it seemed that lighter-skinned people were all the rage in our largely black middle-class suburb.

I once asked my mother, who like the rest of family has a caramel-brown tone, if I was adopted. She pulled out ultrasound images from a scrapbook to assure me I was not. And later, she created a poster of chocolate-toned African Americans, like Iman and others, to show me I was beautiful.

As thankful as I was for her reassurance, I thought she was doing her motherly duty and still struggled to find something about me that was beautiful. I thought about those trips to the hairdresser, how special they made me feel, and so I turned to my hair for acceptance. People had always made a big deal about my longer-than-average black-girl hair. It was special when my mother allowed me to wear my hair "out," because on those days I could truly swish and sway my hair with the best of my lighter-skinned peers.

At Duke University, I was glad I didn't have to wear extensions or a weave. I grew it longer than ever, thinking it would allow me a better chance of getting into a sorority I was interested in. But by my junior year, I realized how long I'd been buying into the mainstream-enforced, black women-accepted notions of beauty. The ruse was exposed, and I was not, after all, like Samson; my hair didn't hold that much power anymore.

Again I questioned, *What about me was beautiful?*

That summer, I wrote a poem celebrating African Americans who had the courage to make strides that included wearing their hair natural in the sixties and seventies. One line read, "I wasn't there but I heard about those who dared to put down the hot-comb for a minute, don a dashiki and look themselves in the mirror exclaiming 'Beautiful.'"

I longed to be like the people I felt so strongly about, people who found their beauty and acceptance in themselves.

The excuse I made to myself was that natural hair was a statement of beauty for another time and place. But deep inside, I was really unsure whether I could ever be beautiful if I discontinued my fourteen-year relationship with no-lye chemical relaxers. I knew I had long been afraid of finding out. So, after a false start my senior year, I thought I would give it another try.

I am going to go natural, I told myself.

The first three months after my last relaxer in November were easy. I had gone longer without a perm before. The real test began in March, when my "waves" grew into full-fledged naps. April came, and my mother and friends at church who, like me, knew no lives without perms or presses, asked, "Lisa, what are you planning to do with your hair again?"

I was confident in my decision to go natural but at times felt like Thoreau's "majority of one." Weeks went by. I pressed on but not without doubt: *Was I crazy? Was this reasonable? Would this allow me to continue to live and work in mainstream America?*

I felt like the world wanted me to just pick up a relaxer and be done with it. But I had to fight; I had to do it. I had to try. By May, I decided to grow my hair gradually and get braided extensions, so no one except me could witness the war being waged between my fragile, permed hair and the stronger natural roots that rose like defiant Zulu warriors month by month.

The situation was metaphoric. As the mercury rose, my roots encroached upon the territory the relaxed hair had held unchallenged for years—my heart. July came, and it was time to take out the micro braids. Once they were completely out, I vacillated between going back to a perm and continuing my quest.

I started to shield my roots from the public view with a scarf. Then on a Friday in August I looked in the mirror, grabbed scissors from a drawer and snipped a little from the back. *Just enough so I can change my mind and get away with it,* I told myself.

I snipped some more. *I can hide this section with a scarf if I change my mind.*

When I was done, I knew it would be an adjustment. I could no longer toss my head to and fro and have my hair swish and sway.

But I could finally really look myself in the mirror, and smile, exclaiming *"Beautiful."* And that was all right with me.

Lisa R. Helem

Disappearing Strands

Love is like a virus. It can happen to anybody at any time.

Maya Angelou

Hair to black people is personal and always something to contend with. My hair was a symbol of my black pride. I forged a bond with myself years ago. I committed to wearing my hair only in its natural state, and gained new appreciation for its uniqueness. Black hair has styling capabilities that few other hair types can accomplish— from cornrows to flat twists, Bantu knots to goddess braids.

We wear these natural styles as a symbol of pride and dignity. More importantly, black hair is a shield of protection, originally given to us by our maker to shade our heads from the searing sun and protect us from the cold of night. Although difficult to deal with most times, black hair is a blessing that was bestowed upon my people, a blessing that is painfully absent to me now.

Nineteen days after my first chemotherapy treatment,

my hair began to disappear. The nurse explained that because of the type of chemo medicine I would receive over the next twelve weeks, I would definitely lose my hair. I became consumed with thoughts of the road ahead of me in my battle with breast cancer.

There I was, wearing an African-style head wrap pretending I didn't feel bald spots forming underneath. I never saw the strands fall; my hair just seemed to dissolve. I could no longer ignore what I felt or the reflection in the bathroom mirror.

My hair was fashioned into two-strand twists. Each twisted section had begun to rise as if my hair was swelling from the roots. Portions of the side and back of my hair had developed baby-smooth bald areas. As my fingers groped through the peaks and valleys, they rested on a twist separating from my scalp.

My husband, Charles, inspected my hair. There was no denying it. I was going bald!

Charles looked at me sympathetically and asked, "Do you want me to cut it?"

"Yes," I replied with a heavy sigh as I sank onto the commode lid.

Charles began cutting my neck-length twists and carefully placing them in a plastic zipper bag. He said I would want to keep them for sentimental value. At that moment, I did not give a damn about those twists of hair. My husband kept softly conveying words of support and encouragement. He assured me that I would be even more beautiful to him without the hair.

He stopped cutting long enough to ask if I was okay. Tears the size of nickels swelled up in my eyes and spilled out over my cheeks. I collapsed against Charles's legs, grabbing him around the waist. He held me close, lifting me up with comforting words that salved my panic and grief inside. We moved to the kitchen where I could sit in a chair, and Charles could finish the haircut using clippers. I sat there in silent shock, paralyzed by the trauma.

After cleaning up, I was emotionally exhausted. I crawled into bed next to Charles, enjoying the warmth of his body next to mine. He kissed the top of my head and forehead several times before falling off to sleep. I lay there waiting for sleep to come. But an uncomfortable coldness invaded my body. The frigid sensation started in my feet and slowly crept up my shins. It felt like death had started its ascent. Anxiety and panic raged in my chest.

With a sudden force, the top half of my body sprang straight up in bed.

I reached over to Charles, gasping for air. "God, please help me, I'm dying."

Charles pulled me down next to him, asking me what was wrong. After the wave of panic settled, I realized I was cold because I no longer had hair—not because I was dying. Although my head was covered with a scarf, my body heat was still escaping from the top.

I had been preparing myself emotionally for the hair loss. Now, how I looked was less bothersome than how I felt. I could wear wraps, wigs or hats to cover my head. What I felt was an absence of protection and strength, my entire body exposed as if I had lost a layer of skin, a vital organ.

As dawn approached, I awoke to a new day with a heightened sense of respect for black hair and its value to our physical existence.

Now, instead of embracing the blessing of hair, I choose instead to embrace the blessing of love, and of life!

Valerie M. McNeal

You Go, Salt-and-Pepper!

No one can figure out your worth but you.

Pearl Bailey

The bible says gray hair is a crown of glory, and I've been sporting that glory since my early twenties.

In fact, my prematurely gray hair, inherited from my father, has always commanded attention and served as a conversation piece that reinforced my youthful appearance. "You look too young to have so much gray hair!" "How did you get your hair that way? Did you dye it?" "I love your hair! I hope my gray grows in like that." "You're wearing that gray hair, girl!"

I received many comments from men who liked it, too, including my husband. He is one of the reasons I never felt compelled to dye my hair. I would respond with a delighted "Thank you!" to these compliments, armed, of course, with the knowledge that the gray hair didn't match my age.

My eighty-something aunt, who gets a rinse every time she goes to the beauty shop, would sometimes complain that my gray hair was making *her* look old! Nevertheless, I took a certain pride in my salt-and-pepper—until, that is, my age began to catch up with it.

The compliments changed, too. Instead of reminding me of my youth, people began to say things to remind me of my age. "I hope my wife ages the way you do." "I wish I had the courage to let my gray hair grow in." Once, when walking with my two young children, I even got the dreaded, "Are these your grandchildren?" The comments I once delighted in were no longer so welcome.

As I approached fifty, I considered dying my hair for the first time. If I was going to get rid of my beloved salt-and-pepper, I was going to make it an event. Since a big bash was being planned for my fiftieth birthday, I decided to do it before then. I was excited, but still a little shaky.

I must have changed my mind a hundred times as I fantasized what it would be like. *How would I look? What if I didn't like it? Or what if I loved it and wanted to bolt to the shop every time the gray roots peeked through? Did I really want to spend that much energy on my hair?*

Finally, I imagined my grand entrance to the party. A hush would fall over the crowd as I, elegantly dressed, appeared in the doorway. There would be spontaneous applause, oohs, ahhs and admiring comments. But this time, the comments would not be about my gray hair, but about the *lack* of it! "Girl, you should have washed that gray out of your hair a long time ago! You look wonderful! And you look so much younger!"

After a few weeks, I arrived at a final decision: I would take the plunge.

When the day of my hair appointment arrived, butterflies swirled in my stomach, and I reminded myself that this would all be worth it. I concentrated on quieting my pounding heart as I explained to the young operator what I wanted.

"Take away all the gray!" I said grandly.

"Why do you want to do that?" she asked.

I was speechless for a moment, and I looked up at her.

"I think your gray hair is beautiful." She looked around the large shop and began to ask the other operators and their customers. "What do you all think?"

One by one they agreed and murmured or shouted their disapproval of a dye job. "No! You'll ruin it!" "There's no way I'd dye my hair if it looked like yours." "Don't do it!" they all said with one voice. The young operator looked at me and said, "See?"

Confused, I pondered this unexpected turn of events. Was it possible that these ladies had some regrets for not making that choice themselves, or were they just being polite, not wanting to hurt my feelings?

Yes, I had always thought my gray hair was beautiful, but how would I feel when the next person on the street said something I didn't think was so flattering? Was I confident enough to walk out of the shop the same way I'd walked in?

On the other hand, I was entitled to make a change if I wanted to. Women change their hair color all the time. It's no big deal! Clarity finally came at the end of this internal dialogue. I realized that it was my decision and mine alone. I could feel myself sitting taller in the chair as I finally told the operator what I wanted her to do.

After she finished with my hair, she spun me around to face the mirror. I realized then that I had made the right choice. I liked . . . no, I *loved* what I saw. I paid the operator and got up from the chair. I thought about my grand entrance later that evening and smiled. I would knock their socks off!

In a nearby mirror, another customer studied her hair and lightly fingered her gray roots. As I headed for the door, she turned to look at me and said, "You go, Salt-and-Pepper!"

Carol Ross-Burnett

I Owe You an Apology

If we don't learn to manage pain by dissolving it or letting it go, it infects the future.

Bishop T. D. Jakes

As I sat with my sistah-friends relaxing, relating and releasing, we began to speak of all the men we had dated or "kinda-sorta" dated. As usual, we segued into an energetic comparison of our "R.D.—relationship drama." We were sharing the woes brought on us by our black men, and I was leading the pack with my male-drama, historical reenactment of "Heartbreak Hotel."

I began with the fact that at age sixteen, I was afraid of their smooth-talking ways and their quick unrefined moves, but by the time I was eighteen they intrigued me; ultimately, they piqued my curiosity. When I was twenty-one they were using the word "love" to spend the night at my house, but I never could get them to stay for breakfast.

We were on a male-bashing roll. "Yeah, girl, he ain't worth a two-dollah bill . . . ain't that right . . . gimme a high-five on that one!"

I went on to add that by age twenty-five we were both in "the game"; they were out to get theirs, and I was out to get mine. "You betta believe, girl, we gotta teach 'em a lesson," one of my diva sistah friends retorted. Feeling like I was putting it down and keeping it real, I then mentioned, "When I was thirty, they were saying that they were *not* looking for Mrs. Right, they were simply looking for Mrs. Right *Now.* Then they would mention that I was 'too nice a person' for them and that they didn't deserve me. . . .Yeah, *right!!!* What the heck does that mean? That ole too-nice thing has *gotta* go!!"

Then it happened, out of the blue something came all over me. I couldn't see straight. I felt a churning in my stomach, a queasiness that was indescribable. I felt a strong distaste in my mouth, like I had been given a spoon of castor oil! I was becoming sickened by this conversation, for what we were saying about black men, *our* black men. My head was spinning, my mouth was dry, and for some unknown reason I could not continue the verbal judo and image-shattering of black men. In that moment, I was convicted with guilt and personal accountability. My head was screaming at me, *What have you done to them, Lisa? What is your role in your miserable B-movie? What should you apologize for?*

This was not cool. I'd been leading the pack! I could have won the "pity party" award with all of the junk I'd thrown out about the black man. Now what? I sat with this internal struggle for what seemed like forever, but was actually about five minutes. I was still, completely consumed with frustration, disgust, confusion and conviction. I began to ask this voice—or was it a feeling?—whatever it was, I asked it for direction, took a deep breath and held on.

What happened next blew my mind. I expected the next words to come out of my mouth to be something like, "I'm strong without them," "I don't need a man anyway," or "They're just intimidated by our strength," but to my extreme surprise and to the astonishment of my true-blue sistah-friends, I broke the "sistah code" and changed directions mid-pity party. I began to apologize to black men, to my black men.

My mind was screaming, *WHAT!!! Why are you apologizing to them? It's them that should be apologizing to you!! Remember when that guy . . . ? Remember the time . . . ?* But my mouth was on automatic pilot and could not be turned off.

"Black man, I apologize for putting you down when I get around my girls and forgetting to lift you up as you deserve to be lifted up.

"I apologize for allowing my insecurities about my shape, my hair or my skin tone to be projected onto you and blaming you for my lack of self-love.

"I apologize for expecting you to teach me how to love myself.

"I apologize, black man, for judging you when I should have been providing you with unconditional support.

"I apologize for pressuring you to adapt to corporate America by my standards instead of allowing you to find your own way and encouraging you to keep going.

"I apologize for not hearing you when you said you just wanted to be friends, assuming I could change your mind, then blaming you for misleading me.

"Black man, I apologize for loud-talking you and making you feel disrespected and unappreciated.

"I apologize for prioritizing my career and business over you, causing you to feel devalued, dismissed and hurt.

"I apologize for talking and yelling at you more than listening to you and allowing you to fully express what's on your mind.

"I apologize for not being that one safe place where you

can let down your guard, stop fighting the world and just be you—with me.

"I apologize for forgetting that you are a king, a descendant of royalty. A survivor, a builder, a confidant, a creator, an entrepreneur, a friend. And that I am your queen—acknowledging you, supporting you, encouraging you and loving you."

I ended my apology by saying, "Black man, you are my partner in this journey and I owe you an apology for forgetting your importance to me. I am honored to be by your side. Any other message I give you is simply untrue."

When I finished I looked around the room into still-glossy eyes fighting to hold back tears. Without speaking a word, we began to embrace each other, one by one, as the tears flowed more freely. We were all ready to stop struggling with the men we loved, our black men, yet not knowing how. We sat, we rocked, we cried, we prayed, we laughed and then cried some more.

Then, as if by magic, our cell phones began to ring one by one.

"Hey, Baby."

"Hey, Honey."

"Whatz up, Boo?"

"Hi, Sweetie."

As if in unison, we all said, "You know, I owe you an apology. . . ."

From that day on, our pity parties changed to just parties and our "R.D.—relationship drama" changed to "R.D.—reminiscing and dancing." And most of all, we began to bring our black men with us.

Lisa Nichols

Sister, I'm Sorry

You really don't know what your true potential is until you've pushed yourself beyond your limits. You have to fail a couple of times to really find out how far you can go.

Debi Thomas

In a crowded hotel lobby in Washington, D.C., with the din of a thousand voices ringing in my ears, the revelation was born. And it was inspired, as often is the case, by a provocateur.

"So, what exactly are *you* sorry for, Mr. Huskisson?" the olive-skinned sister asked, referring to a video I'd helped produce called, "Sister, I'm Sorry: An Apology to Our African-American Queens." Her whispery voice bore a playful and lyrical tone, teasing and prodding and probing all at once.

I responded the way men frequently do in such situations: I froze. It was the kind of question we brothers hate for sisters to ask—the kind to which any reaction is furiously wrong. You know, questions of the "Does my butt look big in these pants?" variety. The wrong answer could be like emotional quicksand—no way to win, no way to survive.

I hesitated, too, because I knew my answer would reveal more than I was comfortable sharing during a chance encounter with a colleague—and I didn't care *how* fine she was, okay?

"I'm sorry that a lack of sensitivity and understanding has caused our relationships to suffer so," I responded vaguely, trying to sound casual and nonchalant.

But my heart was *thump-a-thump thumping* double-time, and trickles of sweat were starting to form across the top of my forehead. Trying to maintain my cool—a must for any self-respecting brother—I turned to wave at a coworker and held my breath expectantly, steeling myself for uproarious laughter or neck-moving disbelief. For the first time in my life, I truly understood the sister sensation, *Waiting to Exhale*.

"Yeah," the brown-eyed provocateur said finally, flatly. "I feel you."

Freed from my anxiety and from the perils of self-disclosure, I wiped my brow, filled my lungs with air and launched a spurt of pseudo-intellectual drivel about the state of male-female relationships:

"Besides the Mars-Venus phenomenon, men and women are socialized differently, so it only stands to reason that . . . *blahblahblah* . . . Accepting that reality, then, we need to empathize more, fully appreciating the social conditions that . . . *blahblahblahblah* . . . At the end of the day, heightened awareness and better communication will help us create a paradigm shift, so to say, that will *blahblahblah.* . . ."

I felt pretty good about this avoidance-behavior response until late that night when, in the darkness of my hotel room, something heavy pressed against my heart: the strain of deceit. My sister had lobbied for a personal, visceral response, and I'd given her superficial psycho-babble. Rather than be bold enough to speak my truth, I'd taken the cowardly route.

So, what was the *real* truth—the unabashed, unvarnished, unveiled truth? What *had* inspired me—heck, what had *possessed* me—to quit a lucrative job after some fifteen years at a big-city newspaper to help produce and promote a video of black men apologizing to black women?

Of course, I knew the answer. I'd renewed my commitment to black dignity, self-reliance, discipline and empowerment in 1995 after joining more than a million of my brothers in a spectacular march and rally outside the Lincoln Memorial in Washington, D.C. As I joined a chorus of strong, black voices reciting the Million Man March pledge, one line stood out for me: "I will never abuse my wife by striking her or disrespecting her, for she is the mother of my children and the producer of my future."

Months later, when I got a chance to help create a video designed to heal male-female relationships and rebuild black families, the idea fit neatly into my rediscovered focus.

Still, that was only part of the story. I knew that my acknowledgement—my revelation—needed to come full circle. What was I *sorry* about—no, what was I *personally* sorry about? I struggled throughout the night, turning and tossing until a voice said: Answer with your heart, not with your head.

That made it *so* much easier . . . *Relax* . . . *Release* . . . *Speak* . . .

"I am sorry that my fear of intimacy made me close my heart to you, making it impossible for us to build a relationship based on unconditional trust, respect and love.

"I'm sorry that my personal ambitions and selfish interests sidelined you when you should have been attended and revered, cherished and exalted.

"I'm sorry that I was not more honest about who I was and what I wanted, forcing you to guess about how to best satisfy me, fulfill me and love me.

"I'm sorry that I was not more focused on your passions, more patient with your ways, and more gentle with your heart.

"I am sorry, in the end, that I have not listened to you enough, kissed you enough, embraced you enough, nurtured you enough, or loved you enough.

"And I'm sorry that I have not been on my J-O-B as a black man, allowing our families and communities to fall into such destructive chaos."

That's what I should have said in that crowded hotel lobby in Washington, D.C.—not just to the sister who asked, but somehow to every black woman within earshot.

Gregory Huskisson

I Am

Mix a conviction with a man and something happens.

Adam Clayton Powell

I am the brown clay God scooped from the sand.
He molded me, then blessed me, with his own two hands.
He breathed life into my lungs and sat me upon the land.
I am God's finest creation and he called me man.
I am the beginning of humanity, intelligent and strong.
My life will be full, and my days will be long.
My mind is the birthplace of philosophy and mathematics,
Position of stars, motions of planets, I know the schematics.
I am creator of civilization and master of architectural
design.
Knowledge, understanding and wisdom flow from my
mind.
In my heart pumps the rich blood of kings and queens.
I am the descendent of those who knew all things.
Adam and Eve, Noah, Moses and Abraham,
The blessed Mohammad, are just a part of who I am.

Formed in the womb of God's most perfect gift,
The black woman, with her perfect skin, full lips and hips.
The angels look down while doing protective duty,
And secretly wish they possessed her beauty.
I am her child, her father, her brother, her lover.
God is the only thing I can place above her.
I am the past. I am the present. I am the future.
I am the beginning. I am the end. I am what moves you.
I am only beginning to understand truly who I am.
I am God's glory and God's love. I am the black man.

Anthony M. Moore

More Alike Than Different

I never considered my race as a barrier to me. In fact, it's become an asset because it allows me to have broader perspective.

James Kaiser

I met Calvin at Camp Unitown. He was our leader. At Unitown teenagers come together to participate in activities that focus on how we are all more alike than different.

Calvin was 5'7", medium brown skin with "locks" to his shoulders and the teens loved him. Calvin possessed a calmness that made you want to be near him. Where you felt okay to be yourself. Calvin spoke straight from the heart. His voice thundered when he told the group stories about acts of racism.

It was a cold and snowy February in the northern Arizona mountains. About sixty kids attended that weekend. Half came from an inner-city school in Phoenix. The other half were from a low socioeconomic community near the camp. Probably about 40 percent of all the teens there were white, 20 percent black, 20 percent Hispanic, 10 percent Native American, and the other 10 percent of the kids were of varied ethnic backgrounds.

They were typical teenagers: loud, unruly, having fun. At first the students didn't mix with each other. The Phoenix teenagers stayed with their group; the rural kids hung with their friends. Everyone was in their own cliques.

We participated in large groups led by Calvin and broke into small groups of six to eight to share individually. The first evening Calvin led us through a scenario of racial injustice and violence. Calvin's story appeared so real in our minds that most of the teens were in tears. Tenderly, Calvin assisted the group in personalizing the inhumanness of any kind of prejudice.

One white girl sitting next to me pushed her head into my chest. She was sobbing. When she lifted her head to look at me, her sky-blue eyes were clear and wide and full of compassion. I kissed her forehead.

In the morning we discussed our different heritages. Calvin told us about individual cultures and described admirable qualities about each one. As he expanded on the honorable attributes of varying ethnic groups he would ask students of that ethnicity to stand as he described their heritage. The last group he asked to stand were kids of mixed ethnic groups. Calvin's voice was passionate. "Here we have brothers and sisters who come from more than one racial background. These individuals came from two parents or parental lines that had different races. Look each one of them in the eyes. See their beauty. Here, my brothers and sisters, is the future of our world."

By the afternoon we heard and watched each other reveal our best-kept secrets. We all shared. No one was left out.

That night we went through a litany of exercises to demonstrate how we discriminate against each other based on sex. Calvin showed us how the belief systems we had been taught verbally or nonverbally affect us. Surprisingly we saw that the girls were just as guilty as the boys in stereotyping others because they were male or female.

Calvin told the boys to stand in rows so that they were facing each other. The girls made a circle around the perimeter of the room. Then Calvin played soft music on his CD player. The music was from cultures around the world—drums, flutes, chants. The directions Calvin gave to the boys were: "Look into your brother's eyes. Do not say a word to him. But with your eyes tell your brother, 'I am there for you. I care for you, and I understand. You don't have to be tough anymore. You can come to me if you need someone to help you remember your commitment.'"

To the girls he said, "Please silently witness the boys making this commitment to each other."

Calvin gave each pair of boys time to connect their eyes and silently make their vow. Then he announced, "Change," and the boys moved up one space to encounter a new person in the row. A few of the "tougher" boys laughed. It didn't take long, though, for them to honor the seriousness of this event. Outside snow fell swiftly as if to solidify their vows to each other. The girls watched in awe as boys became men that day.

Afterwards, Calvin told these young men to hug every person in the room. With each hug I said a silent blessing. Earlier that day most of these guys had been strangers to me. It felt to me like they each received my blessing with honor.

Now it was the girls' turn. Calvin instructed us to take the men's place in the middle of the room. The men encircled us. As Calvin played music created by great women from all around the world, he told us, "Look into your sister's eyes. See her beauty. Tell her how beautiful she is. Tell her with your eyes, not words. Promise her you will be there for her when she needs you. Remind her to respect herself."

Powerful emotions built up inside of me as I gave each girl a silent message using only my eyes. I felt such compassion.

Calvin called, "Change," and I met a new pair of eyes. I looked into brown, black, blue and green eyes that evening; each time I saw beauty and grace. I felt proud to be among these girls, like I was taking part in a sacred ceremony. The snow kept falling.

As the weekend came to an end, I felt like I had grown two inches taller. Before we boarded our buses to go home, we made a large circle and stood in the snow hand in hand. There was no separation of skin colors, schools or cliques. Calvin, with his openness and tell-it-like-it-is manner, had somehow transformed a group of immature teenagers into men and women of integrity.

I thank Calvin for the gift he shared with us that weekend. In my mind he is a real twenty-first-century hero.

Mary Cornelia Van Sant

The Nod

True friendship comes when silence between two people is comfortable.

Dave Tyson Gentry

I got it this week while attending a workshop at the University of Iowa. I hadn't gotten it in such a long time; it refreshed me, the way a cool douse of rain in summer, the first lick of a Popsicle, a smile from a baby refreshes.

The nod.

It came from a gentleman about five years my senior. His russet face was splattered with tiny brown freckles like my grandmother's. He offered it to me as we passed each other on the stairs.

I did not know him. I had no idea if he was an instructor or student or the parent of a student. I didn't know if he was a maintenance man or a scholar on loan from another university.

But I knew the nod.

I knew it from working in corporate America for some twenty-plus years. It's the acknowledgment African

Americans of my generation give in passing when we don't know each other, yet do. We don't know each other by name, age, social security number or any other demographic you could select on a page or check in a box. We know each other through mutual troubles, collective struggles, shared triumphs.

Once when I was running an errand at work with my coworker, she noticed the nod.

"Do you know all of those people?" she asked.

The quip at the tip of my tongue was a popular phrase of the time: "It's a black thang. You wouldn't understand."

I didn't say it, though. Instead, I just said, "No," and kept my black thang to myself. But it truly is a black thang—an African American thang.

There's reverence in that thang, that Black Thang. That nod.

There is respect, reciprocity and recollection as long as the middle passage. That nod remembers that before there were suits and paychecks, there were chains and marches. Before there were fringe benefits and paid time off, there were sit-ins and freedom rides. Before there was EEO, affirmative action and sensitivity training, there was the lash.

There are black codes in that chin. The amalgam of Martin and Malcolm is in that gesture. There are big black fists saluting in Mexico City in that movement. That nod.

The kids nowadays have an up nod—a quick jerk from the bottom to the top. It's hip like, "What's happenin'? What's up?" I like ours better. It moves the same way a prayer moves, down toward the soul, toward the Earth, toward the heart. It's slower, more dip than scoop as if we're laying something down rather than yanking it up.

The nod is a signal, an acknowledgment. It answers yes, yes, yes to unasked questions: Were you there when it became illegal to discriminate? Do you remember when they wouldn't hire us? Was it hard for you to climb the corporate ladder?

It is the celebration of an incredible feat. A monumental undertaking. That, despite everything . . . we've made it this far.

This week, on the stairs, I returned the man's nod and smiled, knowing that even on an Iowa campus, like in corporate America, our connections to each other thrive.

Kim Louise

Soothing the Soul of Racism

It is critical that we take charge of our own destiny and stop waiting for some unknown being to come along and wipe racism from the face of the Earth.

David Wilson

As an activist, someone who is constantly on the front lines for racial equality in the world, my spirit was tired, overwhelmed with the work, hopeless that a real change would ever manifest. In an effort to recharge my spiritual battery, I registered for a cultural retreat, Moonsisters Drum Camp for Women in Northern California.

I believed being around the sacred instrument would renew me, connect me to the ancestral energy I needed to continue my work. I'd be around other black women who were doing similar work. Perhaps they could offer some suggestions on how I could serve my community without depleting myself on every level.

When I arrived, I became immediately resentful. Over 70 percent of the participants were white women. Here I was in my late thirties, and this was the first opportunity I'd had to develop a relationship with a major part of my ancient African heritage: drumming. The term "white privilege" spun in my head until I found out that in order to attend the camp, white participants had to attend a special antiracism training workshop. I was impressed that these women were willing to do this, to pay for it even, to ensure that they wouldn't bring overt racism into a sacred healing space.

The white women offered to help with my bags, show me to my cabin. Although they were kind and welcoming, I wore a scowl on my face: a mask for the fear and mistrust I felt.

We each went around the room introducing ourselves, explaining why we had chosen to attend the drum camp. I told the group I came to try to find a spiritual solution for the race problem in America. After the introduction, two white women approached and said they wanted to support me in any way they could to end racism in America. I was moved but not convinced.

I am what my ancestors called a "seer." I have always had the ability to hear the voice of spirit. This is not a 1-900 kind of connection with the spirit world; it is a gift from God to help me in my journey. During a drumming session, a young woman asked me to do a spiritual reading for her. I'd never sat in spiritual counsel with anyone white. But I intuitively felt led to work with this woman.

She came to my cabin at the arranged time. During the reading, my ancestors directed me to wash her feet with sage and holy oil. I thought I was hearing things. They couldn't be serious. After what her ancestors had done to mine, she should be washing my feet! I followed the directive, reluctantly. Later it was revealed to me that her ancestors were among the whites who helped free the slaves through the Underground Railroad. My lesson was in motion. The spiritual reason I'd been brought to this retreat was steadily being revealed.

The camp workshops included various drumming sessions and collective healing circles. We built a community altar, and each woman placed a sacred object on the shrine that represented her vision for personal healing. It was a powerful altar that embraced practically every religious belief system and cultural background. Our altar was a bridge to healing across the races, a bridge we would all cross before the weekend was over.

The closing ceremony was a culmination of the stories and lessons we had exchanged throughout the retreat. The woman whose feet I had washed was giving her testimony on how the retreat had changed her. Suddenly, she looked over at me and apologized for what her ancestors had done to my ancestors. In all my thirty-four years, no white person had ever acknowledged my pain as a black woman in relationship to the enslavement of my ancestors. I fell to my knees and sobbed uncontrollably. So did every black person in that room. One by one, each white person apologized to every black person in the room for what their ancestors did. We hugged each other, linking arms and bodies. I felt a white light surrounding us. And for that moment, we were no longer white or black, Christian or Yoruba; we were human beings united under one God.

There were ten watermelons on the shrine. The organizers cut and distributed slices to refresh us from our intense healing session. The woman I'd bonded with over the weekend brought over a slice to share. When she handed it to me, the watermelon slipped from her hand. We caught it just before it hit the ground. However, it split open in the process and when it did, a perfect heart fell out and sat between our fingers.

The entire group sighed in awe of the way that spirit

recognized the healing we had brought about. We cried again. The healing was complete. I took off a beloved cowry shell bracelet that I'd been wearing the entire retreat and placed it around her wrist. Cowry shells are a symbol of African wealth; worn to symbolize the return to our original greatness.

"Sisters forever," I told her as I fastened the bracelet around her wrist.

We smiled and parted, connected forever by the drums, our human hearts and the spiritual soup of God. And today, I don't assume anything about a person because of their race. I wait for their spirit to show me who they are.

Ta'Shia Asanti

Cold Hands, Warm Heart

God did not create two classes of children or human beings—only one.

Marian Wright Edelman

Lottie slowly shuffled into the multipurpose room of the nursing home where I conducted weekly group therapy sessions for women having trouble adjusting to their new residence. Lottie looked especially down today, and I wondered whether she was feeling uncomfortable after having shared some very personal experiences the previous week. "Airing one's dirty laundry" was considered taboo in her generation, perhaps even more so in her particular culture.

"I'm sorry I'm late," she mumbled, almost inaudibly. "My arthritis kept me up all night. And I'm so tired that I'll probably nod off during group. Maybe I should just leave."

"That's okay, Lottie," I responded reassuringly as I patted the empty chair next to me. "I saved you a seat right here, and I promise if you start snoring, I'll give you a little nudge with my elbow."

Everyone laughed . . . except Lottie. She didn't even smile. Gosh, I thought, *She really does seem depressed.* This tall, matronly woman was almost fragile today. Her eyes pleaded for something I could not comprehend.

"Please join us," I implored, patting the seat again.

Lottie hesitantly ventured across the room towards me, turned, and lowered herself cautiously into the chair. She let out a gasp of pain that made everyone wince.

"Oh, I'm sorry, sweetie," I said. "You really are having a rough time, aren't you?"

She looked at me and raised her two dark gnarled hands for me to see. They were shaking. In fact, it seemed as if her whole body was almost trembling.

"My hands are soooo cold," she whimpered like a little girl, "and they hurt soooo much."

"Let me warm them up for you." I scooted my chair even closer, took both of her hands in mine and laid them in my lap. To divert attention from her, I began talking to the other women in the group about how they had been doing this past week. I gently massaged one of Lottie's hands, then the other. My instincts told me something was going on with her—something far more serious than arthritis and a sleepless night. I made a conscious decision not to ask her to disclose anything today. I would offer to spend some time alone with her after the group ended to make sure that she was okay.

My mind kept drifting back to what Lottie had previously shared. Several residents had been talking about recent visits from their children and grandchildren. Someone commented that they had never seen anyone visiting Lottie and asked if her relatives all lived out of town.

Mrs. Burton whispered, "I don't think she has any kids."

Lottie overheard her and responded, "Actually, I've had thousands of children in my lifetime."

Everyone stopped talking and just stared at her, waiting for an explanation. Lottie continued, "I never married, but since I'd always loved children, I decided to become a teacher. Before I came here, I would occasionally run into a former student at church or the grocery store. They always recognized me and came over to chat. But now . . . well, probably no one even knows I'm here. Besides, they have their own lives and their own families to take care of."

Mrs. Roberts asked about Lottie's siblings, cousins, nieces, nephews . . . didn't any of them live in Louisiana? Lottie paused, and then said she had lost touch with all her relatives. This undoubtedly made no sense to anyone in the room. Lottie was such a bright, interesting, sweet, caring woman. Surely, anybody would be thrilled to have her in their family and would want to keep in touch with her as often as possible.

I didn't want to pressure her to reveal more than she was ready to, but I also wanted to provide an opportunity for her to process something painful if she felt the need to do so. "You've lost touch with your family?" I asked. "Is that something you'd like to talk about?"

Lottie swallowed, dropped her eyes, and said softly, "My mother died during childbirth, and I think my father somehow blamed me for it. I guess that's why he gave me to his parents to raise. Then he was probably lonely, so he got married again pretty quickly. He and his new wife had a baby within a year, so I actually had a half-sister close to my age.

"Anyway, my grandparents weren't thrilled about my being dumped on them and having another mouth to feed. I remember that even when I was little, I was so very good, never caused any problems and helped around the house as much as possible. I didn't want to be a burden, but they always made me feel like one. Anyway, they both died of influenza the same month I turned thirteen.

"None of the relatives liked me much or wanted me, so

my father had no choice but to take me in. I had seen his family occasionally over the years, but didn't know them well. Of course, I understood why my stepmother resented having to live with another woman's child, but I never knew why my sister hated me so much. And it's sad, because we could have been such friends."

After a long pause, Lottie went on. "I wanted them to be proud of me, so I studied diligently in order to be accepted into college. When my sister heard my plans, she suddenly announced that she wanted to attend the university, too. My father immediately told me to get 'that college idea' out of my head because tuition was expensive and he had already promised my sister that she could go instead of me. I was brokenhearted, but reluctantly started taking typing, shorthand and other business courses so I could at least work in an office instead of cleaning houses or being a nurse's aide.

"Right before I graduated from high school, an army recruiter talked to the senior class about serving our country, then getting the GI bill—like how the government would pay for veterans to go to college and all. So the day I turned eighteen, I signed up. They sent me to Washington, D.C., where I did clerical work for four years.

"After my discharge, I returned home, found a part-time secretarial job, enrolled in classes and eventually earned my bachelor's degree. My sister had changed her mind about college, so at the time I was the first black female to ever graduate from that university. Anyway, I ended up teaching ninth grade in an inner-city school for the next thirty-three years.

"And, in a nutshell, I finally gave up trying to have a relationship with my relatives. But that's okay," she added with a smile to convince everyone (including herself). "I had an endless supply of kids in my classes who needed all the TLC they could get."

After Lottie had so openly discussed her past, I kept wondering what part of her story she kept concealed. She seemed so sad, and it felt like there was a major puzzle piece missing. *Had she ever been in love? Did she lose her soul mate in the war and vow never to marry? Had she bounced back from a near-fatal illness?*

I struggled to refocus on what the other residents in my group were saying. I glanced at everyone in the room, then over at Lottie. She had tears streaming down her face. "Oh, Lottie!" I gasped in surprise. "You must be hurting so much! Maybe we should get a doctor."

"No," she purred softly. "Actually, I'm much better now. In fact, I don't remember when I've felt so good. Do you know that you have been holding and massaging my hands for almost an hour now?"

I stole a glimpse at my watch. "Gosh, I—I didn't," I confessed. "I was just . . . "

"Thank you," she interrupted me. "That was incredibly healing. Do you know that tomorrow is my eightieth birthday, and I've never once had anyone hold my hands like that?"

"Oh, Lottie, I'm so sorry," I stammered, trying not to let my voice crack or my tears flow. *How could anyone be so grateful over something so little? I hadn't done anything!* For one of the few times in my life, I was speechless.

"You've probably noticed that my eyes are light blue," she suddenly interjected.

"I—I actually hadn't," I responded apologetically, really seeing them right then for the first time.

"Hmmmm," Lottie crooned. "That's one of the first things my people notice. You see, my mother was a white woman. In those days, interracial marriages were not welcome, nor were their biracial offspring. I was never accepted into either family because of that. Even though my skin is dark, complete strangers could take just one look at my blue eyes and know my past. It's almost as though people tried to make me feel ashamed of it, ashamed of who I am."

Lottie gazed into space. "When I was about eight or nine, I was hiding behind this fence and watching a white woman playing with her young daughter in a park. The child fell down and started crying. The mother raced over, scooped the little girl up in her arms, hugged her tightly and smothered her with kisses. I memorized that lady's face. I've never seen a picture of my own mother, so from then on, throughout my whole life, every time I've been sad or scared, I just closed my eyes and imagined that lady. I pretended that she was my mother and that she was always there to comfort and protect me—just like she did with her daughter that day."

The words I wanted to say did not come. Lottie smiled peacefully. "Just last night I was thinking that I'm almost eighty years old, and I've never known what it is like to be comforted when I'm hurting. And now I do. You didn't even realize it, but you just gave me the best birthday gift I've ever had."

My God, I hadn't done anything!

"Oh, Lottie," my quivering voice responded, "may I please give you a hug?" We both stood up. I don't know if I held her or she held me, but it felt so good.

Behind me was a long line of other teary-eyed women, waiting to hug their new friend. I overheard Mrs. Burton whispering in the background again, this time planning a surprise birthday party . . . something with a "sisters" theme.

Karen Waldman

5

PRAISE, WORSHIP AND PRAYER

*A*lways continue the climb. It is possible for
you to do whatever you choose, if you first
get to know who you are and are willing to
work with a power that is greater than ourselves to do it.

Oprah Winfrey

I Heard the Voice of Jesus
Saying Still to Fight On

As we are liberated from our own fear, our presence automatically liberates others.

Marianne Williamson

Almost immediately after the protest started we had begun to receive threatening telephone calls and letters. They increased as time went on. By the middle of January, they had risen to thirty and forty a day.

From the beginning of the protest both my parents and Coretta's parents always had the unconscious, and often conscious, fear that something fatal might befall us. They never had any doubt about the rightness of our actions, but they were concerned about what might happen to us. My father made a beaten path between Atlanta and Montgomery throughout the days of the protest. Every time I saw him I went through a deep feeling of anxiety, because I knew that my every move was driving him deeper and deeper into a state of worry. During those days he could hardly mention the many harassments that Coretta, the baby and I were subjected to without shedding tears.

As the weeks passed, I began to see that many of the threats were in earnest. Soon I felt myself faltering and growing in fear. One day, a white friend told me that he had heard from reliable sources that plans were being made to take my life. For the first time I realized that something could happen to me.

One night at a mass meeting, I found myself saying: "If one day you find me sprawled out dead, I do not want you to retaliate with a single act of violence. I urge you to continue protesting with the same dignity and discipline you have shown so far." A strange silence came over the audience.

One night toward the end of January I settled into bed late, after a strenuous day. Coretta had already fallen asleep, and just as I was about to doze off the telephone rang. An angry voice said, "Listen, nigger, we've taken all we want from you; before next week you'll be sorry you ever came to Montgomery." I hung up, but I couldn't sleep. It seemed that all of my fears had come down on me at once. I had reached the saturation point.

I got out of bed and began to walk the floor. I had heard these things before, but for some reason that night it got to me. I turned over and I tried to go to sleep, but I couldn't sleep. I was frustrated, bewildered, and then I got up. Finally I went to the kitchen and heated a pot of coffee. I was ready to give up. With my cup of coffee sitting untouched before me I tried to think of a way to move out of the picture without appearing a coward. I sat there and thought about a beautiful little daughter who had just been born. I'd come in night after night and see that little gentle smile. I started thinking about a dedicated and loyal wife, who was over there asleep. And she could be taken from me, or I could be taken from her. And I got to the point that I couldn't take it any longer. I was weak. Something said to me, "You can't call on Daddy now, you can't even call on Mama. You've got to call on that something in that person that your daddy used to tell you about, that power that can make a way out of no way."

With my head in my hands, I bowed over the kitchen table and prayed aloud. The words I spoke to God that midnight are still vivid in my memory: "Lord, I'm down here trying to do what's right. I think I'm right. I am here taking a stand for what I believe is right. But Lord, I must confess that I'm weak now, I'm faltering. I'm losing my courage. Now, I am afraid. And I can't let the people see me like this because if they see me weak and losing my courage, they will begin to get weak. The people are looking to me for leadership, and if I stand before them without strength and courage, they too will falter. I am at the end of my powers. I have nothing left. I've come to the point where I can't face it alone."

It seemed as though I could hear the quiet assurance of an inner voice saying: "Martin Luther, stand up for righteousness. Stand up for justice. Stand up for truth. And lo, I will be with you. Even until the end of the world."

I tell you I've seen the lightning flash. I've heard the thunder roar. I've felt sin breakers dashing trying to conquer my soul. But I heard the voice of Jesus saying still to fight on. He promised never to leave me alone. At that moment I experienced the presence of the Divine as I had never experienced Him before. Almost at once my fears began to go. My uncertainty disappeared. I was ready to face anything.

Dr. Martin Luther King Jr.

Bedtime Blessing

It is better to walk in the dark with God than to run in the light alone.

Bobby Jones

"I'm tired, Lord," I said as I walked up the stairs leading to the hallway of the kids' bedroom. My circumstances weighed heavily on my normally cheery disposition. It had been six months since I was laid off from my job. I knew the letters by heart. "Thank you for your interest in our company. We will keep your resume on file and if your skills match our needs . . . blah blah blah." The job search thing had gotten under my skin. After all, I have a pretty impressive resume, and I'd never before had a problem getting a job.

I plopped down on the floor at the top of the stairs and dropped my head into the palms of my hands. It had been two years since my marriage ended. I was wrestling with being single, again. This job hunt made me want to pull my hair out. And on top of that, the bills were due and unemployment wasn't quite cutting it.

"Mommy!" the kids called out.

I pushed past my feelings of fear, uncertainty and frustration, got up from the floor and made my way to the kids' bedroom.

"What story would you like to read tonight?" I flipped through a book I thought the kids would both enjoy.

"Mommy, let's read about the animals!" Cameron stood up on the bed and waved one of his favorite animal books.

Courtney, my two-year-old, clung to her doll as I picked her up and sat on the bed next to Cameron.

As I read, their eyes widened with excitement as if they'd never heard this story before. I silently wished I could look at my life this way, too.

They pointed at pictures of the animals and identified which they liked best.

"Mommy, which animal are you? This is me," Courtney said as she pointed at a giraffe.

I pointed at a colorful bird, "That's me."

Cameron interrupted, "No, Mommy. You can't be that bird. That bird looks afraid. Look at his face. He's afraid. Mommy, you're not afraid, are you?"

"Uh." Tongue-tied and amazed at the profundity of my four-year-old, I stared at him, perplexed by the depth of his question.

"Fear not, Mommy, for God is with you," Cameron reassured me with a smile.

I felt a flame of hope ignite inside me. The kids played in bed as I sat there and reflected on the conversation I'd just had with God on the stairs a few minutes ago—and the one He had just had with me through my young son.

Sure, I had lost my job, but it was a job that I no longer enjoyed. The reality of divorce permeated my mind with clouds of uncertainty and fear, but then I thought of how much time my ex-husband invests in the children and what a great partnership we've formed since the divorce.

The bills were due and my expenses far exceeded my income, but every month God provided and met the needs along with a few wants.

After the kids were bundled into bed, I kissed them goodnight and turned off the light. I gazed into their bright eyes once more.

"God loves you, Mommy," Courtney said with the excitement only a two-year-old could possess.

My heart smiled as I reached into her eyes and grabbed a mustard seed of faith.

Catina Slade

Walking by Faith

I am not a special person. I am a regular person who does special things.

Sarah Vaughan

One Sunday morning at the end of an inspiring sermon, my pastor told the congregation, "I want everyone to do something nice for an elder. It really does take a village, and as good Christians, we must take care of our elders. Go out, read to an elder, take someone for a ride, cook dinner, spend time with an elder this week."

Oh, good, I thought. That should be easy; I can do something special for my mother. Maybe I'll take her to dinner along with another family friend. It shouldn't be too hard.

Then my pastor put a special touch to the assignment. "Make sure that you do this for someone you don't know."

Oh well, I'll figure out something later, I told myself. My stomach growled as I drove out of the church parking lot and headed toward the market. I put the challenge out of my mind and started mentally planning my Sunday dinner.

As I was putting groceries in the car, I noticed an older man, a bum, stooping and fumbling with a large trash bag. When I closed the car door, a voice reminded, "Help an elder this day."

So, I leaned out the car and said, "Excuse me, do you need any help?"

"Oh!" the old man turned and looked up, startled.

All of a sudden, it felt important to help this man.

"Sir, can I help you? Do you need a ride?" I asked, sounding a little more urgent.

"Well, yes," the old man said. "I do need some help. I bought more than I thought, and I don't know how I'm going to get all this home."

Now I really started to pay attention. He was taking all his smaller bags and putting them in a large trash bag and I got the impression he intended to carry his large bag on his shoulders.

"I can give you a ride. It's no problem," I said.

"Oh, I live far," he stated.

At that point, it really didn't matter where he lived, I knew that this was a divine assignment, and I would have taken him to the moon without hesitation. I stepped out of the car to help him with his groceries, heavy with canned goods, and started loading them into my car.

His name was Hank, and he lived only a few miles from the market, but with his bags it would have been a long walk. As we reached his home, I helped him with his groceries to the door, and he offered to pay me for the ride.

"No, I was glad to help you."

I told him about the assignment and asked for his phone number.

"I would like to call you sometime this week, just to say hello," I told him. He gave me his number, and I drove off with the promise of calling him.

When I called the next week, Hank answered the phone.

"Hello," he said. "I am so very glad that you called. You just don't know what you did for me. You see, I lost my wife a few years ago, and it has been so hard on me. I'm eighty years old and I have a car I can't drive anymore because my eyesight is so bad. Nobody has ever offered me a ride unless I pay them."

The words were tumbling out of his mouth. "I didn't know what I was going to do," he continued. "I had been struggling with my groceries for about an hour, wondering how I was going to get home. I wanted to catch a taxi, but didn't want to leave my bags. I was getting so upset, I just cried out, 'God, please help me.' It seems like right after that I heard a voice say, 'Excuse me, do you need any help?'"

I took Hank to church with me the following Sunday, and we became friends in the weeks to follow. I had many rich conversations with Hank, and the experience had a profound effect on me because it was a major lesson in obedience. You see, my first thought was that he was a bum, but then I remembered my pastor's words—or I wonder, *Was it the voice of God that I heard?*

Deborah Bellis

God Listens to Even the Smallest Prayers

The more you are aware of God's unchanging love, the safer you feel in the world.

Susan L. Taylor

My daughter was fourteen at the time. She had accepted Christ into her life when she was seven. Now, seven years later, she was questioning her faith.

"Mom, I don't think God is with me anymore," she said one day.

I asked her why she felt that way, and she said she couldn't hear God talking to her, almost as if He didn't notice her at all anymore.

My heart ached for her as I listened to this young child—my child—share her feelings of being abandoned by God. I gave her a hug and searched my mind for the right words to reassure her.

It just so happened that she was planning and saving for the annual youth camping trip. The camp coordinators made camping fun; they had energetic speakers, lots of food, late night expeditions and fun crafts. Kids from all over the country met every year, renewing friendships and making new ones. And each year the camp coordinators added extras like a gift shop, special crafts and extracurricular activities for which there was a small fee. Knowing this, all the kids brought extra spending money.

I thought the camping trip would be a great time to renew her friendship with God and I told her to ask God to speak to her while she was at camp.

"How will I know it's Him and not just my own thoughts?"

"God has a way of speaking to us that we just know it is Him and not just our own thinking," I explained. She looked skeptical, but agreed to give it a try.

Over the next few days my heart was heavy for her. I knew it was very important for her to hear from Him now. I pleaded with Him to speak to her.

"Mom!" she called when she arrived home from camp. "You won't believe what happened! You remember I only had fifteen dollars to spend for crafts and things, right?"

"Yes, I remember."

She continued excitedly, "Well, I bought some friendship bracelets for me and my friends, and I made a craft. I decided to save the last four dollars so I could do another craft. The first morning of camp, I asked God to speak to me just like you said, and during the second session the speaker talked about giving to missionaries. He said they had a hard time out there in the field and they needed all of us to help out. And even though we couldn't be there, we could help by sending money.

"Right then I felt God wanted me to give to missions. Mom, I really wanted to do the craft. It was all the money I had left, but I didn't care. I knew it was the right thing to do, so when the time came I put the four dollars I was saving in the basket. I felt good inside.

"And then, that afternoon, during mail call, the leader

called my name. Mom, I was surprised because we only have four days at camp and I've never gotten mail before. And guess what? It was a letter from you with four dollars in it! Mom, how did you know?"

"I didn't know! A few days before you left for camp I prayed for God to speak to you in a special way, where you would know for sure it was Him. After I prayed, I felt a strong urge to take all the money from my pocket and mail it to you. At first I thought it strange, but I knew God wanted me to do it and it had to be mailed that day."

"Mom, God is so awesome! He asked me to give all the money I had to help someone else, and then He sent me money to do my favorite craft! He listens even to the smallest prayer, doesn't He?"

"Yes, my love, indeed He does!" My heart raced with gratitude that not only had God listened to her smallest prayers but that I had been obedient to His smallest messages as well.

Ray Driver

A Miracle for My Heart

It's pretty hard for the Lord to guide you if you haven't made up your mind which way you want to go.

                                    Madame C. J. Walker

Imagine a boulder jarred loose from its solid rock foundation after a series of earthquakes. Can you see it perched precariously on a crumbling, rocky overhang midway down a steep mountainside, one aftershock away from violent descent and disintegration into millions of tiny fragments? If you have a mental picture of that, then you can visualize my marriage from 1991 to 1996.

After nine sometimes challenging but mostly wonderful years, my standard response to any cheerful, "Hi, how are you?" was a flat, "Hey, just trying to stay married." And I wasn't trying to be funny. I was just keeping it real. When had reality evolved to this? I had to dig deep to resurrect our first reality, the happy one, the beginning. . . .

Our first official date at a restaurant ended with us hanging out at his mother's house with his sister and her boyfriend. Lots of talking and laughing, meaningful glances, teasing, testing. But more than anything, I remember feeling incredibly comfortable and connected. Somewhere near the end of the evening, this funny, spiritual, musical, ambitious, solid-rock-steady, bold, beautiful black man became the brand-new owner of my heart.

Gradually, the tart aftertaste from my previous relationship was invaded by the fresh sweetness of our three-year romance. We laughed and played, kissed and cuddled, shared and dreamed. I didn't have to wonder what heaven was like. Being with this man was the closest I'd ever come to being on hallowed ground.

Now, don't get me wrong. Naturally, I'd always understood God as holy and Creator, but I'd never experienced Him as friend and companion. I realize now that if there had been a simpler, less painful way for me to learn that my God—not my fiancé—was to be the number-one man in my life, events would have unfolded differently.

So what was all the talk about "Marriage is work"? Marriage was marvelous! I didn't know who all the other women in the world had married, but I had a prince! That's why I was careful not to rock the boat, not to say or be anything that might jeopardize this miracle on Earth. I was determined that nothing would separate us—not careers, or children, or "growing apart," or "irreconcilable differences."

I wanted it to be a perfect marriage, but I didn't understand that perfection grows from the seeds of humanness, watered by divine grace. How could I possibly know that the turbulent waterfall we were headed for eventually surfaced in pristine pools of calm, clear, deeply peaceful waters? I had read that God's strength was made perfect in our weakness, but I had to live it to learn it.

It was the mid-1990s. I was oblivious to politics, the economy, world events, whatever. I only knew that I had

forgotten what it meant to be a vibrant, versatile partici-
pant in a meaningful life. Everything that could possibly
go wrong in our marriage gradually did. I suddenly found
that my duties as a wife, mother, homemaker, RN, and
church deaconess were performed with robotic obligation,
completely devoid of joy or purpose. God seemed to be on
extended vacation, and I sure hoped He was having fun,
because I definitely wasn't.

In fact, if this was to be my life, I was no longer interested. How had my failing marriage come to represent my
self-esteem, my accomplishments, my entire world? And
when exactly had my emotional whirlwind of anger,
resentment, irritability and depression settled into a
mindless state of numb indifference? It would take a
miracle for my heart to live and breathe and thrive again.
And that is exactly what God had in mind.

By the time my husband invited me to hear him play
with a jazz band one evening at a local function, I didn't
care enough anymore to have any man in my life, divine
or otherwise. God, however, was a sweet and faithful
song, looking beyond my faults to see my need. Even as I
refused my husband's invitation, ignored the flicker of
hope that faded from his eyes as I claimed to be without
a babysitter, angels must have been hastily dispatched to
do the Master's bidding. While I returned to my magazine, he finished loading up his instruments and paused
at the door.

"If we can't support each other anymore, there's no reason to stay together. If you really don't want to go tonight,
it's okay. But I already packed a bag, and I won't be back
after the concert."

He couldn't possibly feel the chill that instantly
descended on my heart and stilled the flow of blood in my
veins. He could only see my brief upward glance, and the
casual shrug of my shoulders. He only heard a flippant

"Okay, whatever," before turning slowly and walking out. I remember the crushing silence that followed the closing of the door. Finally, it could all be over. Why wasn't I relieved? What was that strange stirring in my heart that in some mystical way made me struggle to catch my breath and order my thoughts? Fear? Indecision? Desperation? Or was it simply the unmistakable fluttering of angels on assignment? I tried to refocus on my ridiculous magazine, but the words blurred into a haze of gray and it fell from my hands.

A silent prayer exploded in my mind, *God, you said you'd handle this and you didn't! I talked to you over and over again about this and trusted you to work it out, but it's falling apart. What about my children? My family? I did my part but you didn't do yours!*

I slid off the couch and collapsed face down on the carpet, knees drawn up under my belly, arms outstretched in abject surrender.

"God, please . . ." For the first time in my life I felt truly connected to the Savior as my lifeline. "God, please . . ."

My humanness was swallowed up in His divinity, His peace was mine.

An intense restlessness suddenly dispelled my calm and compelled me to my feet, willed me to the phone. Three attempts. Three failures. No babysitter. A jumble of disconnected thoughts: *Maybe my marriage wasn't meant to work? Why can't I just read my magazine? I don't want him to leave! But it's too hard; I already tried. It's too soon to give up; it could work. Swallow your pride. You know you still love him, and you saw his eyes, he loves you back. But I'm so tired.*

The shrill ringing of the phone vaporized my thoughts. "Hello?"

It was a close family friend. "Is there something you'd like to do tonight? I can babysit for you if you want."

"What?" How was this possible? (Obviously my faith

was quite a bit smaller than a mustard seed.) "I thought you were at a program tonight," I whispered. "Well, for some reason I think it's more important that I babysit for you. Do you want me to come?" A surge of excitement. Crazy hope. "Yes!" He didn't see me slip silently into an empty seat in an unlit corner, but his eyes periodically swept the room, purposeful, persistent—things I'd always loved about him. When he found me his face lit up like the sun. He grabbed the mike and announced to 150 people that "a very special person has just arrived, and I'd like to ask my beautiful wife to please stand."

Even as my tears threaten to spill over at this moment, I would be lying if I said it was easy after that night. We would return to the brink of collapse more than once. But that night we both knew that God had engineered a miracle to keep us together. And today, two weeks from our twentieth anniversary, I am still amazed at the shift in my chest when I see him across a crowded room, at the ache in my gut when I miss him and hear his voice on the telephone across the miles, at the way I bask contentedly in the warmth of his eyes and the sweetness of his kiss.

And I never cease to wonder that my own personal God loves me enough to send angels on a mission to transform hurt into healing, and grant me a miracle for my heart.

Karlene McCowan

A Lesson Learned
in an Answered Prayer

*I learned to really believe—and you can add a
thousand more reallys—that the Lord loves me
and wants only the best for me. That is an
absolute. I made mistakes and I will again. I
know I may step out of the light and go off and
make the biggest mess in the world. But I always
know that I can step back into the light!*

Della Reese

Some years ago, I taught at a small Christian school in
Yonkers, New York. Most of our students commuted daily
from the Bronx-Harlem areas. A group of African American
parents convinced that private education was the only way
to spare their children from the often forsaken inner-city
public system had started the school years before. Even
though the parents of most of our students claimed no particular religious affiliation, they respected the fact that our
school days always began with Bible class and prayer.

One day during our regular devotional, my eighth-graders and I were discussing the Ninth Commandment as recorded in the Bible in Exodus 20:16: "Thou shall not bear false witness against thy neighbor" (KJV). A lively discussion about lies and lying ensued. Most of the children concluded that lies were harmful because they open the door for mistrust.

Suddenly Shari's interjection gave the discussion a different spin, "But what if someone is about to rape me, Mrs. Richards?"

Faced with our silence she added, "I honestly don't think God would want something bad like that to happen to me. So if I tell the guy that I have AIDS, so that he doesn't rape me, would that lie be such a bad thing?"

All eyes turned towards me. Shari's reasoning seemed logical enough to refute all previous conclusions.

"Well," I began slowly, "a lie is a lie. And that would definitely be a lie because you do not have AIDS. But if you ever find yourself in such a situation, or in any situation of danger for that matter, I think your best bet is to pray."

"Pray?"

"Yes. There are some situations that are definitely out of our control and we need to ask God for help. A lie like that may not help, because what if that doesn't matter to him or he doesn't believe you?"

The kids all shook their heads in deep thought.

I continued, "I honestly think that the best thing to do is start praying, aloud if you can, but pray."

Bible class ended, and we moved on to other topics, yet little did I know that this answer would prepare one of my students to face a most horrifying experience.

The following Monday morning I was startled from my sleep at 3:30 A.M. by the phone. It was the principal.

"I'm on my way to the hospital. . . . Donald's family was robbed at gunpoint last night. I'll be bringing him to school today, but you need to keep an eye on him. He might experience some after-effects during the day. His mother is in shock."

At the time, Donald and his mother lived in the Bronx— a part of the city often notorious for its elevated crime rates. I could not go back to sleep after hearing this, all the while envisioning terrible scenes of what could have happened.

Upon my arrival at school, I went straight to the cafeteria. Donald ran to me; we embraced, and he started crying. Seeing and feeling his pain, I started crying also. I took him up to the classroom, where he recounted his nightmare.

Donald was having dinner while his mother prepared to style a client's hair, when three men, dressed in dark clothing and heavily armed, burst into the apartment. They laid the client on the floor and pointed a gun to her head. One of the intruders also put a gun to Donald's head. The three men yelled at his mother, telling her to hand over the "merchandise" or else they were going to kill Donald. By then, another gun was placed at his head.

Donald's mother did not know what they were talking about and kept crying and pleading that she did not have anything or know about any merchandise.

Obviously intent on recovering the merchandise, they locked the victims in the bathroom. Meanwhile, the men trashed the house in search of the alleged merchandise.

The captives could hear loud cursing and furniture and lamps breaking. One of the gunmen insisted that whether they found the merchandise or not they had to kill the hostages because their faces had been seen. The two women cried uncontrollably, gripping each other in agony, certain they were going to be murdered.

In the midst of their despair, Donald said, "Momma, if I die, I want you to know I love you. But I need to do this now. I need to pray." He climbed into the bathtub, knelt and started praying.

Donald never told me what he prayed that night. Yet the petition of a thirteen-year-old boy, who had learned to pray in school, touched the heart of God. Donald's family did not profess or support any particular religious denomination. His only religious exposure was at school. Donald said that he prayed for a long time until they realized that there was silence in the house.

They dared to turn the lock. With the door open, to their dismay—and relief—they saw the house was trashed, but the invaders had left.

"Teacher," Donald said at the end of his story, "I remembered you said the best thing to do when we're in trouble is to pray. God answered my prayer."

The police could not understand why they were not murdered. It would have been a "clean job" since no one else in the neighborhood claimed to have heard or seen anything.

Later that day, with Donald's permission, I retold his experience to the class. The kids were shocked, and they all rallied around Donald. Each time prayer was offered special mention was made of him and his mother. On a weekly basis, we sent handmade cards and candy to Donald's mother to encourage her and to show our support. Yet the lesson remained unquestionably reaffirmed.

Norka Blackman-Richards

Let the Church Say Amen!

It's no disgrace to start over or to begin anew.

Bebe Moore Campbell

When I received my acceptance to medical school, I was excited to begin my medical training, but frightened to be moving far from my hometown. My son was just four years old, and I was looking at spending four years in a new city in which I didn't know anyone. Growing up in the church, I wanted to seek out some supportive, kind people to connect with. My search led me to a small church located just a few minutes away from the medical school. The church was in a dilapidated building with sparse grass and modest trees. Little did I know that the building would be in sharp contrast to the warmth and love inside.

"Hello! Hello!" We were greeted by the usher, an elderly man with a down-home voice. His eyes brightened at our arrival as if welcoming old friends. I asked to sit in the last pew because I was shy and wasn't quite sure if this would be our new church home. I knew it would allow a quick exit if this was not the place for us.

But as the service progressed, I looked over at Jonathan clapping his small hands and swinging his feet gleefully to and fro. The music was lively and my soul, too, was exploding with the spirit and vigor of the people around me.

Then the pastor asked, "Are there any visitors this mornin'?"

I looked down at Jonathan who looked up at me and then I looked at the congregation. They all knew who the visitors were—the mother and son in the back of the church! No hiding for us!

Holding my son's hand, I stood. "Good morning. My name is Melanie and this is my son, Jonathan. We just moved here a week ago and we are looking for a church family."

"Church family?" The pastor echoed my words, "Did you hear that? This young mother is looking for a church family!"

The congregation clapped and smiled, shouting, "Amen!"

We felt so loved and received. We knew this was right where we were supposed to be.

During the next few months we attended service every Sunday. On Saturdays, we would be home studying and playing. Every once in a while, we would be surprised by a church member's visit. He or she would ring the bell, usually with a fruit basket or some other goodies in hand. "Melanie, I was just thinking about you and thought you would like this. God bless you." During finals week, I would receive calls of encouragement, "Sister Melanie, God is just blessing you. You hang in there. We are all praying for you." And I would get the motivation I needed to keep on studying. There were many offers for babysitting. Going to church was often just the reminder I needed to be grateful, especially for the opportunity to be a single mom pursuing a medical career.

During my next year of school, I had difficulty getting money for textbooks. I went to church and prayed on it, meanwhile trying to think of using the money I did have to copy the pages I needed from my classmates.

During one Sunday service, the pastor announced that there was a family that was in need. He said that he wasn't quite sure what the need was, but God had placed it on his heart to say that he felt we needed to collect money for this family, that those who could contribute should. His words touched my heart. I imagined a family that must be struggling, perhaps barely making ends meet.

I looked into my purse and saw two dollar bills. It was all I had in my purse, but I placed it in the tray praying for God to take care of that family in need. When the offering was collected, I felt so good to give to someone who really needed it. I didn't worry about trying to buy my text-books; I felt blessed with all I had—my health, my son, the opportunity to be in school and the wonderful, loving, giving church family I had. If any of these people were in need, I wanted to help them.

After the money was collected, the pastor said, "Church, I know you all will probably agree on this. We have a family right here in this church that could really use this money. Melanie, would you and Jonathan come up front and get the blessing God has provided for you?"

My eyes welled with tears as Jonathan and I walked from the back pew all the way up towards the front. My pride almost didn't allow me to take the money, but our need was stronger. The church members applauded and smiled at us, nodding their heads and praising God for our family and the ability to help us.

When we got home, Jonathan and I counted the money. Over two hundred dollars, it was enough to cover my textbooks just fine. I didn't know the blessing would be for me, but I learned that when we try to be a blessing for others, we can't help but be blessed by the process. Amen!

Melanie M. Watkins

Life After Death

I used to hurt so badly that I'd ask God "Why, what have I done to deserve any of this?" I feel now He was preparing me for this, for the future. That's the way I see it.

Janet Jackson

Pregnant and sixteen seemed to be the norm in the inner city of Cleveland, Ohio. After all, everybody was doing it—getting pregnant, that is. Why should I be any different? Because I was a straight-A student with anticipations of traveling the world! My head was always stuck in a book, dreaming of the day that I would cross over into the life that was so eloquently described on the pages of Dick and Jane. How was I to know that other individuals had the capability to shatter dreams? Coming from a family of ten children, six boys and four girls, my parental time was limited. So the majority of my counseling and advice came from those who had already surrendered, unbeknownst to me, to mediocrity.

"Girl, you ain't going to ever get to Alaska to see the

ice-blue glaciers so quit your dreaming, not to mention that there aren't any black folks in Alaska."

"The Great Wall of China, you're joking, right?"

"Girl, you had better get your head out of them books."

"But why?" I would always ask, only to hear the same response.

"Girls like you get pregnant, drop out of school, get on welfare and die. That's the extent of the life and times of an inner-city ghetto girl like you. So put your hopes and dreams away and take a sip of this Wild Irish Rose. It will help you to forget all about your dreams." And that it did.

Pregnant, out of school and following the path most traveled, I found myself living without a dream. Gloria Pointer came kicking and screaming into the world on February 28, 1970. Yellow as a rose with three different shades of hair: blonde, red and brown.

"Girl, where in the world did you come from?"

Inquisitive from birth, she seemed to have eyes of great expectations even from behind the glass that temporarily separated us in the maternity wing of University Hospital.

Gloria and I were more than mother and daughter. Because we were assigned the task of growing up together, we were more like friends. She seemed to think much more highly of me than I did of myself. I struggled constantly with dreams forsaken, early motherhood and walking through the dark path of the dreams of another. It was Gloria's love and belief in me, even as a child, that always seemed to be the glue that held it all together. Maybe it was her eyes of expectancy that always seemed to pierce my soul, eyes that encouraged me to strive, if not for me, then for her.

Before long, though, I was swinging from the chandelier of destruction. Drugs, violence and a life of crime seemed to grip my conscience like a hangman's noose around my neck. Life was sucking me under, and it was pulling Gloria along with me. How could I save her when I couldn't seem to save myself? In the midst of everything else, I was pregnant again with my second child, Raymon. He narrowly escaped death at birth because of my lifestyle consumed with street life and neglect. Twenty years old with two kids, and one with those wide eyes of expectancy that continued to pierce my soul even when it was filled with mind-altering chemicals. *How is this possible? How had such big dreams dissolved in the twinkling of an eye? Is there anyone out there who could possibly hear my pleas—"Save me"—before total destruction consumes not only my dreams but also the dreams of those who look at me with eyes of expectancy?*

One day, my father—who had watched through eyes of devastation the rise and fall of his fourth child—assigned a friend to me whose task was to hold me and not let go, to snatch me back from the gates of hell. He found this task to be tedious because, even though I wanted help, I was not coming along willingly. After all, "they" said this was my destiny, right? One day, after I had hit bottom, he told me about someone who could help me to get free and walk on a path full of light. His name was Jesus.

Reluctant at first, I resisted with the mini-might I had left within my dying soul. But one day I said, "Yes." The brightness that followed my conversion was blinding; a world once full of darkness, despair and hopelessness looked new. Yes, life was good again. I began to grow as a Christian, the first to walk through the doors of the church when they swung open to welcome weary travelers such as myself. My questions were finally beginning to be answered. God was the answer that I was looking for, and he was the missing link. He was the one who could show me the way out.

We were on our way to the land of milk and honey, a land where dreams do come true. Yes, life was good. My endless tears seemed to dry up, and Gloria, who was always there for me, filled my ears with her dreams. But her dreams did not include the Eiffel Tower or the Great Wall of China. Her dream was simple: a better life for her mother, a life that wasn't filled with tears or worry over bills.

Her plan was to marry a rich basketball player and have enough money to make my life better. She was going to repair our home, fill it with new carpeting, new furniture and everything that would make my life happy. "Don't worry, Momma, I'm going to make it alright."

How could one child love someone like me so much?

Yes, everything was going to be okay. I had followed all of the rules and was next in line for a miracle. Then came a knock at the door of my heart: an early morning telephone call informing me that Gloria was missing.

"Missing." The word seemed to echo throughout the room. "What do you mean, missing?"

"Well, Ms. Pointer, Gloria was to receive a perfect attendance award this morning in a special assembly and she has not arrived at school," I was told.

"What? Well, I suggest that you get off the phone and go find her!" was my shocked response.

Moments later the phone rang again. It was the principal of the high school informing me to call the police.

Call the police for what? I was thinking. *When I see Gloria later she is going to have hell to pay for giving us all such a scare!* Nevertheless, I dialed 911.

After a short while, police officers were knocking at the door advising me to sit down.

"We found a body," is the last thing I remember hearing. In a fetal position, curled on the floor, I seemed to be floating between consciousness and false reality.

Chastising myself for lying there helplessly when they hadn't said that the dead body was Gloria Pointer, the girl with eyes of expectancy, I forced myself up from the floor.

But the punch came again, fiercer this time, because with it came the news that indeed it was Gloria. Raped, murdered and discarded like an animal beneath rickety stairs of steel, surrounded by piles of filth.

A child isn't supposed to be left lying in such filth, not a child with eyes of expectancy. A child is not supposed to be murdered at the age of fourteen—not an innocent child, minding her own business, walking to school to receive an award. Didn't those eyes expect me to protect her as the final blow was laid to her head rendering her lifeless? Once again, as a mother I had failed.

Plunged into an unexpected reality, catapulted into an arena for which there was no script, life became a fight for existence. All of my reasons for living were gone.

Okay, whoever you are, I believe you now, ain't no ice-blue glaciers nor snow-capped mountains in my future. I agree that I am destined to be just what they said, "An inner-city single parent on welfare without a dream."

However, I had forgotten something—something that seemed to shine even through the darkness of despair. That something, that someone, was Jesus. When Gloria's body was finally ready for viewing, I went alone to the funeral home. I wanted to ask for her forgiveness in private. I wanted to let her know that her murder would not, by the grace of God, be in vain. How could someone just kill a child and walk away? Once again, I was back to asking questions. Once again an injustice occupied my entire view. No longer did I see her lying neatly dressed surrounded by the satin of a mahogany coffin. The only thing I could see was the injustice of it all. That injustice forced me to ask the question, why? From that point, grief took a backseat and a new dream slid behind the wheel— the dream of a better world, a safer world for children.

Could this dream become a reality? It could, according to Philippians 4:13, which states, "I can do all things through Christ which strengtheneth me."

So, I began a letter-writing campaign under the guidance of the Holy Spirit in search of a well-known celebrity who would grace our inner-city ghetto with his or her presence and cry aloud for an end to the violence against innocent children. Each letter described in detail exactly what they should do upon arrival. They should use the status that God had given them to persuade folks to leave our children alone. Time passed without positive response, but the delay of the arrival of such a celebrity only fueled me to occupy their role until they showed up. I wanted them to visit schools, do television shows, radio shows, anything and everything that would get the message across. So, off I went to all of their appointments, proclaiming that I was just the voice "crying in the wilderness," the real person would come after a while. In the meantime, hear me. I know that I am nobody but a mother with a murdered child, but listen as I describe firsthand the agony of it all. Listen as I proclaim the devastation of dreams delayed. Look as I describe Gloria's eyes of expectancy that no longer look to me as her mother. Can anyone please tell me how to wake up from such a horrendous nightmare? No you can't, so until the answer to that question arrives I must continue walking toward the light, which is the only thing that can offer me hope.

As time passed, don't you know, I became the person that I was looking for! Honors and awards began to follow my desire to make the world a safer place for kids. Former President Bush appointed me the 908th Point of Light in the nation's 1,000 Points of Light; I was inducted by former Governor George Voinvoich into the Ohio Women's Hall of Fame. Suddenly I became, as some might consider, a celebrity, a voice to be heard.

My voice cannot save Gloria, but the feelings of failure have diminished through the work that God has given me to do toward saving others. It is as if Gloria is smiling down upon me from heaven, and I can hear her saying to God, "See, I told you my mother could do it."

Today, I am a much-sought-after spokesperson regarding violence prevention and safer communities. As the recipient of national awards, including the 2001 Essence Award, and recently appearing in *Ebony* magazine, I find that my life is filled with national speaking engagements, consolation of families that have been victimized by crime, interviews and tons of traveling. And yes, I finally did go to Anchorage, Alaska, to behold the beauty that was written in the books.

I was invited recently to speak at a prison in Mansfield, Ohio. At the end of my presentation the inmates were permitted to ask me questions. The crowd numbered around three hundred, so you can imagine my surprise when a hand from the rear was raised high.

"Ms. Pointer," he said, "You may not remember me but you made me some Rice Krispie treats when I was in the fifth grade. I was wondering if I could give you a hug?"

Making a difference to each other, that is what it is all about. Perhaps it was God's plan all along for Gloria to be the reason I would be pushed to meet His eyes of expectancy and fulfill my real destiny. Isn't it funny that dreams still do come true—often with an expense, but always to the glory of God?

Yvonne Pointer

$\overline{6}$

LESSONS
LEARNED

*E*very experience has a lesson.

Wally "Famous" Amos

BOONDOCKS. ©1999 Aaron McGruder. Distributed by UNIVERSAL PRESS SYNDI-
CATE. Reprinted with permission. All rights reserved.

Confessions of an Ex-Con

*The longer I live, the more deeply I'm convinced
that the difference between the successful person
and the failure, between the strong and the
weak, is a decision.*

Willie E. Gary

"By the power invested in me by the State of
Washington, I hereby sentence you, Dennis R. Mitchell, to
two consecutive twenty-year terms with the Department
of Corrections."

Talking about dissin' a brother! Without forethought,
my immediate instinct was to leap out of my chair and
inflict my own pound of justice upside His Honor's head.

Fortunately I found myself cut short of my goal and
face down on the floor as several sheriff's officers finally
tackled me to the ground and led me out of the court-
room in handcuffs, kicking and screaming obscenities.
When the good officers wrestled me into the elevator out
of sight, little did I know that they were going to give me
something to scream about: wall-to-wall "counseling"!

The next day the headline read, "Man Screams and Yells!"
Much to my dismay this series of events was only the
beginning. Soon I would find myself in a holding cell with
five thousand skinheads—well, it *seemed* like five thousand
skinheads. Needless to say, my odds of surviving didn't
look too bright, and off to the hospital I went. By the time
I was finally able to open my eyes, I would find out that
things were going to get worse for a player.

That bus ride to Shelton Penitentiary was about seven
hours long, and although I had a lot of experience being
in the back seat of law enforcement's cars, it was a totally
different experience; my bondsman couldn't help me
now. As we pulled up to my new home and the gates
swung open, I looked around and saw barbed wire
around the joint. Behind me, the gate closed and locked.
Inmate onlookers were watching as the new chain came
in, some just to see who they knew and others to see who
they wanted to "get to know," if you get my drift. The
gangs are always waiting just like vultures, watching for
their next prey.

That was back in 1979. From then on my life was filled
with fighting, partying, drug and alcohol abuse, and
denial. Run DMC had just hit the airwaves with rap music
and "my song" was, "Don't push me 'cause I'm close to
the edge."

I decided 1981 was going to be my year. After all I just
knew at most I would spend a couple of years locked up
and be back in the hood kicking it live as always. I had
stopped getting in trouble or at least not getting caught
for it, and I found myself in front of the parole board.

"Come back and see us again in two years!"
I was stunned and dazed! It felt like I had just gone fifteen rounds in the ring with the great Muhammad Ali
during his prime years. The pain was so intense I wanted
to cry, but big boys don't cry, especially in prison.

Take it like a man, I thought to myself while my inner child was in tears. In prison, if you get caught crying it's a sign of weakness and there is always someone watching you, waiting in the trenches, lurking in the darkness behind the cold hard steel, waiting for you to show your weakness.

I staggered out the door as the parole board almost knocked me out with that left hook. I needed some fresh air to clear my head, so I went to the big yard to walk around the track. "Don't push me 'cause I'm close to the edge. . . ."

For the next year, I continued to drift along with no road map or sense of purpose. Then, one Friday night, three days before my birthday, I was lying in my cell watching TV. Suddenly my name boomed over the intercom: "Mitchell, Charlie 3-25, report to the sergeant's office!"

My son Little Dennis, whose fifth birthday we had celebrated, had been murdered by an impaired driver. All I could think of were our daddy-son phone calls when Little D would sing my favorite song, "I love my daddy all the time, all the time."

Monday on my birthday, two armed guards escorted me home to Spokane to attend the funeral at my mom's church. That's right—I am the son of a preacher woman.

I entered in leg irons shackled to my waist and my wrists. I felt like dead man walking; after all a part of me was dead, a very special part.

As I made my way up to the casket and saw Little Dennis so peaceful and so handsome, all the anger, rage, hurt, guilt, bitterness and remorse vanished and I thought to myself, *What would Little D want?*

Immediately I knew that he would want his daddy to be the absolute best he could. As tears filled the wells and flowed down my face like a torrential Niagara Falls, my eyes closed and I heard him singing, "I love my daddy all the time, all the time."

After the funeral I said good-bye to my family, friends and those who came to pay their respects. On that dark, cold and lonely road back, I decided to get involved in the "Scared Straight" program to deter young people from making the same mistakes I had.

Soon I found myself going to the library, reading books; one was called *Think and Grow Rich.* That book said for every adversity comes the equivalent of a greater benefit. I remember thinking to myself, *Where's the benefit?* I definitely had tons of adversity; adversity was my lifestyle back in the day.

Then I heard about a guy in California into that positive-thinking stuff, so I wrote to him explaining my situation and in a few weeks I got a call to the mailroom. I had received a package. Inside was a four-cassette audio album titled "How to Outperform Yourself Totally" by Mark Victor Hansen!

Listening over and over, I stared out into the sky through the broken windows from my cell. I remember thinking to myself, *I sure would like to be able to motivate and empower people in a positive way.* Back in the day, growing up in the hood, the only motivation I knew was fear motivation: You'd better, or else! What a radical paradigm shift this was for me. The more I listened as Mark sprinkled the prosperity seeds into my fertile mind, the more I became excited! I had never heard anybody like Mark before. I thought, just possibly, I could be somebody who could make a difference.

Then I thought to myself, *What a great testament to Little Dennis's memory—going to schools when I got out and sharing my story and talking about the insidious effects of drugs, crime and alcohol abuse. After all, I've been there and done that and look where I ended up!*

For the next several years I immersed myself in a

personal development retreat. No longer was I going to serve time; I was going to make time serve me. Prisoner number 265212 was going to take charge of his life and his destiny. Finally on December 24, 1987 after spending eight and a half years doing hard time, I was paroled. My prayers were answered. Free at last, free at last, thank God almighty; I was free at last!

Now it was time to put up or shut up, so I went to work speaking everywhere I could. Articles started appearing in newspapers and my speaking career was launched. In 1990, I founded, hosted and produced my own TV talk show, *Choices*, where I had the opportunity to interview stars of the big screen like Edward James Olmos, Ellen Travolta Bannon, LL Cool J, The Guys Next Door, Sir Mix-A-Lot, Yolanda King and others.

My life has been about overcoming seemingly insurmountable odds. As I tell my story—whether it is on the news, to an audience of six or several thousand people—I share my earlier life as an example of what not to do. I also let all my brothas and sistahs know that no matter how bad things are, you've got the power within you to turn it around. If I can change and turn my life around from gangs, drugs, crime, prison and the ultimate tragedy of all, losing my son, anybody can do it!

Take my word for it: Being out there representing with the right attitude is the only way to go.

Dennis Mitchell

Making Mistakes Is Natural

Mistakes are a fact of life. It's the response to the error that counts.

Nikki Giovanni

Making chocolate-chip cookies made me "Famous." Losing the company that made my name a household word made me wonder if life would ever be the same again. Despite my missteps in business, I found that my life got better and I got stronger.

Many people who know I started Famous Amos Cookies don't know I'm finished with Famous Amos. It's a long story that began in Hollywood but didn't have a Hollywood ending, and it's why I say making mistakes is natural.

I started Famous Amos Cookies in March 1975 with a little help from my friends. Others believed it was a risky business. My shop on Sunset Boulevard was the first retail store in the world to sell nothing but chocolate-chip cookies.

Even I was amazed that a forty-year-old amateur cookie

maker could achieve such swift success. The first year, I grossed $300,000. I had christened myself "Famous Amos" before I actually became famous, and out of this sweet success was born "the King of Cookies, the Father of the Gourmet Chocolate-Chip Cookie Industry, the Face That Launched a Thousand Chips."

I have always believed that chocolate-chip cookies are special and magical. Just the thought of chocolate-chip cookies evokes emotional feelings and revives happy, caring, loving and heartfelt memories. Chocolate-chip cookies were a way of life for me before I turned them into a way to make a living. I had used my home-baked chocolate-chip cookies as my calling card in the entertainment business. A bag of free cookies always meant a warm, friendly welcome for me, although it didn't necessarily mean that my clients got the jobs.

After two years in business, Famous Amos was grossing $1 million. A *Time Magazine* cover story in 1977 called me one of the "Hot New Rich." *Newsweek* called me "the Progenitor of the Upscale Cookie, the Greatest Cookie Salesman Alive." Of course, I accepted the accolades even if they went too far.

Batch followed aromatic batch. Famous Amos expanded from coast to coast. I was the nut who brought nuts to Nutley, New Jersey, when I opened a Famous Amos bakery there in 1976. It wasn't long before my bewhiskered brown face was to cookies what the pale-faced Quaker was to oatmeal and the Colonel was to chicken.

I was hotter than a baking pan straight from the oven. It seemed I could do no wrong. In 1979, I made $4 million and in 1980, $5 million. I had more than 150 people working to fill those cute little cookie bags and never-enough cookie tins with three and a half tons of handmade, fresh-baked cookies a day.

Within five years, my face, my trademark battered

Panama hat, and my simple embroidered Indian pullover shirt had become known far and wide. In 1980, I donated the hat off my head and the shirt off my back to the Smithsonian Institution as icons of the entrepreneurial spirit that is as American as chocolate-chip cookies. Here was proof that a black high-school dropout from a broken home in Harlem could still make it in this country. For a while it seemed like a cosmic, never-ending experience. But like all sugar-induced highs, it didn't last.

In 1985, my cookie empire began to crumble. I was promoting it like crazy and having good fun, but I forgot one little thing. I forgot to put a good management team under the flying carpet. The financial side was flying without a navigator, and before long, outside investors had begun chipping away at my stake in Famous Amos Cookies.

I brought in the Bass Brothers from Texas as investors to pump more capital into the company, reducing my stake from 48 percent to 17 percent. The deal didn't last long, and another group bought out the Bass Brothers. My equity slipped again, and by that point, I was no longer involved in the day-to-day operations.

The new group was losing money and wound up selling out to Bob Baer, the founder of Telecheck, and his two sons. In 1987, the company was in the hands of its third owners in two years. I had no stake in the company by then, but I still had an employment agreement that paid me $225,000 in salary and expenses to promote the company.

In 1988, the Baers sold the company to a venture-capital group based in San Francisco. When that group sought to lessen my salary, I felt unwanted and unwelcome. In my lectures, I advise people to move on if they do not like the people they are working with. Since that's what I was dishing out to others, it had to be good enough for me. On March 1, 1989, my contract with Famous Amos was terminated, and I left the company I founded with nothing.

To secure my freedom, I signed a "divorce decree" that included a two-year noncompete clause, which expired at the end of 1991. Another agreement, which I had mistakenly thought would expire with the noncompete agreement, gave Famous Amos the rights to my name and likeness in any food-related business. The company hadn't failed me. I failed it. The lesson was humbling. I had passed on the name "Famous Amos" to people I had no feelings for. I was no longer "Famous Amos." To me, "Famous Amos" had been more than just a name. I did not know it at the time, but I was beginning a journey that would help me discover who Wally Amos really is.

After leaving Famous Amos, I launched a career in lecturing, doing for a fee of $5,000 or $7,000 what I had been doing as a spokesperson for the cookie company. I gave inspirational, motivational lectures to colleges, corporations, professional associations and conventions. I also did some consulting. It was bread and butter, but it was never as sweet as flour and sugar and butter with chips of chocolate mixed in.

After the noncompete clause expired, I started a new company, Wally Amos Presents Chip and Cookie. I couldn't use "Famous Amos," of course, but I could use Wally Amos, because that's my name, and I thought it sounded very Walt Disney-ish to say "Wally Amos Presents."

In December 1991, *People* magazine asked Hawaii correspondent Stu Glauberman to do a "Where Are They Now?" story about me. The February 1992 story described how I was embarking on Chip and Cookie, the sequel to Famous Amos, and how my fresh-baked cookies and my Chip and Cookie dolls and books and T-shirts were catching on at J.C. Penney stores in Hawaii.

That story attracted a lot of attention—including some at the Famous Amos Cookie Company headquarters. In

April 1992, they responded with a lawsuit.

In my book *Man with No Name,* I recount how the new owners of the Famous Amos Company dragged me into U.S. District Court to try to prevent me from using my name and likeness in any business. I told myself that this was a case I couldn't possibly lose and that they couldn't possibly rob me of my name. Once again, my sense of what was right was wrong. The court ruled against me, and the upshot was that I could not use my name or the word "Famous" with the name Amos in connection with any cookie, beverage or restaurant business. I lost the case, my name, and the Chip and Cookie venture. But I did not lose my family, my positive outlook and myself. I learned that you don't need a name to sell cookies; you need a cookie that tastes good. So I started the Uncle Noname Cookie Company.

In March 1995, I celebrated the tenth anniversary of losing management control of the Famous Amos Cookie Company. Why celebrate these mistakes? Because I'd learned from them. I learned that mistakes usually happen for a reason. I learned that a business needs a skilled, experienced management team. I learned that I should have spent more time doing what I was good at—marketing and promoting and glad-handing—rather than trying to do all the things I wasn't good at. I also learned how vital it is to be focused and disciplined.

When I was in show business, I sat in on many recording sessions and television tapings. Whenever a performer missed a note or flubbed a line, the producer or director would chat sanely with the artist and/or the backup musicians and roll the tape again. "All right, Take 14, rolling," the producer might say. It was just a mistake. Why is it that when someone makes a mistake in business or in personal relationships, it's cause for anger? Humans aren't perfect—even if they're singing stars, movie stars or cookie bakers. We all make mistakes. We're all in a state of training, a state of becoming—becoming a better worker, a better student, a better parent, a better spouse, a better friend or a better person.

I remember the time I caught a worker who had burned a rack with twenty trays of cookies. I settled down and explained to the worker the cost involved in sacrificing twenty trays of cookies on the altar of carelessness. I told the worker to do another take—more carefully. Patience and understanding and sound advice can go a long way in guiding and encouraging employees and friends through their mistakes.

Another thing I've learned from my mistakes is that it's important to work from your strengths. Don't spread yourself too thin. Focus your time and energy on the things you do best. Leave the rest to the other members of the team.

When all is said and done, mistakes are the process through which we in turn create success. Mistakes create the foundation for our life. That foundation is experience, which in turn creates the light that leads us into our future. That light is called wisdom.

Now things have come full circle. I have launched another cookie company, Aunt Della's Cookies, named after my aunt, Della Bryant, who first made chocolate-chip cookies for me at age twelve. Life continues to get sweeter and sweeter.

Wally Amos and Stu Glauberman

The Race We Run
Is Not About the Finish Line

*When I went to the playground, I never picked
the best players. I picked guys with less talent,
but who were willing to work hard, who had the
desire to be great.*

Earvin "Magic" Johnson

It's hard to say no to Superman.

When Chris, my younger brother, was five years old he
wanted to enter a thirty-yard dash at "Fun Day," a City of
Dallas summer youth program. It was a project that was
designed to give kids alternatives to hanging out on street
corners during summer vacation. Chris, who insisted
everyone in our family call him "Superman," had always
been fascinated by running, jumping and, yes, flying.

Each time we went to the park he would stand along
the sidelines hypnotized as he watched the older kids
race. And although he didn't really understand the con-
cept of running a race—or so I thought—he somehow

knew that the atmosphere of competing and doing your best provided one of the greatest feelings in the world. For three weeks, he had run over to me, panting and out of breath, with the same question, "Can I run today?" For three weeks my answer had remained the same, "We'll see." That tired, worn-out phrase my parents used on me whenever they didn't know exactly how to say no with good reason.

On this particular day I caught a glimpse of the sparkle in Chris's eyes. He wanted, no, *needed,* to run in a race, so I agreed to give him his shot.

As one event finished and they geared up for the next one, I learned that the other two kids in Chris's race were seven and nine years old. I had wondered why they looked so much bigger and more developed than my gangly five-year-old shrimp of a brother who'd just lost one of his front teeth.

Oh, no, I thought. *He's gonna get creamed. He'll hate me for letting him sign up!*

I jogged over to the starting point, thinking I should pull Superman from the race. Maybe encourage him to run with kids his own age. But something in the child-of-steel's spirit told me age was nothing but a number in his mind.

The official called for the runners to take their marks, and I told Chris I would be waiting for him at the finish line and that I'd be proud of him no matter what happened. I laid a big sloppy kiss on him and sent him to the starting blocks, certain I was making a big mistake.

The race began, and Chris took off as if he'd been shot from a cannon. And just as I'd imagined, the two older kids, one to his left, the other to his right, were leaving him in the dust. All of the spectators were going crazy, cheering for all three kids. I jumped up and down, waving my hands, wearing a smile as wide as Texas.

Chris kept his eyes on me and continued to run his little heart out. Finally, he crossed the finish line, leaping into my arms.

"Way to go, Chris," I said, holding back a fountain of tears. "You were soooo good, baby! You ran so hard! I'm proud of you."

He hugged my neck so tight I was sure it would snap. With his sweaty face buried in my neck, he kissed me, pulled away and asked excitedly, "Did I win?"

Surely, he thought he must have won as hard as I was smiling. I laughed but never thought twice about my answer to his question. Instead, I continued to flash my megawatt smile, took one look at the gleam in his eyes and the joy spilling out of his chest, and said, "You sure did, baby. You sure did."

Fran Harris

[EDITOR'S NOTE: *The author of this piece took the lesson of determination and joy her brother taught her that day and went on to earn a spot on the Houston Comets' first WNBA championship team in 1997.*]

Bondage of Fear

Few are too young, and none too old, to make the attempt to learn.

Booker T. Washington

As you read this, I want you to know and be aware that there are thousands around you who can't read it.

I grew up from the 1940s to the 1960s and attended school during segregation. Some of it was good and some not so good. I realized at a very early age I did not, could not, read like other children. During my early years in elementary school I learned what terror was—not the world terror we know today, but just as real and just as powerful to a seven-year-old little boy.

I think back to those days, sitting at my desk, staring at my reading books, *Oh no, the guy behind me just stood up. I'm next.* As he is reading I try desperately to remember the words just as he is saying them. I can't do it. Why do I have to do it anyway? They are going to laugh at me again; the snickering has already started, because they know I am next. This, they think, is their time to get a good laugh. I remember thinking, *Oh, please don't let her say I'm stupid again. I have to remember the story; oh, if I could only remember each word as it is written, then they won't know I can't read.*

That is when it started, my amazing ability to memorize. I found that I could listen while others were reading so I then could memorize what they were saying. This allowed me to slide through school. In high school, I learned to find ways of getting out of school. I found that I could swim and dive. I was the best in town at that time, winning many ribbons and trophies. I had found a way to change their laughing and smirking into cheers and support! I could only do this through my school years. I would soon be faced with real life. I was beating many records in swimming; however, back then we of the darker skin were not recognized as much in sports.

Then it came to me that I could play drums—this became my "safe place." In joining the marching band I learned that this, of course, would allow me to be excused from many different classes. After all, the band had to practice a lot and go to different sporting events and participate in parades. Then I found myself at graduation day. Standing there I just remember feeling how grateful I was to have it over, not caring that I could not read any better than a second-grader. I was free now to go and live life, or so I thought. I did not realize what the bondage of not being able to read had done to me.

By the mid-eighties, I had spent the last twenty years in and out of bands, traveling around, taking jobs that ranged from flipping hamburgers to sweeping floors. During those years, I learned to dull the fear and the feeling of being dumb by drinking and doing drugs. One night, I was playing drums on a riverboat in St. Louis. I was drunk and pretty high, and did not realize that they had the drummer positioned on a pedestal above the rail; I was jamming, and then all of a sudden I threw my hands up in the air and flipped backwards into the mighty Mississippi River. I sobered up right fast! This made me glad to have my swimming experience.

I married and moved to Michigan, where I was faced with having to change my driver's license. I remember asking myself, *Why did my wife have to ask to see my license? Why couldn't she just mind her own business?*

Finally, tired of hearing her mouth, I pulled out a worn piece of paper from my wallet. As I handed it to her it started to crumble in her hands. She looked at the expiration date that showed 1966, and although it was from the State of Michigan, it was now 1985. She looked at me bewildered, because she had met me in California and knew I was from Alabama.

I remember asking myself, *Why can't she just leave me alone?* I remember thinking, *I can't tell her; she will know how dumb I am. I can't share this secret with her. I love her so much, and why can't she just leave me alone? I have to get a drink, then I will be able to talk. Maybe she will just go away! She won't leave me alone. I can drive so why do I need another license? She will know why I always bring things to her to fill out. It has been years of this, and she does not need to know after all these years that I just can't read. I hate the pain I am placing on her. What did she ever do to me but love and support me? She gave me four great kids; I trust her with my life and yet I can't trust her with my secret. I can't take it anymore. She has to be told, and then she will leave me alone. If she chooses to leave me, so be it.*

I remember taking her to our bedroom and closing the door behind me. I was so scared. I didn't want to lose my family. They were all I had. I had to tell her; the fear was raging in me. I could feel the devil himself inside of me trying to explode, "Don't tell her," he kept saying. I couldn't listen. I had to tell her. I remember falling on my knees in front of her, grabbing onto her as if my life depended on it. I was crying now, and she was bewildered; I saw fear in her face. She had no idea what I was about to tell her and she was expecting the worst things imaginable. I silently prayed, *God, please give me strength,* while visions of my classmates making fun of me haunted me. Then, I looked up into her tear-stained face and said, "I can't go get my license because I can't read!" She looked down at me for what seemed an eternity. She pulled my hands to raise me to my feet next to her and wrapped her arms around me, and we cried together. After much release of the years of hiding my secret, she took me and sat me on our bed. We talked for a long time. I was so thankful to have it out.

That night, when the children were in bed, my wife came to me with our youngest son's reading book. He was in second grade. Who would have known that I would have a chance to start all over again? My wife took me back years so I could start again when I thought my life ended. There was no laughing or teasing. No one else even had to know, just us.

I have my license now, and I keep it up to date. I can read anything put in front of me, though it may take me a moment or two. My children all know of my being consumed with the spirit and bondage of terrible fear. I now no longer drink or do drugs; you see I no longer have anything to hide or to numb. I am free of the one thing that kept me in bondage. God has truly brought me out of my Egypt!

As you read this, please pray for all those around you who you may or may not know, are stuck in the bondage of not being able to read. I've learned that "Reading is freedom."

Howard E. Lipscomb Sr.

From the Mouths of Babes

*What lies behind us and what lies before us are
tiny matters compared to what lies within us.*

Oliver Wendell Holmes

I remember the phone call vividly. I was busy at work
as a financial planner when one of the leading African
American businesspeople in Harrisburg, Pennsylvania,
called me. I listened intently as he told me about an opportunity to enter a competition that would enable me to
travel to Malawi, Zimbabwe and South Africa and participate in a study exchange program. It was clearly the
chance of a lifetime. As an African American, I was very
excited about the opportunity to go to Africa and learn in
Malawi and Zimbabwe. However, it was 1985, and
apartheid, South Africa's inhuman system of legalized
segregation, was the law of the land. If it had been anywhere else in the world I would have agreed instantly to
apply for the trip. However, because it included a visit to
racially stratified South Africa, I was very concerned about
even applying.

For the rest of the week, I could not concentrate on work. I felt an emotional and intellectual inner struggle. As the son of parents who had grown up in the segregated South and marched with Dr. King, I was very conscious of the racial struggle in America. My consciousness forced me to ask myself some difficult questions. *Would I be supporting this horrible system if I went? Or would I be missing an opportunity to educate the racists in Africa and inform the people at home if I did not go?* I decided to apply for the trip because I felt that I would be a more effective change agent if I participated. I was fortunate to be chosen to go. However, I was the only African American going out of six participants.

I will never forget how nervous, anxious, excited and scared I was during the seventeen-hour plane ride to South Africa. I could not sleep, because I was trying to anticipate what I would experience during my stay there. *Would I be discriminated against? Was my life in danger? Would I stay in the homes of black or white families? Would the black Africans be happy or disappointed to see me? Would I learn the real reason that apartheid is so important to the government? What would life be like in Malawi and Zimbabwe?* I don't recall many details of the plane ride. However, I do remember tears coming to my eyes when I first saw African land. I was returning to the land of my ancestors. I felt a strange connection to the land that was both frightening and wonderful at the same time.

This trip taught me about nature, politics and prejudice. On the sand of Lake Malawi I had one of the best views in the world of a comet that comes around once every seventy-six years: Halley's Comet. I made history by becoming the first nonwhite to set foot on the floor of the Johannesburg Stock Exchange during trading hours. I watched history in the making as one of the few Americans to witness the coronation of the king of Swaziland. In addition, I learned about the struggle of African blacks during numerous secret—and eye-opening—discussions with members of the banned African National Congress. The trip was not without some very painful experiences. I was denied admission to two movie theatres because I was black. I saw restaurant signs that clearly stated that blacks were not allowed to eat there. I heard numerous white South Africans defending the system of apartheid. These experiences drained my spirit. I was beginning to believe that prejudice and hatred are so ingrained in both individuals and families that change was impossible. Just when I was about to give up all hope for reducing prejudice, a ten-year-old girl changed my view of humanity.

I had been looking forward to staying at the home of the former South African ambassador to Bolivia for most of the trip. For the first time I would have the chance to have an off-the-record conversation with someone who had been an influential member of the South African government. I remember thinking, rather naively, that I might have a chance to convince him of the economic and political advantages of dismantling apartheid.

I arrived about an hour after the ambassador and his family had finished dinner. I was exhausted. The trip to their home was very long and difficult. Fortunately, we were able to wear jeans and T-shirts on the trip instead of the official suits we were usually required to wear. As anticipated, the ambassador and his wife were the most courteous and gentle white South Africans that I had met. However, I was surprised to find that they had a very energetic and outgoing ten-year-old daughter who, immediately upon my arrival, attempted to persuade me to play some games with her. Even though I was tired, I gave in to her demands to play word games. She was clearly a very bright young lady who was sizing me up. Naturally inquisitive, she asked me about the domestic chores that I performed in America, attempting to compare me to their family maid and gardener. I spent that evening describing what life was like in America and how it differed from life in South Africa.

The next morning I came to the breakfast table wearing the official business suit that was required for our formal visits. Seeing me in a business suit and recalling our conversation of the previous evening, the girl turned to her father and bluntly said, "You know, Daddy, black Americans aren't any different than white South Africans."

It was in that instant that I realized that the only people of color that this young lady, and most white South Africans, had ever taken the time to speak with were family servants. I was the first person of color that she had ever spoken with who had the same level of education and exposure as her parents. Clearly, racial segregation in this country was based solely on ignorance about people of color.

This innocent young child made my trip to South Africa worthwhile. She taught me that there is hope for the world. She was living proof that perceptions and prejudice can be changed by exposure. She realized that you should not judge someone until you get to know them. Who would have thought that one comment from a ten-year-old would change my life forever? So often the best lessons in life come from "the mouths of babes."

Since that breakfast I have spent much of my life trying to improve society by increasing the exposure of people of all ages, races and religions to each other in an effort to reduce prejudice and discrimination.

Little did I know at the time that this trip would change my view of the world—and perhaps change the world's view at the same time.

Dale G. Caldwell

Her Little Light Shined

If your faith can't move mountains, it should at least climb them.

Queen Mother Moore

It was the last place I expected to see an American—especially an African American. And I had no idea how she would soon transform our lives.

On a mountaintop in the Alps, I had come to conduct a wedding ceremony in my adopted country of Switzerland. A young black woman extended her hand as I entered the centuries-old chapel.

"Hello, I'm Brenda, the gospel singer for today."

"Oh, American?"

"Chicago," she answered.

"Boston—um, Arthur and I'm the minister."

She was very nice, but I wondered if gospel would go well here. This, after all, was one of the most conservative corners of old Europe—a place where women first won the right to vote in 1971 and strangers find an uneasy welcome. My stomach tightened as I wondered how Brenda would be received with her gospel style. This was a church where people sit stiffly, do not smile much, and do not clap to the rhythm of any kind of music.

It is also a country where people of color are not always greeted with kindness. Discrimination or outright insults are not uncommon. Now, as my stomach tightened once more, the bride marched into the church and I muttered a quiet prayer that the wedding guests would be kind to the girl from Chicago.

As she stood to sing, the congregation sat motionless with blank faces and I grew even more nervous, but Brenda was undaunted. She gave them gospel as the little village had never heard it before. She closed her eyes, reached down into her soul and took us from the valley to the mountaintop.

By the time her song, "This little light of mine, I'm gonna let it shine" was finished, she had shined enough to light up the stodgy Alpine faces. She sang with such talent and emotion that the normally reserved Swiss couldn't help clapping and joining in, and that day, a transformation took place.

In that magical moment, we knew it was all possible— possible to learn from each other, to love each other, to let the little light shine in every heart.

As if she knew it, she showed us in song. "I love you no matter what," and they loved her back. When she was finished, the congregation stood smiling and clapping like blacks in church in a steamy Alabama town.

Later, as I was packing my car to leave, a boy said to me in German, "That American woman . . . I don't know what she said—but I believe it!"

We all believed. And one little Swiss village will never be the same because her little light shined.

Arthur Bowler

7

MAKING A DIFFERENCE

If anybody's going to help African American people, it's got to be ourselves.

Earvin "Magic" Johnson

A Magical Moment with Ali

It's not what you take but what you leave behind that defines greatness.

Edward Gardner, founder, Soft Sheen Products

In more than twenty years as a sports columnist, I have met and interviewed a who's who of greats, including "The Greatest" himself, Muhammad Ali.

My greatest memory of The Greatest happened shortly before Ali lit the Olympic flame at the opening ceremonies of the 1996 Summer Olympics in Atlanta.

The living legend and African American hero—no, *American* hero—shuffled into the room for an autograph show in the cavernous Anaheim Convention Center, his feet sliding forward slowly and carefully in the unsteady gait of an old man missing his cane.

Ali was only fifty-four years old. Fifty-four going on ninety-four, it seemed. Parkinson's syndrome had caused a new "Ali Shuffle."

Still, he remained indisputably the people's champion. When the doors for the National Sports Collectors

Convention opened two hours before his noon appearance, fans rushed to get into a line that grew to three hundred before The Champ's arrival. Meanwhile, Hall of Fame baseball and football players sat nearby, lonely, with capped Sharpie pens.

Ali's hands never got a rest, never stopped moving, even when he wasn't signing endless autographs. His hands shook so uncontrollably it looked like he was constantly shuffling a deck of cards. More "Ali Shuffle."

And yet from the moment he began signing the cursive M until he had dotted the lower-case I, the earthquake in Ali's hands magically calmed. Indeed, his signature was smooth and true. Perhaps his neurons and synapses were programmed with a computer-like keystroke after signing his name a million times.

But Ali was no robotic signing machine. He smiled whenever, which was almost always, an autograph seeker paying $90 to have a flat item signed—a whopping $120 on a boxing glove—called him "Champ" or said, "It's an honor to meet you."

A steep price for a squiggle of ink? Not at all when you consider one man in line called it "a religious experience."

And every time a camera raised, Ali, his face still "pretty" and his body still muscular and almost fighting trim in a tan golf shirt, would rise out of his chair, slowly but gracefully and without assistance, to pose with a clenched fist held beneath the fan's chin.

When I had learned Muhammad Ali would be in town, I made plans to take my then-six-year-old son to see him, just as my grandfather once took my dad to see the larger-than-life Babe Ruth in a hotel lobby.

Beforehand, I schooled the boy about Ali, telling him again and again how he was "The Greatest."

With the handy excuse of me working on a column for the next morning's newspaper, we hung out right beside

The Champ for half an hour as he signed glossy pictures and magazine covers and boxing gloves. Finally, I told my son it was time to leave.

He disagreed.

"Not yet. I've gotta say hi," he whispered, and loudly.

Ali heard the little boy's protests. The great man turned around and instinctively the little boy stepped forward and extended his right hand. Ali, who had shaken adult hands almost femininely with just his manicured fingertips, took the small hand gently into his big paw and this time it did not look awkward or weak or sad.

And, for the very first time in thirty minutes, the man who used to "float like a butterfly" broke out of his cocoon of total silence.

"Hi, Little Man," Ali whispered, spreading his arms wide open.

The six-year-old Little Man, who back then was quite shy, instantly stepped forward and was wrapped in a clinch.

But it turned out the real Kodak moment was yet to come.

After a standing eight count or maybe even a full ten seconds, Ali freed the Little Man and then held his right palm out in the universal "give me five" position.

The boy, who usually slaps hard enough to shatter metatarsals, gently slapped Ali's extended palm before then holding out his own tiny palm for The Champ to return the gesture.

Ali took a swipe . . .

. . . and missed.

At the very last instant, the Little Man, as he still likes to do, pulled his hand away like a matador's red cape teasing a bull.

"Too slow," the Little Man whispered, his two missing front teeth causing the words to lisp slightly. Like, *"Tooooth*

looow." Like Ali's own soft voice that now lisps slightly.
And like two six-year-olds they laughed together at the prank.

While still roaring in delight, Ali once again opened his arms and my son once again stepped into them, except this time the shy boy squeezed back, and tightly, as though he were hugging his dear Grandpa. Ali's eyes caught mine, and I swear to this day they twinkled.

It was an end-of-a-movie fade-out and roll-the-credits hug. A full thirty-second hug. A worth-the-hour-and-a-half-drive-in-Southern-California-gridlocked-freeway-traffic hug.

A hug from "The Greatest" that the Little Man still remembers warmly, and surely will until he is an old man.

As we walked away hand-in-hand after saying good-bye to Ali, my son stopped and looked up at me and said through a Christmas-morning smile in his missing-teeth lisp: "You know, Dad, you were right—he really is The Bestest."

Woody Woodburn

Big Men, Big Hearts

Character is power.

Booker T. Washington

On the weekends I work in a coffee store in an old cigar factory in the historic area of Tampa. Sometimes kids from the projects stop by for candy sticks, and if I'm not too busy, I let them weigh out coffee and grind it, fill the jars with candy and even run the cash register.

A few weeks ago on a big football weekend, Omar, a bright little ten-year-old, came by to visit, and I gave him some chores to help pass a rainy day. In mid-afternoon, a giant of a man appeared in the doorway, and Omar was goggle-eyed at his size.

"I bet he's a famous football player," I whispered to him.

Omar giggled.

The big man approached the counter with a wide grin on his ebony face.

"What you gigglin' at?"

"I told him you were probably a famous football player," I explained with some embarrassment.

He held out a hand as big as a ham hock with a gold ring on his middle finger.

"Can you read that?" he asked Omar.

Omar twisted the ring so he could see it better. "Pitts-burgh Steel-ers," he read slowly.

"That's right," said the man and turned his finger sideways. "Can you read this?"

Omar squinted. "Super Bowl Champion!"

A light clicked in my less-than-athletic brain. "You know who this is?" I nudged Omar, hardly able to contain my excitement. "This is Mean Joe Green!"

Omar looked at him quizzically. Then his face lit up. "Do you know Franco Harris?"

I glared at Omar. "I bet you'd like Joe Green's autograph, wouldn't you?" I prodded.

"Yeah, sure," said Omar while I rummaged for paper and pen. "How could I get in touch with Franco Harris?"

Joe grinned. "He's staying at the downtown Hyatt. Call his room and say you're a friend of mine."

Joe signed his autograph and handed it to Omar.

While nudging Omar a reminder to say thank you, I said, "Give me that autograph, and I'll put it in a candy bag so you don't get it all crumpled up." I laid it on the shelf for safekeeping and turned to thank Mr. Green myself before he moved on to another store.

"Why in the world would you ask about another player when you had Joe Green right here?" I snapped. "That was downright insulting!"

Omar shrugged and said innocently, "I like Franco Harris."

"I'm surprised he even bothered to give you an autograph!" I glared at him.

I returned to helping customers. The day ended with a flurry of business, and Omar, thoroughly chastened, departed abruptly, leaving his autograph behind.

The next Saturday he appeared again. "I forgot my autograph."

"I know," I said, pointing to the shelf. "It's still up here where I put it for safekeeping."

I reached for the bag thinking, *He is only ten after all. Maybe Joe was big enough not to have been offended.*

Omar reached into the bag to look at his trophy once more.

"There's something else in the bag," he said, puzzled, handing me a second piece of paper. Because I'd been off-duty since the prior weekend myself, I, too, was surprised to see something other than what I had personally placed in the bag for Omar.

I opened it and read out loud:

"Omar . . . sorry I missed you. Franco Harris!"

Omar's eyes lit up with both disbelief and excitement as he took the paper to see for himself.

These two big men—with equally big hearts—apparently came back into the store after my shift to leave a special surprise for a young boy. Mean Joe Green isn't so "mean" after all—quite the contrary!

Phyllis W. Zeno

Guess Who We're Playing

Especially do I believe in the Negro race, in the beauty of its genius, the sweetness of its soul.
                                    W. E. B. DuBois

Growing up in white-bread America during the 1960s and early 1970s, I didn't meet a black person until I was a sophomore in high school. Other than a few Asian kids and a handful of Hispanics, I attended school and hung out with white kids. Diversity was not part of anyone's vocabulary who grew up in the then predominantly white suburbs of Los Angeles.

Playing for the sophomore football team, I suddenly came face to face with black America one Thursday afternoon, when we played the team from Manual Arts High School. Most of us had never heard of Manual Arts High School, and even fewer of us had traveled to *that part* of Los Angeles where Manual Arts was located.

When we were told that Manual Arts was an all-black school we thought our coaches must be crazy. We figured we stood no chance against them. They would be bigger, faster, stronger and better than us. Not to mention, most of us were scared of blacks.

During practice the week of the big game, our coaches kept emphasizing that the players from Manual Arts were no different than we were. We were told that they put their pants on the same way we did, and if we tackled them hard enough, they would feel pain the same as we would. None of us were buying into the daily pep talks by the coaches. Most of us were convinced that what we really needed was to take out a life insurance policy prior to Thursday's showdown.

When game day arrived, we were getting dressed in the locker room when the football team from Manual Arts arrived. Strolling through the boys' locker-room door around forty players poured in, all black, all talking, laughing and carrying on as if they were attending a birthday party. Most of us just stopped and stared at them, marveling at how much bigger than us they were. Even before we hit the gridiron, we were convinced of our opponent's superior speed, strength and ability. In all honesty, we were also staring because for many of us, myself included, this was the closest we had ever gotten to a black person. Besides their size and apparent superior physical strength, I was immediately impressed by how "loose" these guys were. Prior to a game, most of our guys were tense and barely said a word, while the kids from Manual Arts actually looked and acted as if they were having *fun*.

During the pre-game meeting, our coaches continued to emphasize that we had nothing to fear. Other than skin color, our coaches proclaimed that we were no different from the kids from Manual Arts. We hadn't believed him in the first place but now that we had actually seen our opponents, the coach's pep talk fell on totally deaf ears.

When we took the field for pre-game warmup, we knew we were in trouble. While our coaches kept yelling at us to keep our eyes on our side of the field and focus on the mission at hand, most of us kept diverting our eyes to the other side of the field. Even during pre-game warmup, the kids from Manual Arts were impressive and fast, very fast. I would like to say that our team pulled off the upset of the year, and that the end result was reminiscent of the championship game depicted in the movie *Remember the Titans*. Unfortunately, the outcome was a 55-0 shellacking at the hands of Manual Arts. The only reason the score wasn't 155-0 is that the coaches for Manual Arts pulled their players back in the second half. If anything, I surmised that black people were sympathetic. As it turned out, Manual Arts was a far better team than us, in more ways than one.

At the conclusion of the game, the players from Manual Arts poured onto the field to offer their congratulations and let us know how well we played. I couldn't believe it. Normally, at the end of the game, win or lose, it's a few quick handshakes with the players from the other team and then it's head for the locker room or the bus—but not these guys. Here they were patting us on the back and complimenting us on our effort, and asking us questions about our school and the remainder of the football season. This was a far cry from the violent, stealing, cheating, lying, lazy people that I had been told made up black America. Then something really strange happened. A number of the players from Manual Arts invited us to walk with them to the bus. Not knowing exactly what to say, most of us said, "Okay."

As we walked off the field, white next to black, black next to white, I started to understand what our coaches had been trying to tell us all along, which is that "They're no different than you are." But in fact, these guys were different. The players from Manual Arts were friendlier, funnier, more mature and a lot looser than most of us white kids, not to mention far superior at the game of football.

They asked us more questions than we asked of them, and they showed a genuine interest in us.

As their players were boarding the bus, the middle linebacker, who had been in my face all day long since I was our team's quarterback, approached me and said, "Hey, next year you guys come to our school and we'll play ball again, okay?"

Somewhat surprised, I quickly replied, "Alright, let's do that."

Somewhere deep inside I knew that would never happen, even though I felt at that moment, and still do to this day, that a bunch of white kids from the suburbs traveling to Manual Arts for a football game would be the best thing that could happen to any white kid who had grown up with little or no contact with people of color.

As the bus started to roll away, the players from Manual Arts leaned out of the windows of the bus and waved enthusiastically and bid us good-bye. At the same time, they were singing a Motown favorite, changing the chorus just slightly and chanting, "Na, na, na, na, Na, na, na, na, Hey, hey, hey, we're number one." As the bus drove out of the parking lot and onto the street, they kept waving to us and singing their re-created Motown fight song. In fact, as the bus got to the end of the street and turned right to head for the freeway, we could still hear them singing as the bus drove out of sight. There we stood, a group of gangly white kids, wondering what the heck just happened.

Back in the locker room, the conversation centered on how nice the kids from Manual Arts were, how well they played football, and how they could have easily beaten us 100-0, if not for an empathetic head coach. Whereas two hours ago we were scared and bewildered by these black kids from Manual Arts, now all we had was respect and admiration for them.

The next night, many of the players from the sophomore team attended the varsity football game. As we normally did, we all sat together in the stands. One day removed from our game with Manual Arts, you could tell that something about us was different. Even though we had gotten our brains beat out just twenty-four hours prior, we were laughing, joking and having a great time. In the second quarter, we burst into song, singing the "Na, na, na, na" song that we had learned from the players from Manual Arts.

One of the adults sitting near us said out loud, "What the heck has gotten into the sophomore football team?"

Another person said, "I don't know what they're so happy about. They lost yesterday, 55-0."

Somehow, it just didn't matter that we had gotten blown out the day before. While people looking in from the outside might think our team lost that day, we all knew that we had gained far more.

Tony Ramos

Reprinted with permission of Stephen Bentley and Creators Syndicate, Inc. ©2003.

My Momma Will Give Me More

As we make it, we've got to reach back and pull up those left behind.

Joshua I. Smith

I was out making home visits that Friday—out visiting families. Managing the load, doing the paperwork and making the visits was a large part of my responsibilities as a caseworker for the welfare department in Michigan. My clients came in all shapes and sizes. I had a strange feeling that afternoon, almost like I had lost the final piece in a jigsaw puzzle I was trying to put together. Every driveway was filled with large mounds of snow; the snow truck tracks were still fresh on all of the streets.

As I approached my client's house, I couldn't help but notice the chipping paint made a small pile in the right corner of the porch. The walkway had not been shoveled in days, and each step I took seemed more difficult than the one before. There was a strong odor of gasoline in the air, and as I looked next door, I noticed a man fiddling with an old car that looked as if it had not been moved from that one spot in weeks.

The wind started to blow again, so I placed my gloved hands on my cheeks to lessen the sting. I stepped onto the porch, reached through a tear in the screen and knocked on the door because there was no doorbell. I stood there in the shivering cold for what felt like an eternity until finally someone answered. The woman and I had spoken several times by phone, and I had advised her that I would be out soon to make a home visit. This was the first time that we had talked face-to-face.

My caseload was heavy and I didn't remember faces very well, but she had the kind of eyes you'd think I would remember forever. They were haunting, almost dim—noticeably absent of the usual vitality that you normally see in young women. Her skin looked weathered and aged—almost grainy. I could tell that she had been crying. Her thin T-shirt was tattered and damp from tears. I heard children's laughter in the background, and I heard a little boy say, "It's your turn." Children never have to worry about where their next meal will come from or whether or not the house will stay warm for another night. Only a mother lives with that worry.

Before I could take a seat to begin my interview, she said to me, "I spent my last five dollars earlier in the week for food for the children. And now, I don't have any food left in my house."

She was out of food stamps and had no other means of buying food until her ADC check arrived at the end of the following week. I looked at my watch; the office was going to close in a half-hour. I didn't have time to run back for an emergency food voucher, so I did the only thing I could do—I took her and the kids to my house. I had not made up my mind about what I would do next, but I knew that it was up to me to make sure that those children had food to make it through the weekend. I needed to give them enough to sustain them until I could get back to the office on Monday.

My mind wandered a little on the short drive to my house—back to Rapides Parish, to my hometown, Alexandria in central Louisiana. My momma taught me to share at an early age, even though I was an only child. I've carried that teaching with me all these years, even on this cold winter's day in 1972.

During the ride, the children pointed at every drop of snow they saw, naming each one and wishing for more. Their mother had put them in their only coats—which they had already outgrown—for the trip to my house. When we reached my home, I invited my client and the kids inside and offered them a seat in the living room. As I went into the kitchen I heard the mother say in a hushed tone to the children, "Now you both sit still and don't touch anything."

I smiled and happily opened my refrigerator door. I always kept a lot of food, enough to feed an army, even though there was just little old me. I pulled out all the food I had. It filled two or three shopping bags. I took the bags into my living room and placed them at her feet. She was extremely grateful, and she didn't know how to accept the food because no one had ever done this for her.

I assured her that I had more than enough and said, "My momma will give me more."

As my great-uncle Steve would always say, "Baby, if you keep your fist always balled up tightly where nothing can get out of it, ain't nothing go get in it either."

For the first time, I saw the wrinkles soften and bright-ness return to her eyes. They were warmed with a sense of hope. She gave me a hug and started to cry. My momma always taught me to give freely, and to believe that God would always provide a means for us to get more. And He always did. I shared that with her as we started on our way back to her home. I have always given freely, and God has continued to bless me.

She was wiping her tears when her children asked her why she was crying. Her reply, "Because God has always provided a way for us. Just when I thought I couldn't go any farther, He sends a sign for me to keep on going."

Then, they turned to each other with a puzzled look on their faces and started talking about everything they were going to eat when they got home. They didn't understand what she meant, but I sure did.

As time went on, I forgot about that cold, blustery winter Friday and the years went by. One day nearly fifteen years later, a coworker stopped me in the hallway at work and said, "You don't remember me, do you?"

I tried my best to remember her face, but we had so many new people in my department I couldn't keep track of all the new employees that hired into the agency. Besides, I had been promoted to management several years back and spent just about all of my working hours coaching my own staff. Well, I don't need to tell you who she was. Deep down in your soul you know who she was. Yes, she reminded me of that Friday afternoon many years before. She was the client I had taken home with me when I was a caseworker. She shared with me how much I had inspired her back then, and she was determined that she would find me one day and surprise me. I was surprised, indeed! While I thought I had just been delivering food that day, it turned out those grocery bags also contained hope and encouragement, and now, she too is in the position to touch others through serving.

Gloria J. Quinney

I Am My Sister's Keeper

The best mirror is an old friend.

George Herbert

The Thanksgiving-Christmas holiday season conjures feelings that I do not have at any other time of year. I live in the Midwest, and there is always a chill in the air and plenty of warmth in the spirit. The contrast is exhilarating, and the stimulation causes my heart to pump wildly from the expectancy of this wondrous holiday season. Inevitably it delivers a joy that is inexplicable. When I was a child, my mother stressed using this season to convey appreciation to those who had impacted your life during the year, and to this day that is the focus of my giving. There is the mailman, the dry cleaners, the person at the corner store who speaks to me, the doctors and their staffs, and the list goes on. I usually find that my energy runs out before I reach out to all those who have blessed my life. But, for years, there was a "forgotten" group that never crossed my mind.

I had lost both of my parents by the time I was

twenty-four, and because I had married and moved away at twenty-one, the distance slowly erased my memory of those people who had been so significant to my "growing years." Time went by, and it was not until nearly thirty-plus years later when I attended a family member's funeral in my hometown that one of the women I had known, Mrs. T., came to me and was overjoyed to see me. I was stunned, and a reality pervaded my soul. It had been eons since I had seen her and many others from my child-hood years.

"Oh, my God," I said to her. "I didn't know you were still with us!"

Her son had died when he was thirty-six, and she was now over ninety years old. She remembered me like it was yesterday. Her son and I were great friends. We had gone through elementary, junior and senior high, and gradu-ated together. Back in that day, every parent looked out for you, and you had the same kind of respect for them as you did for your own parents.

This encounter rocked my very being. I had run into several other elders in recent past years, but none matched *this* connection. When I saw my first Sunday school teacher from my home church, he nearly cried. I promised him I would write. And I did. I had seen others from time to time whose emotional response was similar and I embraced each and then wrote them. But the depth of the lesson did not hit me until I followed my Spirit in reaching out to Mrs. T.

It was the holiday time, and as usual, I was reflecting on the year. I realized I had not written to Mrs. T. for a few months, so I decided to give her a call. She answered the phone and was quite excited about my being on the phone. Now she does not like talking long distance no matter who is paying for it. She always says it costs too much, so you have to hurry through your conversation. I got the gist of how she was doing and that things were going well except for a "little arthritis." Her demeanor always reminded me that life was about the business of living and giving. She was still driving others around who needed her help. She started telling me about her church's anniversary and how thrilled she was to be wearing a long dress and going to one of the city's finest hotels. I listened, smiled to myself and hung onto the wisdom of her every word.

As soon as I hung the phone up, I began to reflect and felt a prompting in the Spirit to order her a corsage for her special event. I told the florist that she was ninety-three, and to make her something beautiful, but simple. I hung up the phone and quietly thanked God for her, the opportunity to show my appreciation, and for the love that we have for our churches. They have always been our refuge.

Two days later on Friday morning, I played my messages and Mrs. T. was on there—very, very emotional. All I could hear was my name over and over—and how shocked she was to get the flowers. I tilted my head to the side and smiled, and felt that feeling that occurs when your giving touches "that place" in someone. I felt as if God had chosen me to be the lucky one to deliver this joy. As I moved about my day, the same Holy Spirit urged me to call her. She could not stop telling me what the gesture meant to her and how surprised she had been when the flowers arrived.

Then she said, "Now why did I have to wait until I was ninety-three years old to get my first corsage!"

In that moment, I'm not sure which of us felt more blessed.

Nikki D. Shearer-Tilford

Meeting Maya

We are almost a nation of dancers, musicians and poets.

Olaudah Equiano (1745?–1801), slave autobiographer

San Francisco is an autumn town, but it was July and it was scorching. I had flown to the Bay Area from San Diego, where I had been living for five years. Being born and raised in Philadelphia, the change from the Northeast to the Southwest coast was dramatic for me. So far, I had found San Diego to be a beautiful but sleepy work environment. I had cut my writing teeth in New York City and was a bit bored in San Diego. I was anxious to fly to Oakland to meet a longtime friend who was in town to promote her first book.

I had been writing seriously for over twenty years and published many times. There were also well-attended performance readings in New York City, Washington, D.C., Baltimore, San Francisco and San Diego. For several engagements, I performed with a band. My writing paid my rent more than once. It lived in me and helped me live.

Somehow during the trip to Oakland, I had an epiphany. I would stop writing the poetry I had loved to write since I was eight years old. I surmised that this would somehow make me feel better and solve the problems I'd been experiencing in San Diego.

When I shared my thoughts about giving up writing, my friend was alarmed. "You *are* poetry!" she said.

"Poetry is for the birds. There is no job description, lousy pay and long hours," I said.

Despite our conflict, we had a wonderful visit. I was very proud of her. For myself, I felt it was getting too late to publish a book. Obstacles such as poor health, mobility and money were preventing me from furthering my work.

After my friend flew back to the east coast, I spent the afternoon with a young married couple. My flight was leaving from Oakland later that evening. On my way to my friends' house in Berkeley, we stopped at my favorite supermarket-deli-bakery. The deli makes a turkey breast sandwich with Swedish lingonberries. The combination of sweet and tart is pleasing, especially on the hard roll that the juice soaks into. This is the food that soothes, preparing me not to be a poet anymore.

At the checkout stood only a stately black woman, half-through purchasing a rather large order. Something seemed to tell her to turn around as I approached the line. She turned. She smiled. Maya Angelou! It was Maya Angelou in line in front of me at Andronico's Market.

Without saying hello, she asked my name. I spoke as if in a Twelve-Step meeting, "My name is minerva [pen name, small 'm,' after the goddess of wisdom] and I am a poet," I said.

By this time my friends had joined me in line. Later, they told me what they were thinking: *"Maya Angelou! Wow, minerva knows everybody!"*

Maya was majestic, even in the Sunday afternoon "buy me" lights of a grocery store. She was regal, leaning over her stick of French bread. Dressed in earth tones, she reminded me of the Earth Mother I imagined her to be.

When Maya Angelou heard me say that I was a poet, she beamed. She placed the divider down for me to put my groceries on the conveyor belt. With a welcoming motion of her hand she said gleefully, "Well, step on up!"

We started to chat, briefly musing about hunger and choices and the price of food. I told her that I was buying snacks for the plane trip back to San Diego. I also mentioned that I visited two women's prisons with my friend to talk about writing. My friend had served time and ended up becoming an award-winning journalist. Maya's reaction was strong. She cried a sincere thank-you and loudly professed that the inmates were her sisters and daughters.

The few minutes we visited together were magical and divine. I wanted to get as close as I could to her side. It was as if we had this sacred space carved out just for us, for this particular point in time—a crossroads in my life.

As Maya Angelou gave the cashier her credit card, I noticed that the cashier and the other shoppers didn't seem to have a clue as to who our national treasure was: poet, actress, singer, professor and so much more. This was the author of President Bill Clinton's inaugural poem: "On the Pulse of Morning." *Well, that's poetry for you,* I thought.

Ms. Angelou was kind enough to write me a message on the back of my pocket computer's manual (the only thing quickly available for her signature).

"Poet on in Joy!" she wrote. And I did.

When I returned to Southern California, I was a writing fool. What wonders have emerged from what at first seemed a chance meeting in a Bay Area supermarket-deli-bakery. Some blessings from God are not in disguise.

minerva
also known as Gail Hawkins

Food from the 'Hood

Success is when your cup runneth over and your saucer too!

Nathaniel Bronner Sr.

I was in junior high school when the verdict came out: The four policemen filmed beating Rodney King were acquitted. South Central Los Angeles exploded in riots. I was outraged at the looting and burning that took over our city. I thought, *Why burn your own neighborhood?*

At the age of fourteen, I had experienced some tumultuous times myself. There were times I didn't know where my next meal would come from, but I had never been driven to the point of violence. The events of that spring made no sense to me.

The next fall I enrolled at Crenshaw High School, one of the most notoriously gang-ridden high schools in South Central L.A. One day, my biology teacher, Tammy Bird, asked a few students to meet her during lunch hour. She introduced us to Melinda McMullen, a business executive who was looking for a way to help rebuild our community.

Together, they proposed that we turn the abandoned plot of land behind our classroom into an organic garden. With Ms. Bird offering extra credit and Melinda offering pizza, it was an offer too good to refuse. For the next few weeks, about a dozen of us spent our time after school cutting down the weeds in the garden, most of them taller than we were. The ground was so hard and dry that we had to take an extra Saturday to prepare the soil. Then we planted herbs and vegetables. Before long, we were growing more than we could eat—so the idea of selling our bounty was a natural.

In September 1993, we held our first official business meeting. We named ourselves "Food from the 'Hood" and decided to use our profits to fund college scholarships.

That April, we took our vegetables to Santa Monica's Farmers' Market, which is in a pretty ritzy part of Los Angeles. At first we felt out of place. People ignored us. I don't think that they knew what to make of a bunch of Latino and African American teenagers at a vegetable stand touting "Food from the 'Hood." Finally, one of the guys bounced out of the booth and walked up to people saying, "Hi, I'm Ben Osborne from Crenshaw High. We've grown some organic veggies that are just too good to pass up!" People started buying our produce like crazy. For the rest of the school year, we had sell-out weekends.

But even with the success of our farmers' markets, we ended the school year with a profit of only six hundred dollars to put toward the scholarships. (Farming is so expensive!) It was clear we had to find an additional route to profits if we wanted to go to college. That's when we decided to go into the salad dressing business. After all, as my friend Karla Becerra said, "We grow ingredients for salads, so why not make what goes on top?"

Our next step was to develop a recipe. Our first priority: low sodium. High blood pressure is a serious issue among minorities in our community. Our second priority: low fat. We wanted to make people healthy, as well as make money! That December, we had a tremendous surprise. Rebuild L.A., a nonprofit organization formed out of the riots, gave us startup funding of fifty thousand dollars. Armed with our seed money, we found someone to manufacture our dressing and made our first large batch. We also used the money to buy office equipment and set up shop in a storage room near the garden. Also, we hired Aleyne Larner, one of our adult volunteers, to be the company's full-time advisor.

I'll never forget our first sales call. It was with the senior vice president of Vons, one of the largest grocery store chains in California. The room was full of men in suits and us—a group of kids from South Central! We told them about our product and how well it would sell, and they agreed to stock it. Other large grocery chains also decided to carry our dressing.

On April 29, 1994, on the second anniversary of the Los Angeles uprising, we announced to the community that Food from the 'Hood's Straight Out of the Garden salad dressing was available in two thousand supermarkets. No one had ever dreamed we could be so successful.

Soon after that, we heard that England's Prince Charles would be visiting Los Angeles. Carlos Lopez, our fourteen-year-old PR manager, wrote and invited him to visit us. We didn't know it at the time, but Prince Charles is a huge fan of organic gardening and has his own company that helps build economic empowerment in the inner cities of England. No one thought that he would come. But a few weeks later, we received a call from a representative of the British consulate saying, "The prince would be delighted."

Three weeks before the prince was scheduled to arrive, our office was vandalized. All of our computer equipment, fax machines and telephones were stolen or destroyed. Some of us burst out crying. But Ben said, "Whatever doesn't kill us makes us stronger." We decided to come back stronger than ever. Many people from the community helped with repairs, and a few businesses donated money to replace the stolen equipment. Our school district even donated a telephone. We were back in business.

The day of the prince's visit finally came. I shook hands with the Prince of Wales! Karla, who used to be really shy, showed him around our garden. There were lots of reporters trying to crowd around, but Prince Charles waved them back and said, "I'm afraid you're trampling on their lettuce." He had lunch with us and ate an entire plate of salad with our salad dressing on it. Then he said, "Your garden is truly remarkable." After the prince's visit, the British consulate gave us a gift: a company delivery truck. We call it the Chuck Wagon.

Today, Food from the 'Hood is ten years old and the biggest success ever seen at Crenshaw High School. Our salad dressings—we now have three flavors—are sold in grocery and natural food stores in twenty-three states. To date, we've had more than 120 student-owners participate in Food from the 'Hood. Most have gone on to pursue higher education. This year, many of us are graduating from colleges all over the United States, including UC Berkeley, Stanford and San Diego State.

I feel like I owe a lot to that quarter-acre plot in back of my old classroom. We all do. The garden is where it all started. Ms. Bird always said one of the most important things about gardening is composting—how you can take leftovers and garbage and turn them into fertile soil for growing great things. Well, truer words were never spoken. I've never seen a bigger waste than the riots—and look what great things we grew out of that!

Jaynell Grayson

One Miracle at a Time

Remember, luck is opportunity meeting up with preparation, so you must prepare yourself to be lucky.

Gregory Hines

In July 1996, I began to lose weight rapidly and was not eating much. I lost so much weight my clothes began to fall off of me. The following November, I experienced a migraine headache for the first time, and it scared me. I went to the doctor to have it checked out.

A week later my nephrologist told me that I had end-stage renal disease. My kidneys were failing and I had to have emergency surgery to be prepared for dialysis—either hemodialysis or peritoneal dialysis.

I went home and jumped on the computer to research renal disease. I discovered that end-stage renal disease is when the kidney does not filter out the waste products in your body. It allows the waste to get into your blood-stream and causes toxicity. Once this happens, a person will eventually die if preventive measures are not taken, such as dialysis or a kidney transplant. I joined the National Kidney Foundation and did research on dialysis. I found out that over 150,000 patients on dialysis with ESRD are awaiting a transplant either from a live donor or a cadaver. I soon went on dialysis and started the search for a kidney donor. I continued to live my life to the fullest. I traveled, played softball and enjoyed my life as much as I possibly could.

Then in December 2000, I did something that would change my life forever: I enrolled in a three-part series of self-development courses. The first class allowed me to discover who I truly am and understand what I am all about. I was able to come to grips with my relationship with my son and realized what I could do to make that relationship stronger.

The second class of this series took place in February 2001. I wanted to take the class, but wasn't ready to shell out the $650 it was going to cost. However, God works in mysterious ways, and something just told me to hand over the credit card and take the class. So reluctantly, I agreed.

Once inside the class, I noticed approximately a hundred people of all races, creeds and colors. I was quite comfortable in the class, but one of the requirements presented a dilemma. The instructor said that no one in the class would receive credit until we were all in attendance for four consecutive days. That meant arriving at 9:00 A.M. and staying until midnight, which created a problem for me because I had to go to dialysis the very next morning at 5:30 A.M. and would not be able to make it to class until after 10:00 A.M.

I had to address the class and notify them of my situation. I let them know that I was a kidney patient and had to do dialysis every Friday morning. At the break, several participants asked me about dialysis and kidney failure. When I explained my condition to them, they were astonished because they said that I did not look sick. My reply to them was that, "Sickness is a state of mind."

During the next few days, people in the class continued to inquire about kidney disease and my condition. On the last day of the class, a student named Patricia Abdullah asked me if I was on the donor list.

I told her, "Yes, because no one in my family was a match, I have been searching for five years to find a donor."

She said to me, "Wouldn't it be great if our class found you a kidney?"

I said, "Sure it would," but I heard that all the time. I knew that she was just being sentimental but that her heart was in the right place. I often heard similar remarks from concerned people who did not necessarily know what to say because they did not know what I was experiencing. I knew that Patricia was like these people—kind and cordial. So I left it at that.

On that last day, we each had to address the class and attempt to explain who we really were and what we stood for as individuals. After I had my turn to speak, I proceeded to leave the class. About two minutes later, one of the assistants in the class yelled at me to come back because Patricia was getting the class involved in finding me a kidney.

I rushed back to hear Patricia say to the class, "Before I speak, I would like to get the class involved in the possibility of helping Mike Jones find a kidney."

The class applauded in agreement, and the course leader said that could be the project for our third class of the series. I could not believe what had happened! I felt elated as I was sent back up to the front of the room to address the class. All I could do was just stand there and cry. It was hard to believe that three days prior we did not even know each other, and now this class of ninety-five people was coming together to help me find a kidney donor. The power and the love in that room just overwhelmed me. The class gave me a standing ovation as I broke down. It was truly an amazing moment.

The next session was the final class in the self-development course. All ninety-five participants showed up on that first day eager to fulfill our project. But there was a problem. Our new instructor said that we could not do that assignment as our main project. He said that everyone had to create their own individual project and work solely on that. I was extremely upset because that was not what we were told in the previous class. Some of the other classmates felt the same way. I was livid and ready to drop out of the class altogether because I felt that I was misled to take this class.

Again, something told me to stay in the class and fulfill my commitment to this group of individuals. You see, I have a thing about keeping my word and having integrity. If I say I am going to do something, then I have to honor that commitment. Since we had to pick our own project, I chose to make folks aware of what it takes to be an organ donor—how they can affect the lives of other people, whether it is by giving the gift of life by being an organ donor, donating blood to help save lives, or being a bone marrow donor so the platelets in your blood can help save a child who may be in need.

Another one of our assignments was learning how to make unreasonable requests. I admitted that I rarely asked for things because it becomes a pride issue for me.

One of my classmates responded by saying, "But Mike, if you had asked for a kidney, maybe you would have one right now."

I said, "True, all they can tell me is no." I explained to

him and another classmate that because of my "O" positive blood type a donor and I had to be a perfect match. As the class came to a close that day, Patricia Abdullah approached me and said, "Mike, I am 'O' positive."

I looked at her and said, "That's nice, so am I."

She looked at me again and said to me, "Mike, I am 'O' positive. Make an unreasonable request of me."

And then it hit me; I was speechless for a moment because I felt that the Lord was saying something to me through Patricia. I then walked up to her, put my hand on her side and said, "Patricia, may I have one of your kidneys?"

She looked at me and said, "Sure, what do I need to do?"

The next morning while I was at dialysis, I received a phone call from Patricia. She told me that she had contacted UCLA and was on her way to get tested. I just prayed that it would be successful.

We did not hear anything about her tests for several weeks. Figuring that was a bad sign, I was disappointed but thanked Patricia anyway for the thought and told her that I would not forget what she had attempted to do. However, UCLA did finally call on Friday of that fifth week and ask her to come back in for more tests. Patricia was confused because we had assumed that we were not a match. The nurse at UCLA said that was not the case. She said that they needed to run more tests to verify their results because the initial test results said that we were a PERFECT match!

A "perfect match" means that the donor and the patient are an exact match in every test that is run—blood-type testing, tissue-type testing and antibody testing. Our test compatibility was six for six, which is perfect. The only thing better is an identical twin from the same cell.

Here is another miracle that shows how the Lord works in mysterious ways. After all the testing was complete and the results were confirmed, the surgery was set for

September 11, 2001—the day of the attacks in New York, Washington and Pennsylvania—and our story just happened to be timely with the events.

Ms. Patricia Abdullah is Irish, Scottish, German, Italian, Welsh, Hawaiian and Arab. She is also a converted Muslim. I am African American, Irish and Creole. Our story gained media attention because the September 11 attacks had raised the profile of the Muslim faith. Fox Television even contacted Patricia for an exclusive interview.

The media was drawn to our story because there was so much diversity surrounding the surgery. We had a white Muslim woman donating a kidney to an African American Christian in a Jewish hospital with a German, South African and Jewish surgical team performing the operation. Talk about a rainbow coalition of people coming together to give the gift of life!

I believe this is proof that we are all God's children. We are all the same on the inside, just different shades on the outside. How else can two people from totally different backgrounds be the perfect match where the only thing closer is an identical twin sibling from the same cell?

I hope that this miracle will help raise awareness worldwide and encourage others to make a difference in someone's life by giving the gift of life—by being a blood, organ or bone marrow donor.

I have been truly blessed to receive this ultimate gift of life. I truly thank Ms. Patricia Abdullah for giving me the ultimate gift that a person can give. Patricia is my sister, and I will love her and cherish her forever. We are taking a dual family photo to show how life has affected two families, two races, two religions and one God.

Mike Jones

Freedom

One of the first questions to be resolved was where I would spend my first night of freedom. My inclination was to spend the night in the Cape Flats, the bustling black and colored townships of Cape Town, in order to show my solidarity with the people. But my colleagues and, later, my wife argued that for security reasons I should stay with Archbishop Desmond Tutu in Bishop's Court, a plush residence in a white suburb. It was not an area where I would have been permitted to live before I went to prison, and I thought it would send the wrong signal to spend my first night of freedom in a posh white area. But the members of the committee explained that Bishop's Court had become multiracial under Tutu's tenure, and symbolized an open, generous non-racialism.

The prison service supplied me with boxes and crates for packing. During my first twenty or so years in prison, I accumulated very few possessions, but in the last few years I had amassed enough property—mainly books and papers—to make up for previous decades. I filled over a dozen crates and boxes.

My actual release time was set for 3 P.M., but Winnie and

Walter and the other passengers from the chartered flight from Johannesburg did not arrive until after 2. There were already dozens of people at the house, and the entire scene took on the aspect of a celebration. Warrant Officer Swart prepared a final meal for all of us, and I thanked him not only for the food he had provided for the last two years but the companionship. Warrant Officer James Gregory was also there at the house, and I embraced him warmly. In the years that he had looked after me from Pollsmoor through Victor Verster, we had never discussed politics, but our bond was an unspoken one and I would miss his soothing presence. Men like Swart, Gregory and Warrant Officer Brand reinforced my belief in the essential humanity even of those who had kept me behind bars for the previous twenty-seven and a half years.

There was little time for lengthy farewells. The plan was that Winnie and I would be driven in a car to the front gate of the prison. I had told the authorities that I wanted to be able to say good-bye to the guards and warders who had looked after me and I asked that they and their families wait for me at the front gate, where I would be able to thank them individually.

At a few minutes after three, I was telephoned by a well-known SABC presenter who requested that I get out of the car a few hundred feet before the gate so that they could film me walking toward freedom. This seemed reasonable, and I agreed to do it. This was my first inkling that things might not go as calmly as I had imagined.

By 3:30, I began to get restless, as we were already behind schedule. I told the members of the reception committee that my people had been waiting for me for twenty-seven years and I did not want to keep them waiting any longer. Shortly before 4, we left in a small motorcade from the cottage. About a quarter of a mile in front of the gate, the car slowed to a stop, and Winnie and I got out and began to walk toward the prison gate. At first, I could not really make out what was going on in front of us, but when I was within 150 feet or so, I saw a tremendous commotion and a great crowd of people: hundreds of photographers and television cameras and newspeople as well as several thousand well-wishers. I was astounded and a little bit alarmed. I had truly not expected such a scene; at most, I had imagined that there would be several dozen people, mainly the warders and their families. But this proved to be only the beginning; I realized we had not thoroughly prepared for all that was about to happen.

Within 20 feet or so of the gate, the cameras started clicking, a noise that sounded like some great herd of metallic beasts. Reporters started shouting questions; television crews began crowding in; ANC supporters were yelling and cheering. It was a happy, if slightly disorienting chaos. When a television crew thrust a long, dark, furry object at me, I recoiled slightly, wondering if it were some newfangled weapon developed while I was in prison. Winnie informed me that it was a microphone.

When I was among the crowd I raised my right fist and there was a roar. I had not been able to do that for twenty-seven years, and it gave me a surge of strength and joy. We stayed among the crowd for only a few minutes before jumping back into the car for the drive to Cape Town. Although I was pleased to have such a reception, I was greatly vexed by the fact that I did not have a chance to say good-bye to the prison staff. As I finally walked through those gates to enter a car on the other side, I felt even at the age of seventy-one that my life was beginning anew. My 10,000 days of imprisonment were over.

Nelson Mandela

And the Walls Came Tumbling Down

The bedrock of individual success in life is securing the friendship, the confidence, the respect of your next-door neighbor in your little community in which you live.

Booker T. Washington

When I saw the new house in Flatbush, I had a hard time believing it was ours.

The three-story brownstone was a far cry from the four-bedroom, one-bath frame house we'd left behind in the Brooklyn ghetto. Our large, three-generation family—there were about twenty of us—needed the extra space.

But, only nine years old, I froze as still as a mannequin when I saw our new neighbors. The men and boys wore long, black coats and round caps the size of small dinner plates perched on their heads, locks of curls peeking out the sides. The women and girls wore short coats over their long dresses. Their white stockings were as stark, cold and grim as their stares.

Our new home stood next door to a Jewish synagogue.

The first morning, we awoke to a surprise. Garbage littered our front steps—our welcoming present. Neighbors stood outside pointing and talking. For the first time, I saw them smile.

My grandparents, called Daddy and Mama by all of us, appeared with brooms to begin the arduous chore of cleaning the mess. As I began to help put the garbage in bags, I spotted a little dark-haired girl peeking at me from behind a woman's skirt. She smiled; I waved—but the woman scolded her in a foreign tongue.

The next evening, a gray-bearded man appeared wearing a round hat trimmed in fur and a white shawl around his shoulders. The same little girl hugged his leg and played peek-a-boo with me and my cousin Naomi while he spoke in broken English to Daddy.

"I don't know what we will do if we don't get help." The rabbi nodded toward the synagogue. "Our maid is suddenly hospitalized and Sabbath services begin in fifteen minutes."

I wasn't sure whether his cheeks reddened from the cold or the embarrassment of asking for assistance. But all of us knew what was coming next because we knew Daddy and Mama.

We spent the evening serving and cleaning in the rabbi's antiquated kitchen. Rebecca—who, we discovered, was mute—stuck to us like glue, crying until she was allowed to dine near us and laughing at our antics. Once, I caught her mother beaming from the shadows. She quickly turned away, but not before I saw the tears in her eyes.

When we were done, the rabbi and his wife, the woman who had at first shooed the little girl away, thanked us profusely. They offered us money that we refused. Without being asked we volunteered to come back the next morning to turn on the lights, which they were prohibited from doing during their Sabbath. Someone else would be there to help later. They stood speechless holding hands as we departed.

In the morning we didn't need an alarm clock. The blaring horn from the synagogue awakened us. We dragged ourselves next door and entered the unlocked back door, turned on the lights and went back home.

An amazing thing happened when we stepped out of the door on Sunday morning. From top to bottom, flowerpots and baskets of breads, cakes and fruit lined the sides of our porch steps. Some of our neighbors, the rabbi and his wife stood at the bottom of the stairs with a sign, "Welcome to the Neighborhood." Rebecca scampered up the stairs and gave Naomi and me flowers and a hug. Because of a good deed and the blind love of a child, at least for that day, there were no walls standing between the Johnson family and our new neighbors. Flatbush felt like home.

Cheryl Dash

A Story of the South Bronx

All work is honorable. Always do your best because someone is watching.

Colin L. Powell

Unlike today's vista of decrepit buildings, dilapidated housing and rusting junked cars, the South Bronx in 1950 was the home of a large and thriving community, one that was predominantly Jewish. Today a mere remnant of this once-vibrant community survives, but in the 1950s the Bronx offered synagogues, Mikvas, kosher bakeries and kosher butchers—all the comforts one would expect from an observant Orthodox Jewish community.

The baby boom of the postwar years happily resulted in many new young parents. As a matter of course, the South Bronx had its own baby equipment store. Sickser's was located on the corner of Westchester and Fox, and specialized in "everything for the baby," as its slogan ran. The inventory began with cribs, baby carriages, playpens, high chairs, changing tables and toys. It went way beyond these to everything a baby could want or need.

Mr. Sickser, assisted by his son-in-law Lou Kirshner, ran a profitable business serving the needs of the rapidly expanding child population. The language of the store was primarily Yiddish, but Sickser's was a place where not only Jewish families but also many non-Jewish ones could acquire the necessary paraphernalia for their newly arrived bundles of joy.

Business was particularly busy one spring day, so much so that Mr. Sickser and his son-in-law could not handle the unexpected throng of customers. Desperate for help, Mr. Sickser ran out of the store and stopped the first youth he spotted on the street.

"Young man," he panted, "how would you like to make a little extra money? I need some help in the store. You want to work a little?"

The tall, lanky African American boy flashed a toothy smile back. "Yes, sir, I'd like some work."

"Well then, let's get started." The boy followed his new employer into the store.

Mr. Sickser was immediately impressed with the boy's good manners and demeanor. As the days went by and he came again and again to lend his help, Mr. Sickser and Lou both became increasingly impressed with the youth's diligence, punctuality and readiness to learn. Eventually Mr. Sickser made him a regular employee at the store. It was gratifying to find an employee with an almost soldierlike willingness to perform even the most menial of tasks, and to perform them well.

From the age of thirteen until his sophomore year in college, the young man put in from twelve to fifteen hours a week, at fifty to seventy-five cents an hour. Mostly, he performed general labor: assembling merchandise, unloading trucks and preparing items for shipments. He seemed, in his quiet way, to appreciate not only the steady employment but also the friendly atmosphere

Mr. Sickser's store offered. Mr. Sickser and Lou learned in time about their helper's Jamaican origins, and the helper in turn picked up a good deal of Yiddish. In time young Colin was able to converse fairly well with his employers, and more importantly, with a number of the Jewish customers whose English was not fluent.

At the age of seventeen, the young man, while still working part-time at Sickser's, began his first semester at City College of New York. He fit in just fine with his, for the most part Jewish, classmates—hardly surprising, considering that he already knew their ways and their language. But the heavy studying in the engineering and later geology courses he chose proved quite challenging. Colin would later recall that Sickser's offered the one stable point in his life in those days.

In 1993, in his position as the Chairman of the Joint Chiefs of Staff—two years after he guided the American victory over Iraq in the Gulf War—Colin Powell visited the Holy Land. Upon meeting Israel's Prime Minister Yitzhak Shamir in Jerusalem, he greeted the Israeli with the words "Men kent reden Yiddish" (We can speak Yiddish). As Shamir, stunned, tried to pull himself together, the current Secretary of State continued chatting in his second-favorite language. He had never forgotten his early days in the Bronx.

Zev Roth

A Few Kind Words

No one rises to low expectations.

Les Brown

What would it take to reach him? His name was Gary. He was sixteen years old. He had already had several brushes with the law and had done time in several juvenile correctional facilities. Now, he sat in my classroom bored and defiant. What would it take?

He had linked up with another young man in the class who had a background that was strikingly similar to his background. His name was Lee. Lee, like Gary, had committed some offenses and done some time. Both of them had brilliant minds. They both had little respect for authority. Gary and Lee would do whatever they felt they were grown enough to do. Sometimes they would just sit in the back of the room and play around on Lee's laptop, composing beats and making up raps. At other times, they would hold conversations and freely use profane language. Some days, they would get up and walk out of class without permission, and then there were those days when the two of them would not bother to come to class at all. I am ashamed to say that I was grateful for those days. Sometimes, the battlefield called the inner-city classroom can be such a draining place that you are thankful to receive a moment of peace, no matter how it comes to you. I knew I had a job to do, but I wondered what it would take.

When the time came to distribute the first progress report of the year, I did so with a little trepidation. I knew that there would be a confrontation because of what I had written on Gary's report in the teacher's comment section. I started off by saying that Gary was very bright. I then went on to say that he could be rude and disrespectful. I even commented on his open use of profanity in the class-room. I approached him, handed him his report and went on to distribute the rest of the reports to his classmates. I watched out of the corner of my eye as he read his report. I noticed no significant change in his facial expression, so I relaxed just a little bit. As I headed for my desk, Gary called to me. I went toward him determined to stand my ground.

"Did you write this?"

"Yes, I did."

"What do you mean, I'm disrespectful?"

"I mean what I say."

"I don't disrespect you."

"You disrespect me every day. You talk over me while I'm trying to teach class. You . . ."

"I don't disrespect you."

"Okay, Gary. But I believe you do."

I walked to the front of the room and attempted to begin to teach class. As I spoke, Gary made sure he was speaking. He matched me word for word, sentence for sentence. It got so bad that I had to stop what I was doing to address him. I asked him to leave, and he refused. The situation escalated to the point where the principal had to come and intervene. I went home from school that day with the question looming larger than it ever had before. What would it take? As I rode to school the next day, I hoped that I would not have to see Gary at all. I was at a loss. I did not know what to do. I felt as though I would never reach him. Though I had pondered the question over and over again, I still did not know what it would take. When I pulled up in front of the school, the very first person that I saw was Gary. I lifted my eyes toward heaven, sighed and asked, "What now?"

A still, small voice responded, "Apologize."

My reaction was, "Apologize? I didn't do anything to him!"

Once again, the still, small voice responded, gently urging me to apologize. I was determined not to apologize but the still, small voice began to give me some much-needed instruction.

"Apologize. He has no one in his life speaking positive things to him. He only gets to hear the negative. He needs someone to speak life to him. Apologize, and speak life."

It was quite a humbling moment, a moment of epiphany, the moment when I finally knew what it would take. It was so simple, yet so profound. All it would take was a kind word.

At first, I didn't know what I had to apologize for, but as I thought about it, it became clear: disrespect. I was to apologize for disrespecting *him*. Though I had started his progress report off with the comments concerning how bright he was, that point never came up in our conversation. Only the negative came up, not the positive. I swallowed my pride and approached the bench where he was sitting munching on a snack cake and drinking a juice.

"Gary?"

"Yeah," he said as he looked up.

"I just wanted to apologize. If you feel I disrespected you, that was never my intention. It's just that you have so much going for you. You are so bright and talented, I would be remiss if I allowed you to sit around and not reach your full potential. Disrespect was never my intent. I am sorry."

He looked at me, and I saw something in his eyes I had never seen before: hope. I walked away from him sensing I had said and done the right thing.

When it came time for me to teach his class, I walked in the classroom and was met by a brand-new Gary. The transformation in him was almost startling. He was attentive. He participated in the class. He asked questions. He answered questions. From that day on, he continued to learn, grow and develop. Our relationship developed to the point where we were able to talk about a lot of things. He came to me often for guidance and direction.

Gary is no longer at our school. He had to leave when his father's military unit was transferred to another state. It happened suddenly—so suddenly that I didn't get to say good-bye. I was hurt when I heard he had left us, but I know he didn't leave us without having received what he needed.

What would it take to reach him? His name was Gary. He was sixteen years old. He had already had several brushes with the law and had done time in several juvenile correctional facilities. Now, he had sat in my classroom bored and defiant. What would it take? All that it took was a few kind words.

Nancy Gilliam

Angels All Around

Every hardship; every joy; every temptation is a challenge of the spirit; that the human soul may prove itself. The great chain of necessity wherewith we are bound has divine significance; and nothing happens which has not some service in working out the sublime destiny of the human soul.

Elias A. Ford

Dorothy Wright's husband, Forrest, shook her hard, "Wake up, Dorothy! Get up! There's smoke everywhere!"

Dorothy coughed, opened her eyes to a gray haze in their bedroom, bolted upright and screamed, "Get the kids!" She grabbed the phone to call 911 but before she could tell them where they lived the line went dead.

"Oh Lord, help us," Dorothy prayed as she and Forrest ran in opposite directions to waken their children: Forrest Junior, sixteen; Danielle, fifteen; Leonard, thirteen; Dominique, twelve; Joe, eleven; Anthony, ten; Marcus, eight; Vinny, seven; Curtis, five; Nicholas, three; and

Ja-Monney, three. (Ja-Monney is her nephew that they've raised since his birth.)

Scared and confused, the children rubbed their eyes and stumbled down the stairs and out the front door. Dorothy counted heads.

"Someone's missing!" she screamed. "Who? Curtis! Forrest, Curtis is missing!"

Forrest ran back into the house and up the steps as smoke poured out the front door. Five-year-old Curtis, who'd been hiding under his bed, struggled into the smoky hallway when he heard his daddy's voice. He couldn't see Forrest in the thick smoke, but he ran right into his daddy's arms. Forrest grabbed him and tore back down the stairs. Halfway down Forrest fell, sprained his ankle and stumbled outdoors.

Dorothy dashed to the neighbor's house. The woman who lived there had been studying all night and had just gone to bed when Dorothy banged on the door. The neighbor finally saw the orange glow through the Wright family's windows and called 911. Within minutes the fire trucks arrived. By now the flames had spread between the walls of the old wood frame house and moved to the second floor.

Neighbors took the children into their homes, but Dorothy couldn't move. As firefighters slammed their axes into the roof, she stood there and watched her dream evaporate. Everything inside that house went up in flames. Furniture, clothing, housewares, linens, photo albums, cash, jewelry, the only picture she had of her mother who had died when Dorothy was a teenager. Everything was gone.

Our dream, Dorothy thought. *How can it end like this?* She and Forrest had wanted so much more for their eleven children than was offered in the inner city. They'd just moved to the suburb of New Milford, outside Hackensack,

New Jersey, four years earlier. They didn't want the kids growing up around drugs, alcohol abuse, fighting and gangs. They didn't want the substandard education or the rundown neighborhoods. What a blessing it was when they found the big frame house and met Diane, their landlord. They convinced her that they were hard workers and that their children were polite, good kids and that they'd take care of her home. The rent was reasonable and the Wright family moved in.

Now as Dorothy stood there four years later watching their dream evaporate into smoke, all she could think about was two things: *Thank you, God, my family is safe!* And then, *Where will we ever find another house for our big family?*

After visiting the hospital to make sure the kids were okay and to get a brace on Forrest's sprained ankle, Dorothy went directly to Social Services in her blue pajamas and sneakers a neighbor had given her. As she stood in line people looked at her like *What's your problem, lady?*

Dorothy didn't care what she looked like. She was a woman on a mission. The only thing the emergency assistance program could do was to put them into a family shelter back in the inner city. Thirteen people crowded into four tiny rooms.

"It was awful," Dorothy told a friend. "So much goes on in a shelter like that. People moving in and out every day. Drugs. Yelling. Women getting beat up by boyfriends. No play area. Nothing for the children to do."

That's when the guardian angels started to arrive. Dorothy's friend Lisa, who owns Alfredo's restaurant, brought dinner for the family every night for four months. Pizzas, spaghetti, garlic bread, fresh salads, lasagna, eggplant Parmesan . . . all the foods kids love. Their neighbors, Jerry and Cynthia, brought a TV to the shelter. Strangers brought brand-new clothes. The kids' teachers brought school supplies, coloring books, crayons. Other teachers from the New Milford high school, middle school and grammar school had fundraisers for the family.

The whole town adopted the Wright family, and the gifts continued all summer. But Dorothy continued to worry about how they'd ever get out of the shelter and back into the wonderful neighborhood they'd worked so hard to get into four years earlier. How would they ever find another house big enough for their family that they could afford?

One day, one of Vinny's classmates came to visit. When little Michael Kontomanolis and Vinny saw each other they just hugged and started crying. Michael said, "Mommy, can Vinny come live with us? We have to help him. He's my friend."

Michael's parents, Pauline and Nikkolas, were so touched by the boys' deep friendship that often that summer they took the Wright children back to their home in their old neighborhood on the weekends.

Dorothy was relieved that her kids could get out of the shelter for awhile, but she said to Pauline and Nick, "You only have two kids. How can you stand so many at once?" Nick would laugh and say, "We love it! It's like a big party when they come over."

Then the biggest surprise of all. One day Pauline said, "Dorothy, Nick and I have decided to buy a house in our neighborhood and rent it to you for four years. Then you can buy it from us. We want you to have your own home. We want you to come back to the neighborhood where you belong."

Dorothy and Forrest couldn't believe it. Why would this couple who hardly knew them before the fire do such a thing for them? Pauline just smiled and said, "We connect through our hearts, Dorothy."

Together Dorothy and Pauline found a two-story Cape

Cod with six bedrooms, a huge living room, big dining room and a finished basement.

The thirteen members of the Wright family moved in in October, just five months after the fire. On moving day the family opened the doors to discover huge "WELCOME HOME!" banners taped everywhere. The neighbors had supplied the house with everything from toothpaste and toilet paper to laundry soap and paper towels, even makeup for the girls.

One couple, Agnes and Ralph, bought twin beds and pillows for all the children. Others brought quilts, sheets and bedspreads for everyone.

Since then, "Aunt Pauline and Uncle Nikkolas," as the children call them, have become like brother and sister to Dorothy and Forrest. They cook out together, share things and spend time together. If you couldn't see color, you'd never know they weren't related.

Every day as Dorothy watches her children come home from volleyball or basketball practice or a yearbook meeting, she thanks God that they have their dream back. Danielle wants to speak eight languages and go to Harvard to be a lawyer. One of the boys wants to be a fighter pilot. Three of them want to be doctors. Dominique wants to be a nurse. Leonard wants to be a technician for NASA.

Dorothy Wright says it best, "With as many guardian angels as this family has, and with the love we have for each other, the dreams of the entire Wright family will continue for generations."

Patricia Lorenz

Otis

Just don't give up what you're trying to do.
Where there is love and inspiration, I don't think
you can go wrong.

Ella Fitzgerald

His phone call had come during a busy Friday after-noon the first week of June in 2000. I had other plans and told him so. "But I'll see if I can change them. I'd like to be there."

"It's just—well, I just wanted to let you know that I'm graduating Sunday. You've always encouraged me to stay in school. You're one of the biggest reasons I'm graduating. I wouldn't have stuck it out if you hadn't encouraged me."

Nearly two years had passed since I'd heard from Otis. When he first started his studies at West Chester University, he contacted me regularly. As in most situations with kids going off to college, as time went by he called less frequently.

"I didn't want to walk down that aisle on graduation

day," he said, "without having a chance to thank you for everything you've done for me."

I barely remember my response because I kept thinking of Otis graduating.

During my early days of reactivating the chess team at Vaux Middle School, I had seen the possibilities in that kid. He was one of the older ones who already knew how to play and was better than most adults. Otis was shy and quite studious.

One thing, though: all through high school he called or came back to Vaux to let us know how school was going.

I wanted to be at his graduation, but I wasn't sure I could make it, so I couldn't promise. I did tell him how excited I was that he was going to graduate.

"You're the first of my kids to make it through college," I said. "That makes your graduation special, you know."

After I hung up the phone, I paused and thought again about Otis Bullock. I felt warm inside after that call. It was finally happening! All those years of urging kids to stay in school and to keep on. Yes, I felt proud of him—the first of my kids to graduate from college. Others would graduate in the years ahead, but Otis would be the first.

I had seen as much promise in a number of kids who had dropped out of school after they left Vaux. Some had been murdered; a few had gotten into drugs and disappeared. Others moved away, and I lost track of them.

These inner-city kids face obstacles that middle-class Americans can't understand. It's more than a lack of money. Some get little support from their families and even less from their peers. Many of those kids have never known a father, and few of them have been inside a two-parent home.

Every day of their lives those kids live in the projects or near one. They know about drugs, violence and prostitution, and they can tell you where to buy a handgun. Most of them either had had someone murdered in their family or could name half a dozen kids in their neighborhood who never lived long enough to reach college age.

"Oh, God, it's so hard for these kids," I heard myself praying as I sat at my desk. "So many pressures from their peers and the pull of their community."

Then I thought again of Otis. He had done it. He had paved the road that others could follow.

Throughout the rest of the day, my thoughts kept returning to Otis's telephone call. In my mind, I could see him lined up with gown and tassel, waiting to receive his degree.

"I have to go to his graduation," I said aloud. I wanted to see Otis graduate—to walk alongside those other graduates and receive his diploma. But even more important, I needed to be there—for me. I had to see hope fulfilled through Otis.

On the drive up, I kept thinking about inner-city kids. As long as they're alive they have a chance to turn their lives around. As long as there are teachers and leaders out there giving of ourselves, we can make changes.

I wasn't the only teacher or leader. There were others—many others—and each of us carried the same burden. We cared. And because we cared, it hurt deeply when we lost a child.

I kept thinking of the funerals I had been to during the past ten years—more than I wanted to remember. Some of those we buried were young—elementary- and middle-school kids who happened to be playing in the wrong place when a fight broke out.

When I was a boy, I had gone to funerals—but they were only for old people. I'd stare at their lined faces and gray hair, and it felt peaceful. They had lived their lives, but these kids were eight, ten or fourteen years old.

They'd never know what life really is. Too many

inner-city kids grew up too fast—if they grew up—seeing the harshness of life on the streets every day. For the ten-year period beginning in 1990, I mentally ticked off almost twenty of my former students who had been murdered. That's something I never thought about when I was studying to be a teacher. No education classes had ever mentioned coping with such grief.

Too many funerals.

The world is larger than North Philadelphia and bigger than the ghettos, I kept saying to myself. *Education is their passport to another world.* As I drove toward the university, I vowed afresh that I would give every child a passport to go wherever he or she wanted to go.

I know I'm impacting lives and careers—and that's encouraging, but I'm just one person. I would have such a short time to impact each of these children. At most, I'd have six years to point them in new directions. That didn't seem long enough.

I had debated about calling Otis before we left Philadelphia, but I decided not to. I wanted to be there and to watch his face the moment he spotted us.

Shawnna and I sat in the shade near the stadium stairs. It was almost one hundred degrees that Sunday, and several people collapsed from the intense sun and heat.

I fidgeted and squirmed until the graduating students marched in procession.

It took me a few seconds to spot Otis. I stared at him, hardly aware that tears had filled my eyes.

When he saw Shawnna and me, his eyes lit up and he grinned. I couldn't hold back any longer. Tears streamed down my cheeks, and I didn't care. Otis had made it! He had beaten the poverty and the drugs and the peer pressure. He was alive and graduating from college. Between the pride and the tears, I paid little attention to the rest of the ceremony.

As soon as the graduation was over, Otis rushed over and hugged us. We made him pose for pictures alone, then with other classmates, with me, with Shawnna and me, with professors. I couldn't get enough pictures of him in his graduation gown.

At least four times Otis thanked us for coming. He couldn't seem to get over the idea that Shawnna and I would drive all the way from Philadelphia to see him graduate.

"When I called, I really didn't expect you to come," Otis said.

"I'm not sure you understand, Otis," I said. "I needed to come to this graduation. I had to come. I've been to too many funerals. I needed to go to a graduation. I need to go to many of them. I hope that many more of my students will give me the opportunity to come and see them graduate and reach their goals and continue to hold to the commitments that they've made to themselves and to me."

When I attend funerals, I weep over those kids and I ask myself and God how I can go to another one. Almost immediately, I find comfort in one thought: *If I quit teaching, if I left the inner city, if I stopped reaching out to these kids, how many more funerals will take place that I might have prevented?*

Then the pain eases. I know I need to keep teaching.

As I looked at Otis, standing there in his cap and gown, more than ever, I knew why I still choose to stay in the inner city.

Salome Thomas-El

Senior Editor's Message:
And the Winner Is . . .

When I was in fifth grade, my teacher assigned us the task of writing an essay for a contest on "What It Means to Be a Good Citizen of the Fifth Grade." I have no memory of what I wrote in my essay, but I suspect I said things like "We must respect each other and be nice to each other," which, now as a citizen of a much bigger classroom, I still believe to this day. I probably added something that pleased my teacher like, "We must follow the rules and do as we are told." I wrote my essay, turned it in and promptly forgot all about it.

One day as I was getting ready for school, my mother started behaving strangely. I had put on my dental headgear which I seldom if ever wore to school and which my parents were always reminding me to wear. On that day, Mom told me not to wear it to school.

Odd, I thought, and took it off as I was told.

Then she told me as I was walking out the door, "If anything makes you nervous at school, take a deep breath and think of the Lord."

Good advice for sure, but *odd again,* I thought.

As my class headed in a single-file line toward the

assembly in which the winners of the essay contest were to be announced, one of my friends said, "Evey, your mom is here. I saw her up by the office."

Really, really, really odd, I thought, starting to wonder if I was in trouble for something. It was then that I started to put all the pieces together. I must have won the essay contest and that was why my mom hadn't wanted me to wear my headgear! She must have come to school to see me read my essay out loud in front of the whole school! My stomach started churning and I was short of breath. There, again, another puzzle piece fit as I remembered my mother's advice. I began chanting the name of the Lord and taking deep breaths in anticipation of what was yet to come.

I did, indeed, win the contest and was called to the front of the cafeteria to read my essay, which I managed to do without any great mishap or embarrassment. As my prize, the school gave me a book about Martin Luther King Jr. with a big picture of him on the cover. At the time, I remember thinking it was an odd prize for an eleven-year-old white girl. Certainly, I had heard of Martin Luther King, but even as winner of the "What It Means to Be a Good Citizen" contest, I couldn't have told you much about him.

Even without reading it, I knew that there was something special about the book. I moved it with me over the years from Southern California to Northern, from Northern California back to Southern. I moved it from California to Hawaii, and I still own and treasure it to this day—now, more than thirty years later.

The gift of that book was a destiny, a planted seed, even more than a book I was supposed to read, or a prize for my essay. Now, as senior editor of *Chicken Soup for the African American Soul,* I am reading essays, stories, memories, triumphs, tragedies and celebrations about what it means to be a citizen of the African American culture. I had a role in selecting the "winners," during two years of reading more than 3,000 raw and unedited stories. But, I am the real winner, honored with the opportunity to look into the hearts and souls of thousands of African American people. I was educated; I didn't know how much I didn't know. I was blessed with a new understanding of the trials, tribulations and successes. I was crushed under the weight of some stories and elevated by the levity of others. I cried from the depths of my soul and laughed so hard tears rolled from my eyes. I was called "Sistah" via e-mail—where the walls of color are invisible, and I glowed, yes glowed, with the joy of connection and acceptance. While some stories made it into the book and others did not, rest assured that they all, *you* all—each and every one—made it into my heart. And I give thanks, for I will never, ever again be an ignorant white girl.

Eve Eschner Hogan

More Chicken Soup?

Many of the stories and poems you have read in this book were submitted by readers like you who had read earlier *Chicken Soup for the Soul* books. We publish at least five or six *Chicken Soup for the Soul* books every year. We invite you to contribute a story to one of these future volumes.

Stories may be up to twelve hundred words and must uplift or inspire. You may submit an original piece, something you have read or your favorite quotation on your refrigerator door.

To obtain a copy of our submission guidelines and a listing of upcoming *Chicken Soup* books, please write, fax or check our Web site.

Please send your submissions to:

Chicken Soup for the Soul
P.O. Box 30880, Santa Barbara, CA 93130
fax: 805-563-2945
Web site: *www.chickensoup.com*

We will be sure that both you and the author are credited for your submission.

For information about speaking engagements, other books, audiotapes, workshops and training programs, please contact any of our authors directly.

Supporting Others

In the spirit of supporting others, a portion of the proceeds from *Chicken Soup for the African American Soul* will be donated to the Tom Joyner Foundation.

The Tom Joyner Foundation only does one thing . . . it helps students continue their education at black colleges. All too often a student will get into college, then encounter financial difficulties that will force them to drop out. The Foundation provides money directly to Historical Black Colleges and Universities (HBCUs) for the purpose of helping these students complete their education.

Each month the Tom Joyner Foundation selects a specific HBCU as the benefactor of funds raised during that month. The money is sent directly to the school and the students. Scholarships are awarded through the financial aid department at the HBCU based on financial need and academic achievement.

Your purchase of *Chicken Soup for the African American Soul* helps the Tom Joyner Foundation create a brighter future for America, its young people and its Historically Black Colleges and Universities. Your support is important, and it is appreciated.

The Tom Joyner Foundation
P.O. Box 630495
Irving, TX 75063
tjf@blackamericaweb.com

Who Is Jack Canfield?

Jack Canfield is one of America's leading experts in the development of human potential and personal effectiveness. He is both a dynamic, entertaining speaker and a highly sought-after trainer. Jack has a wonderful ability to inform and inspire audiences toward increased levels of self-esteem and peak performance.

He is the author and narrator of several bestselling audio- and videocassette programs, including *Self-Esteem and Peak Performance, How to Build High Self-Esteem, Self-Esteem in the Classroom* and *Chicken Soup for the Soul—Live.* He is regularly seen on television shows such as *Good Morning America, 20/20* and *NBC Nightly News.* Jack has coauthored numerous books, including the *Chicken Soup for the Soul* series, *Dare to Win* and *The Aladdin Factor* (all with Mark Victor Hansen), *100 Ways to Build Self-Concept in the Classroom* (with Harold C. Wells), *Heart at Work* (with Jacqueline Miller), *The Power of Focus* (with Les Hewitt and Mark Victor Hansen) and *Chicken Soup for the Soul Life Lessons.*

Jack is a regularly featured speaker for professional associations, school districts, government agencies, churches, hospitals, sales organizations and corporations. His clients have included the American Dental Association, the American Management Association, AT&T, Campbell's Soup, Clairol, Domino's Pizza, GE, ITT, Hartford Insurance, Johnson & Johnson, the Million Dollar Roundtable, NCR, New England Telephone, Re/Max, Scott Paper, TRW and Virgin Records. Jack has taught on the faculty of Income Builders International, a school for entrepreneurs.

Jack conducts an annual seven-day Living Your Highest Vision Training program. It attracts entrepreneurs, sales professionals, corporate trainers, professional speakers, and others interested in creating and living their ideal life.

Look for Jack's latest book *The Success Principles* on the shelf in January 2005.

Self-Esteem Seminars
P.O. Box 30880
Santa Barbara, CA 93130
phone: 805-563-2935 • fax: 805-563-2945
Web site: *www.jackcanfield.com*

Who Is Mark Victor Hansen?

In the area of human potential, no one is more respected than Mark Victor Hansen. For more than thirty years, Mark has focused solely on helping people from all walks of life reshape their personal vision of what's possible. His powerful messages of possibility, opportunity and action have created powerful change in thousands of organizations and millions of individuals worldwide.

He is a sought-after keynote speaker, bestselling author and marketing maven. Mark's credentials include a lifetime of entrepreneurial success and an extensive academic background. He is a prolific writer with many bestselling books such as *The One Minute Millionaire, The Power of Focus, The Aladdin Factor* and *Dare to Win,* in addition to the *Chicken Soup for the Soul* series. Mark has made a profound influence through his library of audios, videos and articles in the areas of big thinking, sales achievement, wealth building, publishing success, and personal and professional development.

Mark is the founder of the MEGA Seminar Series. MEGA Book Marketing University and Building Your MEGA Speaking Empire are annual conferences where Mark coaches and teaches new and aspiring authors, speakers and experts on building lucrative publishing and speaking careers. Other MEGA events include MEGA Marketing Magic and My MEGA Life.

He has appeared on television (*Oprah*, CNN and *The Today Show*), in print (*Time, U.S. News & World Report, USA Today, New York Times* and *Entrepreneur*) and on countless radio interviews, assuring our planet's people that "You can easily create the life you deserve."

As a philanthropist and humanitarian, Mark works tirelessly for organizations such as Habitat for Humanity, American Red Cross, March of Dimes, Childhelp USA and many others. He is the recipient of numerous awards that honor his entrepreneurial spirit, philanthropic heart and business acumen. He is a lifetime member of the Horatio Alger Association of Distinguished Americans, an organization that honored Mark with the prestigious Horatio Alger Award for his extraordinary life achievements.

Mark Victor Hansen is an enthusiastic crusader of what's possible and is driven to make the world a better place.

Mark Victor Hansen & Associates, Inc.
P.O. Box 7665
Newport Beach, CA 92658
phone: 949-764-2640
fax: 949-722-6912
Visit Mark online at: *www.markvictorhansen.com*

Who Is Lisa Nichols?

Lisa Nichols is a dynamic motivational speaker and advocate of personal empowerment. She is the founder and president of Motivating the Masses, Inc., which provides transformational workshops for adults, and the founder and CEO of Motivating the Teen Spirit, LLC which is recognized by many as the most comprehensive program available today for teen self-development. Motivating the Teen Spirit has impacted the lives of over 35,000 teens, prevented over 850 suicides, reunited thousands of teens with their parents, and influenced more than 575 teen dropouts to return to school. The program provides services to the educational system, leadership programs, juvenile justice system and youth serving agencies.

Lisa is also a motivational speaker, delivering powerful and thought-provoking seminars to standing-room-only audiences of empowered women, entrepreneurs, investors, parents, educators, juvenile justice employees and adult youth advocates. Her no-holds-barred messages include powerful energy, personal testimonies and eye-opening interactive processes. She is known not to leave a dry eye in the house as she moves the audience towards giving themselves permission to be completely comfortable with who they are. Her personal coaching to CEOs, entrepreneurs, investors, principals, pastors and parents helps get people clear on their vision, their roadblocks, their power and their possibilities.

For her work and dedication, Lisa has received the 2003 Trail Blazers Entrepreneurs award, LEGOLAND Heart of Learning award, and the Emotional Literacy award. November 20th was proclaimed by the Mayor of Henderson, Nevada as Motivating the Teen Spirit Day. Lisa was born and raised in Los Angeles and loves to dance, swim, skate, play laser tag and read. She and her son, Jelani, live in Southern California.

Please visit *www.AfricanAmericanSoul.com* for continuous updates, events and African American resources.

Web site: *www.AfricanAmericanSoul.com*
E-mail: *mtts@ureach.com* or *Lisa@AfricanAmericanSoul.com*
For information regarding
Motivating the Teen Spirit or
booking Lisa as a speaker: 858-376-3700

Who Is Tom Joyner?

Tom Joyner is one of the most influential, inspirational, and dynamic personalities in the country. The native of Tuskegee, Alabama, is founder of REACH Media Inc., the Tom Joyner Foundation, *BlackAmericaWeb.com*, and host of the nationally syndicated *Tom Joyner Morning Show*. This four-hour, drive-time radio show offers a daily dose of information, entertainment and tons of pride for his nearly eight million listeners in 115 markets around the country.

In the mid-1980's Joyner earned national recognition as the "Fly Jock" when he hosted both morning and afternoon drive time shows. Everyday, for nearly eight years, he flew between two cities in order to host his shows, earning him more than seven million frequent flyer miles. In 1994, he syndicated the *Tom Joyner Morning Show* as part of the ABC Radio Network and in 2004, REACH Media Inc. took over ownership of the show that has garnered the largest audience of any urban radio program.

Joyner's efforts over the years have been widely recognized. He has received the Good Samaritan Award from the National Broadcasters Education Foundation (NABEF), and he is an inductee into the Radio Hall of Fame. *Savoy* magazine named him their 2002 Person of the Year, and he is a four-time winner of the Billboard Award. His Tom Joyner Foundation, which has raised more than $25 million, helps fund students in need who are attending Historically Black Colleges and Universities across the nation. Joyner's wife, Donna Richardson, is a world-renowned fitness guru. His two sons, Thomas Jr. and Oscar, are integral parts of his business.

Learn more about Tom Joyner at:
www.blackamericaweb.com.

Who Is Eve Hogan?

Eve Eschner Hogan, senior editor of *Chicken Soup for the African American Soul*, is an inspirational speaker and the relationship advisor for *www.dreamMates.com*. She is the author of *Way of the Winding Path: A Map for the Labyrinth of Life, Intellectual Foreplay: Questions for Lovers and Lovers-to-Be, Virtual Foreplay: Making Your Online Relationship a Real-Life Success,* and coauthor of *Rings of Truth.* Founder of Wings to Wisdom: Tools for Self-Mastery, Eve facilitates personal and spiritual growth workshops. She writes an advice column for newspapers and Web sites guiding readers to create healthier relationships. She possesses a rare and deep understanding of human behavior and is a true example of the principles she shares. Her charismatic style captivates listeners, igniting people's enthusiasm and joy for life.

Eve has been featured as a relationship expert on Lifetime TV, *Iyanla, The Other Half* and in *Cosmopolitan, Men's Health* and *Bride* magazines. Her special interest is in helping people discover their own inner resources, thus expanding their strengths and life skills. She leaves her audiences empowered with the skills to effect positive change in their lives. Eve lives on the island of Maui with her husband, Steve. Together they run Makena Coast Dive Charters, enjoying the underwater world of Hawaii.

Look for Eve's latest book, *How to Love Your Marriage,* on bookshelves spring 2005.

Wings to Wisdom: Tools for Self-Mastery
P.O. Box 943, Puunene, Maui, HI 96784
phone: 808-879-8648 • fax: 808-879-8201
E-mail: *Eve@HeartPath.com*
www.EveHogan.com and *www.MauiUnderwater.com*

Contributors

Several of the stories in this book were taken from previously published sources, such as books, magazines and newspapers. These sources are acknowledged in the Permissions section. If you would like to contact any of the contributors for information about their writing or would like to invite them to speak in your community, look for their contact information included in their biographies or visit *www.AfricanAmericanSoul.com*. The remainder of the stories were submitted by readers of our previous *Chicken Soup for the Soul* books who responded to our requests for stories. We have also included information about them.

Faith Adiele teaches nonfiction at the University of Pittsburgh and travel writing at the Iowa Summer Writing Festival. Her books include a memoir, *Meeting Faith: The Forest Journals of a Black Buddhist Nun in Thailand* (Norton, 2004), and a mystery-thriller, *The Student Body* (*www.thestudentbody.com*). Contact her at *www.pitt.edu/~adiele*.

Dr. Jarralynne Fletcher Agee is a psychologist working at UC Berkeley in the Department of Workforce Development. Her passion centers on helping others develop their best selves in their career and personal lives. She achieves this through print, in-person and radio consultations with people from across the U.S. She lives in California with her husband Robert and two sons, Trey and Quest. To contact Jarralynne, e-mail her at *ageesoul@yahoo.com*.

For over a decade, **Wally Amos** has been the national spokesman for Literacy Volunteers of America, Inc., in addition to also actively supporting and working with other charities and causes. The recipient of many honors and awards, Wally Amos received an honorary Doctorate in Education from Johnson & Wales University. His autobiography, *The Face That Launched a Thousand Chips*, was published in 1983. His most recent book is titled *Watermelon Magic: Seeds of Wisdom, Slices of Life*. In it, he uses watermelon as a metaphor for life, sharing his personal path to wisdom, humor, joy and a positive outlook on life.

Darrell (Coach D) Andrews is the founder of Darrell Andrews Enterprises and FamQuest, Inc. He is a motivational speaker, trainer and author of the book *How to Find Your Passion and Make a Living at It*. He can be reached toll free at 1-866-4-COACHD x108 or through *www.daenterprises.com*.

Ta'Shia Asanti is the recipient of the Audre Lorde Black Quill award, the Kathleen Morris award for contemporary fiction and is a celebrated poet, fiction writer, activist and journalist. She is also the author of the acclaimed book, *The Sacred Door*. Asanti's Web site is *www.sacreddoor.com*.

Leslie Esdaile Banks is a graduate of the University of Pennsylvania's Wharton undergraduate program and Temple University's Masters of Fine Arts in Filmmaking program. She is currently the author of over eighteen novels and many novellas in literary genres as broad as romance, women's fiction, crime/suspense and horror. She lives and works in Philadelphia with her husband, Al Banks, and children. Please e-mail her at *writerle@aol.com*.

Judy Belk's essays and short stories have appeared in various literary magazines as well as in the *New York Times, Washington Post, Wall Street Journal* and on National Public Radio. In 2000, she was awarded a fellowship to Hedgebrook, a retreat for women writers on Whidbey Island in Washington. You can reach her at: *jbelk3@earthlink.net*.

Deborah Bellis is a newborn-baby nurse in the Los Angeles area. She is presently writing an interactive workbook for first-time parents. She provides consultations about infant care and enjoys writing about life experiences. Her articles have been published in local newsletters. She is a caregiver for her mother. E-mail her at: *dabellis@earthlink.net*.

Stephen Bentley, creator of "Herb & Jamaal," first became interested in cartooning in grade school as a means to increase his popularity. Later Bentley realized he could make a living with his craft. The six-year-old comic strip blends characters that represent different sides of Bentley's personality with current societal issues. Born and raised in California, Bentley currently lives in Southern California with his wife and daughter.

Norka Blackman-Richards is passionate about teaching and writing. She currently teaches for the City University of New York. Norka is actively seeking a publisher for her teaching memoir, *Confessions of an Immigrant Teacher*. She lives in Queens with her husband, Warner. Please reach her at *NorkRich12@aol.com*.

Arthur Bowler, a U.S./Swiss citizen and graduate of Harvard Divinity School, is a writer and speaker in English and German. His work has appeared in several bestselling inspirational anthologies. He is currently seeking representation for his book *A Prayer and a Swear*. Contact him at *www.arthurbowler.ch*.

As a renowned professional speaker, author and television personality, **Les Brown** has risen to national prominence by delivering a high energy message which tells people how to shake off mediocrity and live up to their greatness. It is a message Les Brown has learned from his own life and one he is helping others apply to their lives.

Isabel Bearman Bucher, wife, mother, friend, writer and teacher, continues her honeymoon with life. At one point she thought that all of her stories had been written—but as it is with a life well-lived, her stories are always beginning and becoming. She loves hiking Earth's great wildernesses, and with her husband and grown daughters, exchanging homes throughout the world. She's finished two books and is starting a third. Please contact her at: *IBBucher@cs.com*.

Dale G. Caldwell is the deputy commissioner of the New Jersey Department of Community Affairs (DCA). He holds a B.A. from Princeton University and an M.B.A. from the Wharton School. Dale has been nationally ranked in tennis and is an avid hymn writer. He is married to Sharon Caldwell.

A native of Southern California, **Tracy Clausell-Alexander** poseses a love for creative writing using her personal experiences to influence her literary works. She is an accountant who enjoys reading and playing the piano. Tracy is the mother of six children, one of whom lives only in her heart. She is working on her first book. Please e-mail her at: *tdclausell@attbi.com.*

Miiky Cola trained as a playwright in London (2003–2004). He is currently developing his student play, "8,000 Manic Seasons" and has written his first play titled "Incurables-Laissez Le Bons Temps Role." Miiky is a native New Orleanian. He enjoys linguistics, cooking and Brazil. Contact him at *colascola@hotmail.com.*

Linda Coleman-Willis is a professional speaker, author of several books and a performance improvement coach. She was the 2002–2003 president to the National Speakers Association—Los Angeles Chapter. Linda enjoys spending "fun" time with her family and friends. Please e-mail Linda at *Lindaspeaks@aol.com.*

Jerry Craft is a graduate of the School of Visual Arts (B.F.A.) and a National Cartoonists Society Award Nominee (2000). His book, *Mama's Boyz: As American as Sweet Potato Pie!*, was named a "Great Book for African American Children." Check his Web site for book, shirts, mugs, greeting cards and children's board games at *www.mamasboyz.com.*

Cheryl Dash is the founder of A Pinch of This—A Dash of That Desktop Publishing. She writes poetry, lyrics and short stories. She has completed a screenplay and is currently working on a novel. Cheryl considers her passion for writing a gift from God. Please reach Cheryl at: *cdash@apotadotdesigns.com.*

Tyrone Dawkins is a motivational speaker, executive career coach and clinical hypnotherapist. He has provided career consultation for executives from numerous fortune companies. He has helped many people change unwanted behaviors and beliefs through private coaching sessions and workshops. His empowerment presentations introduce people to their unlimited potential.

Mel Donalson received his B.A. from Bates College, M.A. from the University of Iowa and Ph.D. from Brown University. A published poet, fiction writer and essayist, he is a professor of film, literature and popular culture at Pasadena City College and California State University, Los Angeles.

Ray Driver, the author of *Jemma's Treasure,* is a homeschooling mother of three and a keynote speaker and workshop coordinator for homeschooling groups and conventions. Born and raised in California, she is also a Christian family counselor for her church, a preschool director and a former state coordinator for a political awareness group.

RuNett Nia Ebo resides in Philadelphia with her family which includes seven grandchildren. She attended Clark (College)-Atlanta University, class of 1972. She went from welfare to work and established her own business as a self-published author of eight books. For more information visit: *www. POETEBO-NET.com* or *www.black-network.com/niaebo.htm.*

Minister Mary Edwards has authored five books. She is founder of The Called and Ready Writers, His Lovely Wife Ministries, M.E.D.I.C. Ministries, and co-founder of Joy of Jesus Ministries with her husband, Rev. Eddie K. Edwards. Voted "One of the Most Influential Women in Metropolitan Detroit" in 2002, she ministers nationally and internationally. E-mail her at *mwwginc@aol.com.*

Gary K. Farlow is a native Tarheel with a juris doctorate from Heed University. His most recent book, *Prison-ese: A Survivor's Guide to Speaking Prison Slang* may be ordered from Loomanics Unlimited, P.O. Box 1197, Port Townsend, WA 98368. Mr. Farlow is in his 14th year of incarceration and welcomes any and all correspondence. He has completed a play dealing with the HIV/AIDS crisis in prison and enjoys reading, writing, classical music and collecting postcards. You may write to him at The Nash Correctional Institute, #0215977, P.O. Box 600, Nashville, NC, 97856.

Greg Franklin received his bachelor of arts degree from Morehouse College where he majored in finance and political science. Greg is a medical sales representative and a professional speaker. He can be reached at *gfranklin7@cox.net*. Greg dedicates this story to his mom, Barbara Franklin, who died of multiple myeloma on May 9, 2003.

Nancy Gilliam resides with her husband and seven children in Philadelphia where she works with Creative Kids. She's the director of Freedom Christian Bible Fellowship Drama Ministry. She's written numerous songs and plays and has published her first children's book, *Thank You, Thank You, Thank You.* Contact her at *nk81dove@yahoo.com*.

Michelle R. Gipson earned both her B.A. in mass media and her M.A. in counseling from Hampton University. She has been published in *Jane, Black Issues Book Review* and *The Atlanta Daily World.* Michelle is currently working as a freelance writer while working on her memoir. Please reach her at *michelle_gipson@hotmail.com* or at P.O. Box 250504, Atlanta, GA 30325.

Thyonne Gordon, COO of the nonprofit youth center *A Place Called Home* in South Central, Los Angeles, attended Howard and Pepperdine Universities for her B.A. and M.B.A., respectively. She currently seeks doctoral candidacy at Fielding Institute and is writing *Chicken Soup in the Heart of the Hood.* Contact: *awriter@comcast.net.*

Farrah Gray grew up in the inner city of Chicago. He started his first business at the age of eight and made his first million at the age of fifteen when he sold his food company, Farr-Out Foods. He is currently the majority owner and publisher of *InnerCity* Magazine, a joint venture with Inner City Broadcasting Corporation, the oldest African American-owned media conglomerate in America. His book about his experiences and the lessons he's learned in his first nineteen years, *Reallionaire: Ten Secrets to Being Rich from the Inside Out,* will be published in January 2005. He can be reached at *publisher@innercity magazine.com.*

Jaynell Grayson is a public relations specialist for IBM Global Services. Food from the 'Hood is a student-owned business located at Crenshaw High School in Los Angeles, California. Company profits provide college scholarships for the student owners, who donate 25 percent of their crop to feed the needy in their community. For more information, contact Aleyne Larner at 323-295-4842. To contact Jaynell, write to: IBM Global Services, Rte.100, Bldg.4, Somers, NY 10589; phone: 914-766-4107; fax: 914-766-8494; e-mail: *jngrayson@us.ibm.com.*

Fran Harris was a member of the Houston Comets' 1997 WNBA Championship team. An author, speaker and former ESPN, Lifetime Television and Fox

Sports announcer, she owns Tall Tree Productions, a multimedia company that specializes in reality, documentary and nonfiction programs. Connect with Fran via e-mail at *frantv@aol.com*. Visit *www.franharris.com*.

Lisa Helem, a writer in New York city, received her bachelor of arts in English and African American Studies from Duke University in 2001. She enjoys laughing with friends, 1970's era music and shopping. Next fall, she plans to attend graduate school. She can be reached via e-mail at: *lhelem@alumni.duke.edu*.

Nicole Hodges Persley is an actress and playwright. She is a Ph.D. candidate in American Studies and Ethnicity at the University of Southern California. Nicole studies African Diaspora theater and performance and loves working with youth. She is currently writing a play about transnational identity. Please e-mail her at *nrhodges@usc.edu*.

Bill Holton is a freelance writer living in Florida.

John L. Horton is a sixty-two-year-old, retired Marine sergeant major. He holds an M.A. from the University of Oklahoma. He is a juvenile probation officer, motivational speaker, youth activist, writer and trainer in Norfolk, Virginia. John enjoys working with inner-city youth and families and doing consultant work.

Wade Hudson's career as a writer spans more than three decades. After his involvement in the civil rights movement of the 1960s, he was a newspaper reporter, playwright and public relations specialist. In 1988, he and his wife Cheryl founded Just Us Books. Mr. Hudson has written nearly twenty books for children. His newest is *Powerful Words*. *www.justusbooks.com*.

Gregory Huskisson has a bachelor's degree in communications from Morehouse College and a master's degree from the Medill School of Journalism at Northwestern University. A writer and a budding filmmaker, Greg is working on a sequel to "Sister, I'm Sorry" in which men tell *their* story. Contact him at *Gjhusk@aol.com*.

Pastor, community advocate, humanitarian, author, songwriter, playwright, conference speaker and broadcaster, **Bishop Thomas D. Jakes, Sr.** pastors what *Christianity Today* calls "one of America's fastest growing mega-churches." Named The Potter's House, this multiracial, nondenominational church has fifty-nine active internal and outreach ministries and more than 28,000 members. For more information visit *www.ThePottersHouse.com*.

Tinisha Nicole Johnson lives in Denver, Colorado. She has her associate degree in business and paralegal and is currently in school full time, pursuing her bachelor's in accounting and finance. Her goal is then to pursue her master's in education. She is a single black mother of one son and is currently working at a finance company in the Accounting/Payments Department. She looks forward to pursuing her longtime dream as a freelance novelist and nonfiction writer.

Michael Jones is a single father with one son. He is a systems analyst in Los Angeles. Mike enjoys softball, jazz and inspirational speaking. He has started a foundation called OMCOL (One Miracle Celebration of Life) and is writing a book by the same name. Please e-mail him at: *Onemiracle911@yahoo.com* or through his Web site at *www.onemiracle911.com*.

Yolanda King is the firstborn child of Dr. Martin Luther King Jr. and Coretta Scott King. As a dynamic speaker and seasoned actress, Yolanda King has performed or lectured in forty-nine of the fifty American states as well as in Europe, Africa and Asia for education, business, religious and civic organizations. She is the co-author of the inspirational book, *Open My Eyes, Open My Soul.*

Landis Lain received her bachelor of arts in 1984 and her juris doctor in 1988. She is an administrative law judge in Michigan. She loves her husband and family, dance and reading. She writes fiction, romance and inspirational women's books. Please e-mail her at *lainl@michigan.gov.*

Upon graduation from Carver High School in Gadsden, Alabama, **Howard L. Lipscomb Sr.** traveled around the country playing in several bands as a drummer. After traveling, he married and settled in Flint, Michigan, where he and his wife raised their family. His life is centered around God and his church, the Family Worship Center Church, as well as the ecumenical movement DeColores, a ministry that provides tools for individuals in their walk in Christ. He is also a dedicated volunteer for incarcerated youth. He enjoys being with his children and grandchildren most of all, but is known to hang out on the riverbank fishing or in the backyard barbecuing.

Patricia Lorenz, an art-of-living writer and speaker, is one of the top contributors to *Chicken Soup for the Soul* books with stories in nineteen of them. She's the author of five books, including *Life's Too Short to Fold Your Underwear* and *Grab the Extinguisher, My Birthday Cake's on Fire* (available at: *guidepostsbooks.com*, 800-932-2145) and *Great American Outhouse Stories: The Hole Truth and Nothing Butt* (available at *www.buybooksontheweb.com*, 877-289-2665). To contact Patricia about speaking opportunities e-mail her at *patricialorenz@juno.com* or visit her Web site: *www.patricialorenz.com.*

Kim Louise is the author of six novels and three novellas, including *Destiny's Song, A Touch Away* and *A Love of Their Own.* She is a sought-after speaker and instructor whose writing has appeared in the *Omaha Star, The Cathartic Journal,* and *Role Call Anthology.* Reach her at: *MsKimLouise@aol.com.*

Ahmon'dra (Brenda) McClendon, president of Brilliance Inc., has an M.S.W. from San Francisco State University and twenty years' experience in the field of human experience services. She is a facilitator with Motivating the Teen Spirit, a teen empowerment program and the creator of "Passionate Living a New Existence," a program of self-discovery. E-mail her at *Ahmondra@aol.com.*

Karlene McCowan received her master of science degree in nursing from Ohio State University in 2002. She lives in West Virginia with her husband and three children. She enjoys serving God, reading, jogging, walking, tennis, music and working with youth. You may e-mail her at: *McKargo@msn.com.*

Valerie McNeal received her bachelor of science, with honors, in Organizational Behavior from the University of San Francisco in 2001. She is currently an account manager at SBC in San Francisco. Valerie is an avid cook. Her current work in progress is a unique cookbook titled *The Dish.*

minerva, also known as **Gail Hawkins**, is a noted poet, editor, teacher and performer. She was on the staff of the National Geographic Society for ten years.

Her book of poetry, *The Wall,* was published by The Inevitable Press. Contact her for poetry workshops, performance, editing or public speaking at *minervapoetry@hotmail.com.*

Dennis Mitchell is a highly sought-after motivational speaker and author who gives life-changing keynotes, seminars and workshops. Since the early 1980s, Dennis has devoted his life to acquiring and sharing the attitudes, beliefs, tools and strategies to help others achieve excellence both personally and professionally. For more info or to book Dennis for a cutting edge program for your event, contact him at 1-888-547-3255 or *www.yesyoucansucceed.com.*

Anthony Marquis Moore is studying computer aided drafting and design at Sinclair College. He enjoys reading, writing and cooking. He intends to continue writing while living in the Dayton, Ohio area.

E. Joyce Moore is a modern-day Renaissance woman. Her passion encompasses all of the arts, but her focus is on writing. After nineteen years with AT&T she chose to take the opportunity to pursue the development of a nonprofit fine arts organization and write her first book, *Gettin' to the Good Wood,* published in December 2003. Please e-mail her at: *director@artists4a.org.*

Dominique Morisseau, writer/actress, Detroit native, has work both in print and onstage throughout metro Detroit, New York and California. Author of two NAACP Image Award-winning plays, Dominique's work can be most recently seen in the ROAR! and Rebel Verses Theatre Festivals in NYC; in *Signifyin' Harlem,* a literary journal; and in her own book of poetry, *Screamin' with My Mouth Closed.* Contact her at *dominiquemorisseau@yahoo.com.*

Always a storyteller, **Herchel Newman** started writing after retirement in 1999. He loves family, humor and romance, so he is a professional wedding photographer. As an Air Force and professional firefighter veteran, he says every day is an adventure someone should write about. Contact him at *ZoomN500@juno.com.*

Evelyn Palfrey writes romantic suspense for the "marvelously mature." Her novels, *The Price of Passion, Dangerous Dilemmas* and *Everything in Its Place,* have appeared on the *Essence* bestseller list. She is an attorney in Texas. Find out more about her at *www.evelynpalfrey.com.*

Myrtle Peterson earned her B.A. from Dillard University in 1952 and an M.S.W. from Columbia University in 1955 with extensive postgraduate study. A mental health practitioner, she retired in 1991 and enrolled in acting school. She has performed in "Caroline's on Broadway" in New York City. She studies autobiographical writing at Nassau County Community College. You may reach her at: *mpeterson@optonline.net.*

Yvonne Pointer is a motivational speaker and author of the book, *Behind the Death of a Child.* She's the recipient of numerous awards, including a 2001 Essence Award and the 908th Point of Light from former President George Bush. Please reach her at: P.O. Box 603456, Cleveland, Ohio 44103 or *yvonnepointer@aol.com.*

Vici Howard-Prayitno is a struggling independent filmmaker and writer who decided to get married and raise a couple of kids to pass the time until she gets discovered. She loves chocolate and compliments. So if you're a fan or producer with a massive bank roll, HOLLA BACK!!! at *Betterwa4u@aol.com*.

Tracy Price-Thompson is the national bestselling author of *Black Coffee* and *Chocolate Sangria*. A decorated Desert Storm veteran and retired Army engineer officer, she is also the co-editor of *Proverbs for the People*, an anthology of contemporary African-American fiction released by Kensington Publishing.

Gloria Quinney is a native of Alexandria, Louisiana, and currently resides in Flint, Michigan. Gloria received her bachelor of arts degree from Grambling State University and her master of arts and master of public administration degrees from Western Michigan University. She is currently CEO of GQ Enterprises. E-mail her at: *G.Quinney@prodigy.net*. Web site: *http://gqenterprisesltd.net*.

Tony Ramos received his bachelor of arts in journalism from California State University at Long Beach in 1979. He is president of the Allied Healthcare Group, a division of Medical World Communications. Tony is married with two children and serves on the executive board of his church, Crenshaw Christian Center in Los Angeles. He enjoys coaching his children in sports and running. Please e-mail him at *tramos@medpubs.com*.

Dorothy C. Randle earned her bachelor of arts degree from California State University Dominguez Hills and her master of organizational leadership with high honors from Biola University in 2003. She is happily married with three children. She plans to author books on training, leadership and development. Please reach her at: *authordcrandle@hotmail.com*.

Carol Ross-Burnett is a gospel singer/songwriter/producer who released her first CD in 2002. She is also a diversity consultant, trainer, author and speaker. Carol holds a bachelor's degree from the University of California at Berkeley and a master's degree from San Francisco State University. Contact her at *crburnett@prodigy.net*.

Zev Roth is a freelance author living in Israel. He has published three books with Targum Press, the most recent one titled. "*10.10.*" His articles have appeared in Jewish Press and World Jewish Review. Zev is married and has seven children. Please contact him at *zevstenten@yahoo.com*.

Nikki D. Shearer-Tillford is a writer and owns a business, The Sacred Mind. Her vision is to create messages/products that speak to the heart and mind. She conducts an annual women's group that encourages expression of unresolved emotions through creativity. She can be reached at *thesacredmind@cinci.rr.com*.

Catina Slade has enjoyed word play ever since she wrote a poem for a childhood friend that served to mend a broken relationship. Her twofold ministry of writing and speaking has allowed her to speak life into the broken-hearted with words of hope and healing. Her two children, Cameron and Courtney, are her rays of sunshine in Los Angeles, where she is at work on her first novel. You may e-mail her at *Bycatina@aol.com*.

Jayme Washington Smalley is a professional musician, storyteller and folk artist living in Augusta, Georgia. She enjoys traveling, cooking and crafting. Jayme has written a collection of short stories titled, *As the Butterbeans Boil*. Please contact her at *smalley@bellsouth.net*.

Mary Spio went on to establish herself at the top of her field, developing core technology applications for major networks including Viacom, BBC, M-NET and a myriad of Fortune 100 companies. The multifaceted Spio also engineered a fun and engaging online dating community, *www.One2OneLiving.com*, to turbo-boost love lives.

John W. Stewart Jr. has worked extensively in the film industry for the past twelve years. Recently, he has resurrected his childhood dreams of writing and entrepreneurship. He is currently working on a screenplay and can be reached at P.O. Box 8153, Universal City, California, 91618 or *jjstewartla@aol.com*.

Lalita Tademy, a California native, was formerly vice-president of a Fortune 500 high technology company. She left the corporate world, immersed herself in tracing her family's history, and subsequently wrote *Cane River*, which was Oprah Winfrey's 2001 summer book club selection. Her Web site is *www.lalitatademy.com*.

Elodia Tate is a writer, speaker and "health coach" who uses the power of storytelling and humor to encourage others to embrace a natural health approach. With Yolanda King, she recently co-authored an inspirational book called *Open My Eyes, Open My Soul* (*www.openmyeyesopenmysoul.com*). Contact her at *www.elodiatate.com* or 209-238-9938.

Salome Thomas-El is author of the bestseller, *I Choose to Stay* (Kensington, March 2003). He is an elementary school principal and national champion chess coach in Philadelphia. Walt Disney recently purchased the movie rights to *I Choose to Stay* (*www.ichoosetostay.com*). Salome Thomas-El lives with his wife and two daughters in Philadelphia.

Mary Cornelia Van Sant, known as Connie, believes that peace on Earth is achievable in our lifetime. Connie believes healing for our world begins in each of our own individual hearts and minds. She has a passion for teaching mindful meditation. This is her second story to be published in the *Chicken Soup* series.

Karen Waldman, Ph.D., finds her work as a psychologist extremely rewarding. She also enjoys writing, music, acting, playing in nature, traveling with her husband Ken, and spending time with their wonderful families, friends, children and grandchildren (Lisa, Tom, Lana, Greta, Alyson, Brian, Eric, Maryann, David and Laura). Her e-mail is *krobens@aol.com*.

R. Jenée Walker, M.D. is a psychiatrist board-certified in child, adolescent and adult psychiatry. She practices in Charleston, West Virginia. She presents workshops across the country with an emphasis on spiritual healing. She is presently writing a book that will serve as a guide to maintaining emotional peace. Please reach her at: *myra.dolan@camc.org*.

Melanie M. Watkins, M.D. is a recent graduate of the Stanford University School of Medicine. She attended University of Nevada Reno where she graduated with high honors. Her work and life story have appeared in *USA Today, Chicken Soup for the Single's Soul, Woman's World Magazine,* and *This Side of Doctoring*. She enjoys writing and motivational speaking. She lives with her son Jonathan in San Francisco, California. You may contact her at *watkinsm@obgyn.ucsf.edu.*

Woody Woodburn is a sports columnist for the *Daily Breeze* in Torrance, California. He was honored for column writing by the Associated Press Sports Editors' national contest in 2003 and 2001, appeared in *The Best American Sports Writing 2001* and is a frequent contributor to the *Chicken Soup for the Soul* series. He can be reached at *Woodycolum@aol.com.*

Phyllis W. Zeno recently retired after twenty years editing *AAA Going Places,* a magazine that goes to 4.5 million AAA members. She is currently writing two children's books, *Look, Find & Learn: U.S. History* and *World History* with her daughter, Linda Williams Aber. She travels all over the world with the Merry Widows, a ballroom dance group she directs. She can be reached at *Phylliszeno@aol.com.*

About the cover artist:

For **Keith Mallett**, painting is a spiritual journey that started in childhood and continues to this day. A painter, etcher and ceramic artist, his subject matter ranges from still lifes to abstracts. In recent years, he has devoted his talents to themes that portray the beauty and strength of the African American experience. His work has been exhibited throughout the world, and has been featured in Showtime's "Soul Food" series, Disney's "The Famous Jett Jackson," TNT's "Second String" and Woody Allen's movies "Mighty Aphrodite" and "Celebrity." His paintings grace the covers of several books, including *Sisterfire,* a collection of poems by Maya Angelou, Alice Walker and Terry McMillan. For more information, visit his Web site at *www.keithmallett.com* or write Keith Mallet Studios, Inc., P.O. Box 151378, San Diego, CA 92175.